ON MY OWN TERMS
One Actor's Journey

ON MY OWN TERMS

One Actor's Journey

Marion,
I am glad our spirits
were brought together at
AFTRA. We can make a difference
in the direction of the industry.
Enjoy the journey!
Adilah
06/17/09

Adilah Barnes

To order additional copies of this book, contact:
Xlibris Corporation
1-888-795-4274
www.Xlibris.com
Orders@Xlibris.com
36973

Contents

Dedication

This book is dedicated to my mother and father, Mosea Lee and Edward Barnes; sister Dorothy; brothers Hollis and Edward; niece Adrienne; and nephews RJ and Eugene.

You have not been forgotten.

Praises for ON MY OWN TERMS *One Actor's Journey*

"An engrossing memoir that presents . . . life's journey with honesty and insight . . . will also touch anyone who has struggled to create . . . teach . . . grow . . . to be a better person . . . learn from mistakes . . . overcome obstacles, or simply to exist in a world that Barnes portrays as challenging, exhilarating and precious—you will find yourself inspired . . . warmth and intelligence and integrity radiate from every page . . . incredibly touching and fiercely honest . . . device of providing life lessons in italics worked well. I found myself looking forward to seeing how you'd present the lesson and then I'd stop and think about it. Little gems."

—Judith Claire Mitchell, *The Last Day of the War*

"Adilah Barnes' frank and unvarnished story about her life and its challenges from Oroville to Oakland to LA, will be a primer for young actors and a good old-fashioned page-turner for the rest of us."

—Sandra Seaton, *The Bridge Party*

"Barnes affords us an intimate written account of her life . . . rends the veil of that mystical community that we know as the film and television industry . . . timely . . . story is so accessible we co-partner on her journey."

—Dr. Kwakiutl L. Dreher, *Dancing on the White Page: Black Women Entertainers Writing Autobiography*

"Informative . . . Entertaining . . . Enlightening . . . I had no idea how the audition process worked . . . book gave me a behind the scenes look at that process . . . Some of the things . . . I already knew just through the process of living life. Others were like a message sent to me . . . reminding me to stop and think about my own spiritual journey. As I read I felt a spiritual quality . . . I enjoyed this . . ."

—*Crystal Ink Publishing*

"Adilah Barnes speaks from the heart in *On My Own Terms*. Packed full of words of wisdom from an artist's life well-lived, the book is an inspiring read for young actors and artists, and a reminder to us all to speak out against racism whenever it appears in our personal and professional lives."

—*Woza Books*

What Others Say About Adilah ...

"Adilah is a woman with tremendous strength, tenacity, love and talent. She is a woman committed to making things happen and she does. We do well to mirror her actions."

—Hattie Winston, *Becker*

"Adilah's passion behind her commitment is rarely seen in show business today. She brings an entire community to witness her success as an actor and producer."

—Anna Maria Horsford, *Amen*

"Adilah is an actress of uncompromising power and intelligence. When she takes on a role, she uses her great director skill as a communicator combined with her natural insight . . . She is a wonder to behold and a delight to witness in film or onstage. I admire her talent immensely."

—Ted Lange, *Love Boat*

"Recognizing that on one's own terms is in sync with being on God's terms, I applaud you for recognizing the path, following it and succeeding."

—Marla Gibbs, *The Jeffersons*

"I have studied with several acting teachers over my forty years as a performer, but none quite like Adilah Barnes. She respects the person I am and does not try to change my spirit. She helps me expand and develop as an actor. Adilah's teaching is not only helping make me a better actress, but through understanding myself better, I am becoming an improved singer and a stronger person."

—Florence LaRue, *The 5ᵗʰ Dimension*

"A journey can not be so bad and even enjoyable if you have good directions . . . Thanks to Adilah for navigating ahead of us and reaching back to share the map . . . I am eternally grateful that I had the pleasure of your teaching. Your lessons have inspired me . . ."

—Don "DC" Curry, *Friday After Next*

"Adilah is intense. She's not easy, but she never gives up on you and pulls out your best."

—Kym Whitley, *College Road Trip*

"Adilah is a radiant, warm and intelligent presence."

—the late Roscoe Lee Browne, *Behind the Broken Words*

Acknowledgments

There are so many I want to acknowledge that surely I am bound to leave some out. First and foremost, I pay homage to my mother, Mosea Lee Barnes. She was my first teacher, and indeed a woman of individuality and grit. She was a major influence in my life and deservedly has received her own chapter in this book. I pray that she will continue to look over and protect me.

I have two fathers—Edward Barnes, who was my daddy; and Theoplis Dennis, my biological father. (At the time of this writing, God bless him, he is still very much alive at 99 years old and still driving his truck!) This threesome had everything to do with my existence, from inception to now. In terms of my nuclear family, I shared my humble beginnings at 3267 Fallbrook Avenue in Oroville, California with my brothers and sisters on my mother's side. I speak now of my eldest sister, Dorothy, the firstborn of the seven of us (I miss you so), Norma, Hollis (I miss you, too), Ora, Ellis, and Edward (and now you are gone.) Although it has been many years since we all lived under the same roof, I thank each of you for contributing to my early sense of family, discovery, and also the life lessons.

From our meager beginnings, we were taught resourcefulness and appreciation for what little we had. I thank my maternal grandparents, both Flowers and Lillian Osby. Had they not had twelve children, I would not be part of the huge tribe I represent. To my aunts, uncles, cousins, nieces, and nephews, you all know who you are. I especially thank my cousin Marilyn Theresa Moore Colvin for writing this book's afterword, and for always being one of my biggest cheerleaders with whom I can share my successes and innermost thoughts.

I thank Aunt Ester for loving me unconditionally, even when I did not know I was related to her. I thank those who were my early teachers both in and out of the classroom, including Mrs. Phoebe Officer, Miss Jimmie Black, and Mr. Roy Johnson, my earliest community leader role models. I thank my early classroom teachers in Oroville, especially Mrs. Chef (thanks for being in the first row to see my solo show when I returned home as an adult to perform), Miss Flynn (you were so ahead of your time in our small town) and Mr. Hughes (you were far more than a French teacher to me.)

I thank those who have met me at every juncture of my life's path including my childhood buddies, Sylvia Warren Alexander, the only person I have been able to sit opposite and read with for hours without uttering a single word; Brenda Jackson Stovall, who shared my teen years with me (remember The Front?); Elaine Thomas (you drove the heck out of that white stick shift Comet of yours); Cynthia Bluford (may you rest in peace); and Mararice Bush Davis (thank God we reunited after so many years); and the many others along the way.

I thank my University of California at Santa Cruz college buddy Jacki Scott, who may singularly know me better than any one person has over the last forty years (we've seen 'em come and we've seen 'em go, haven't we?) You taught me how to say "I love you" freely, and how to be comfortable giving and receiving a hug. Now I hug everybody. I thank my other UC Santa Cruz buddy, the late Eric Thomas, for being an inspiration to me and all those whose lives you so lovingly touched. (What a legacy you left behind from your short life.)

I thank all the men I have loved from my core and who have most influenced me, including Faruq Azikiwe (thank you for introducing me to higher consciousness and joining me in union to bring our son Tariq into this world), Samuel Archer Lee (forgive me for being too young and inexperienced to know how to love you back), Mychal Chambliss, James Brooks, and the rest of you who allowed and encouraged me to take a risk in this thing called love. Whether you were in my life for a season or a lifetime, you know who you are.

I thank my dear friend and director, John Henry Doyle (you *did* put me on the Bay Area theatre map.) I thank other Bay Area acting buddies, including DeBorah Pryor, Charli Smith, Alicia Nelson, the late LeOna Harris, Kellmar Gonzales and Brandi Swanson and so many others who knew me way back in the trenches when we were all cutting our teeth as actors.

I thank every person who believed in me, especially those like Dr. J. Herman Blake (thanks for guiding me to UC Santa Cruz) and I thank those who knew me in Project Upward Bound (that program is like the American flag to me.) You saw me as a diamond in the rough and recognized my worth, perhaps even more than I did at age sixteen. I thank Lij Kerai, who studied with me and who has become a caretaker of my home whenever I am on the road (thanks for loving and taking care of my Rottweiler, Booch, who has now passed on, and for our brief stint with my puppies, "The Spice Girls".) I thank every single other student of mine, including Toni Braxton, who has entrusted me with their souls and spirits during their most vulnerable states as they have further developed their creativity.

I thank those who have been a part of my professional team, having contributed to my career in so many ways. They include my agents over the years: current agents Steven Neibert and Tracy Mapes, Michael Linden Greene, Azeem Chiba, Kristene Wallis, Jenny

Delaney, and Jeffrey Leavitt. I thank Allison Queen. You have been a wonderful publicist over the years, willing to write a press release announcing any little happening in my life, whether of public interest or only of interest to you and me. You've worked passionately and tirelessly on my behalf to promote me, and I appreciate and love you for that.

I thank those I have mentored over the years, who have helped me remain accountable as a guide and mentor. They include Sauda Johnson, Yael Reed Wachspress, and Sasha Pemberton. I thank my godson Sterling Ardrey Baty, and his mother, Stephanie Ardrey, for allowing me to have a small hand in his life. I am very proud of the professional young actor Sterling has become.

When it comes to this book, I thank all my celebrity friends who gave personal quotes that speak to my character including Toni Braxton, the late Roscoe Lee Browne, Don "DC" Curry, Marla Gibbs, Danny Glover, Anna Maria Horsford, Florence LaRue, Ted Lange, Delroy Lindo, Kym Whitley and Hattie Winston. Thank you all for believing in me as worthy of your public validation. In that number, I especially thank my friend, Ella Joyce, who passionately read my entire manuscript twice and then meticulously chose each word and spoke from the heart in this book's foreword. (I knew I could count on you to call it as you saw it, and you did.)

I especially thank Rebecca Gallegos for being the catalyst who guided me to my first and primary editor, Audrey Richardson, who worked intimately with me on this book from Utah without ever meeting me eye to eye. (We *will* meet in person.) Says Audrey, "You really didn't need me to do this book." It is true that ninety-nine percent of what is written in this book has originated from my own chosen words, but Audrey's positive spirit and availability kept me on track. Even when I was distracted, I knew I was accountable and that I could always return to our telephone editing sessions. Without her, this book might still be dancing around in my head. (Thanks for everything, Audrey.)

Joining us in the last stage of this book were editors Meredith Harris, K. D. Greene, Amy Wachspress and English professors and friends playwright Sandra Seaton (thanks for giving me the opportunity to work with Ms. Ruby Dee in the staged reading of your play, *The Bridge Party)*, Dr. Kwakiutl Dreher and Dr. Judith Claire Mitchell who helped push me the rest of the way up the hill by giving me that last read of my "galley copy" for final edits to move this book on to the publishers. (Whew, I thank you!)

Thanks also to those who offered touching "blurbs" (or quotes) after reading my galley copy that make me feel my book does have something to say including words from the above mentioned professors and editors and writers Crystal V. Rhodes and Kathy Z. Price.

Many thanks also to Vesper Osborne (your time spent adding your meticulous edits to my manuscript was so appreciated), Etoy Ridgnal, Chaka Ra, and my niece Venita Jacobson, who also took the time to read and give written proofs early on, long before my book went to the publisher. All their comments made a huge difference. Thanks also to my childhood friend Sylvia Warren Alexander for her thoughts on the manuscript in its early stage while we were on our Caribbean cruise.

I thank those around the country who have joined my book junket tour to make sure we reach as many people as we can. My team leaders in the Washington D.C/Maryland area include Patrice Jenkins, Mararice Bush Davis; Marcia Ellis, and Venita Jacobson; in Los Angeles, Christine Burton, Deirdre Weston, Meme Kelly, Teri Akpovi, Smeralda, Zorana Edun Caldwell, Rainier Kenny, and Justin Parkinson; in New York, Adrian Hill and Michael Angel Johnson;

in Atlanta, Gayle Watts, Jennifer Spradling, Assuanta Collins, Lynda Price, and Lorita Harrison; in Sacramento, Edward Lewis, Marilyn Colvin, Leilani Thomas, and Sheila Hawkins; in the Bay Area, Sylvia Warren Alexander, James Brooks, Patricia Warren Gregory, and Alicia Nelson; Sandra Pemberton in New Jersey; Don Williams at the University of California at Santa Cruz, and Brenda Jackson Stovall and Patti Murrish of Oroville California.

I saved the best for last. I thank most of all my son Tariq (thanks for putting up with an imperfect mother) and grandson Malik Isaiah (Grandma's boy), whom I am proud to call my immediate family. You have both loved me unconditionally and patiently. I love you both so very much.

I thank every single person I have ever met who has in some way left their mark on me. I thank all my unnamed role models, both those publicly known and those known in my memory and heart. For those whose names are not listed and you feel you deserve to be, you are listed in my heart. Thanks for understanding my limitation of memory and space.

Foreword

I want to get straight to the point. Adilah thinks outside the box.

She provokes us to think outside the box.

On My Own Terms takes us on a wonderful, personal journey through the eyes of a Black woman into the unique yet familiar perspective of making it as a Black actress. Her experience is unique and even peculiar to so many simply because she *is* Black in America, *and* a woman in the world.

This book is a *must-read* for any young Black actor or actress who is serious about acting, making a living at it with integrity, and making it their life's work. It's not about stardom, even though the writer has many varied personal relationships and interactions with stars. It's about the integrity and the joys of working, with its highs, lows, disappointments, frustrations, desires, fears, hopes, and dreams that are shared by so many who are Black.

On My Own Terms is not only to be read by those who are Black. It is also to be read by those who are young of any race or culture, to gain a reality check and understanding of the sacrifices to be made for this acting world you dare to enter.

It's not to be read by just the young, either. For those experienced veterans who have been around awhile, it is a wonderful jaunt down memory lane, reminding us old birds and hawks of why we went into this business in the first place. Adilah renews the spirits for those of us who have been burned, and made to feel like our noses are pressed up against the window pane, looking in, wishing we could join in, but feeling locked out.

The reader learns of the exciting beginnings of the Los Angeles Women's Theatre Festival, and Adilah's own successful solo play (which is inspiring), and you come to understand just how entities like this are born and destined to become great. The birth of Adilah's own show can inspire us all to renew our commitment to our dreams and life's pursuit of our performance art.

Adilah has inspired me personally as an artist and a writer to write some of my own stories for other actresses to learn from, having worked in her *Wisdom Wednesdays* writing workshop. *On My Own Terms* gives me personal inspiration and courage to continue to take control of my own opportunities as an actress, to give and teach through my work.

One of the most exciting and illuminating moments of her book was when her solo play provoked an intelligent question of thought and compassion from an Anglo audience member who was obviously moved by her performance: "How can we erase racism in this country?" *Now, that's what theater is all about!* That's exciting. That's what makes a difference when it's all said and done: provoking people to thoughts and dialogue they need to have in order to learn from one another.

I thank Adilah for writing this book and mentioning plays that people don't know or have forgotten, for they are not being revived with any regularity on the Great White Way or even in Equity Regional Theatre. It took us until the year 2005 to name a Broadway Theater after a Black playwright, and I personally resent the fact that America only wants to recognize one. At some point, our young Black intellectuals eventually research these matters and are always shocked when they dig up our colorful, buried literary history—the archived Black actors and playwrights associated with that history.

Adilah is part of that colorful history. She invokes the names of great Black playwrights and actors, not just one. She archives and memorializes some who have since passed on. Adilah's book makes a valuable research tool for that very reason.

Adilah also reveals how truly exhausting chasing our profession can be and the hindsight of sacrifices that must be made and weighed along the way, which is equal to great advice.

I am personally honored to write Adilah's foreword. I consider Adilah to be a successful business artist, the rare artist; the one who has great artistic skill, aesthetic taste, teaching ability, and creativity, accompanied by great business acumen. That rare artist and teacher is Adilah Barnes.

Adilah has successfully blended art, business, and integrity in *On My Own Terms*. How wonderful of her to share her artistic soul with us. I especially enjoyed her "entrepreneur" story at age eleven. It made me smile, because it seemed so prophetic for the Adilah she was destined to become and the one I've come to know and admire. I especially enjoyed the space she shares when she answers the questions from the audience about her choice of characters. She exhibits the genteel patience to educate others even in the face of their own emotional anger, due to their own ignorance. Her "quiet tone" regarding that situation teaches us "class."

Yes, Adilah's book is moving, informative, entertaining, educational, and insightful. But what is of paramount importance to me is its *archival* nature. Who else to tell our stories but one of us?

Adilah shares her encounters with us as she interacts with those who are destined to become stars and those who are already stars. There are so many wonderful things I can say about *On My Own Terms*, but you, the reader, will experience her words for yourself.

There is no real contemporary guide for Black women making it in this particular business. This is as close to anything you might read which is personal and honest.

Not many Black actresses even share their very real and intimate experiences and how those experiences affect them deeply. As we are trying to succeed and establish our careers, we raise children, experience death of loved ones, face prejudice and racism, and deal with decisions of marriage and other things that affect us and our loved ones.

So we are joyous as we read and champion the constant courage and determination that Adilah shows in mounting her own dreams and continuing to do so.

She did it. She did it with dignity and love for the craft. She did it *on her own terms,* and the reward was great. Yeah!!!

So enjoy the journey, and allow Adilah's insights and life triumphs and tribulations to entertain you, inform you, and cause you much pause for reflection.

Ella Joyce

Introduction

Not every working actor is a household name. I am a testament to that truth. I represent a cadre of actors who have carved out a niche in "the industry" without the luxuries and distractions of fame.

As Bill Ball, founder of the American Conservatory Theater (ACT) in San Francisco, once told my acting class, "Fame is more trouble than it's worth." Although arguable, what is certain is that it is possible to find some measure of creative fulfillment and personal satisfaction without all the trappings of that sought-after thing called *fame*. Since most actors will never know fame, my voice speaks for the unsung, yet deserving artist.

My story is a humble one.

In the late 1980s, students of my American Conservatory Theater Summer Training Congress class presented me with a beautifully bound white journal with dried flowers on the cover. Inside was a slip of paper they had all signed. They let me know the book was mine to make use of when I decided to write my own acting book. I thank them for the vision of this book before I saw it.

As I discuss within these covers, those planted words seemed very, very far away. At that point, I had no intention of writing a book of any sort. Yet my students planted the seed.

Fast forward to 2008.

I share in this book my personal journey as an actor who first stepped foot onstage at the tender age of sixteen. In writing this book, I was not led to write a traditional "how-to" acting book, but rather a book that chronicles my story of over four decades. Perhaps, by example, this book will still qualify as an acting book of sorts and hold some measure of inspiration for others.

I have not sought fame or wealth. However, I have sought to maintain my status as a working actor committed to projects I am proud of. I especially want to speak to those reading this book whose sense of integrity carries more weight than "making it" in the business. I do understand your challenge.

At its essence, this book is meant to center around my own journey as a creative being. Whatever may be learned about my personal life is incidental and intended mainly to connect my artistic dots along the way.

I have also chosen to protect many I mention. Some I do not want to identify by name because it would be unkind. For that reason, some are mentioned without reference to any name. In other cases, I do not want to overstep the privacy of others because it would not have furthered *my* story.

Many thanks to anyone who picks this book up and stays with it until the last page. If I am able to engage any reader from start to finish, perhaps I have succeeded in my attempt to reach out and touch another.

Here is *my* story.

Chapter One

Sixteen

You must begin wherever you are.
—Jack Boland, Founding Minister,
The Church of Today

We were an unlikely royal family: me, an African American queen, flanked by my Anglo king, our blonde, blue-eyed daughter, and her African American suitor. There we were, all in our mix-matched majesty.

The play was A. A. Milne's *The Ugly Duckling*. It was the summer of 1966. The place was Project Upward Bound at California State University, Chico, and this was my very first play. In this college preparatory program for "disadvantaged youth," we were given the choice of two electives. I only remember the one I chose.

Drama was mine.

Aside from my Oro Vista Baptist Church's Annual Easter and Christmas recitations as a child in Oroville, this was my entry into what would become my lifelong profession. I had no idea as a teen that acting would become my career calling as an adult.

Before that summer, my sights were set on becoming an English teacher. I often brought together neighborhood kids during the summer months, where I would cut up pieces of recycled paper and play the teacher. Looking back, I don't remember anyone ever challenging me for my coveted role. It was just understood that I was the teacher, and they were not. I never became an English teacher but I did become an acting teacher.

What a blessing it was to know my calling to teach at such a young age.

In *The Ugly Duckling*, I was simply satisfied playing the lead role of the queen in a world of make believe. I was allowed to magically enter a period of time foreign to me. My costume reflected a long-gone era, and I spoke in a cadence unlike my own. I embraced the heightened language with open arms.

I can still see my mother sitting in the front row of our makeshift theatre leading the audience in applause composed of family, friends, and Upward Bound staff and students. On the "stage" was her baby daughter. She was proud of me and her smiling face made me feel proud, too.

I had never experienced anything quite like the joy of being onstage. At that point in my life, my creative outlet had been writing short stories, a solitary expression; or participating in church programs at church. Now, here I was, with an ensemble of would-be young actors testing the waters of theatre. I loved every minute of the imagination, attention, and escapism of my newfound world.

Larry Dick, our director, chose a form of non-traditional casting I later came to know as "color-blind" casting. Young and idealistic, Larry cast each of us based on talent, not race. I did not realize then that I had entered theatrics in a very evolved way.

I did not know then that casting based on talent rather than other considerations would not always be the norm.

I would come to perform in other "color-blind," non-traditionally cast plays from time to time, such as Charles Dickens' *A Christmas Carol* at the American Conservatory Theater (ACT) in San Francisco. In that production, as Mrs. Cratchit, I looked around the dinner table at my rainbow tribe of ethnically diverse children who surrounded me during each performance.

In Shozo Sato's production of *Kabuki Medea* at Berkeley Repertory Theatre, I was made-up nightly in white face. I played a Japanese chorus member and wore a colorful satin kimono. When asked if I wanted to color my neck white, I declined because I wanted it to be known that one of the actors was, in fact, Black.

Kabuki Medea came to be the most physically demanding play I have ever performed in. There were long stretches where the chorus stood motionless in stylized Japanese positions, feet angled, and knees slightly bent onstage with our backs turned to the audience. We internally occupied ourselves as we looked at a beautifully painted canvas of Japanese trees on the upstage wall. We listened and patiently waited for our "cue" to move.

Offstage, we learned a very long and complex Japanese dance as part of our rehearsal process. At each rehearsal, Shozo added another movement to the very intricate and spiritual dance. The dance was never meant to be performed onstage. Its purpose was to strengthen our concentration through movement, increase our appreciation for the Japanese culture, and to create a stronger sense of ensemble.

I never excelled at the intricate dance, but I did my best.

This production was also one of the most spiritual plays I have ever performed in. We "cleansed" the stage floor as we stretched our way across it. Before the theatre doors opened, we gracefully moved on our hands and knees like four-legged animals with towels, as shown by our director. Our stage cleansing was a symbolic gesture honoring our sacred space.

A Christmas Carol and *Kabuki Medea* made clear to me that audiences would accept any reality presented them onstage, as long as the actors believed the same. In *A Christmas Carol*, I recall affluent, primarily Anglo, audiences stiffening as my Anglo stage husband, played by Ed Hodson, lovingly kissed and embraced me onstage each performance. I also remember feeling them relax in their seats as they accepted our reality.

They believed because we believed.

In *Kabuki Medea,* I received my highest compliment when a petite and hesitant older Japanese woman approached me after one performance.

She lit up as she shyly blurted out, "Now *you* were Japanese!"

Despite those wonderful early experiences, I later learned I could not always expect color-blind casting in the real world of make believe.

I still wonder from time to time whatever happened to my very first acting teacher and director, Larry Dick. I never saw nor heard his name after Project Upward Bound. I recently googled him, but the Larry Dick I found was not him. I thank him on these pages for providing a safe environment to freely create in my first play.

He taught me that anything was possible onstage.

Without such a warm introduction to theatre, I am not sure I would have continued on my path as an actor.

As an acting teacher myself, I try to meet my actors where they are. I see myself as having a metaphoric chain full of keys. Each key opens the creativity of actors in different ways. I always respect and honor the vulnerability and trust actors place in me. Much damage can be done to actors by a teacher who does not understand how fragile the ego may be. As the adage goes, "You can get more with honey than vinegar." That adage sometimes makes the difference in unlocking creativity within an actor. My hand is firm, yet nurturing.

Upward Bound was my bridge to the performing arts, and, as theatre often can, it strengthened my sense of self-confidence. Theatre was a healing vessel for me.

In fifth grade, a part of me lost sight of who I was when I was struck with petit mal epilepsy. Unsure of myself during that very painful time in my life, I retreated inside myself.

My symptoms caused an involuntary and momentary trancelike state. I would lose awareness of myself, my surroundings, and of time. I had no warning of an oncoming episode, but I always knew when I had just come out of one. I was left feeling lightheaded, hot, and disoriented. My toes gripped themselves inside my shoes so intensely, they ached in pain afterwards.

Petit mal epilepsy was at once terrifying and embarrassing. I could never remember what happened during each brief time lapse. Misunderstood, the disease also attracted ridicule. I felt a brand of shame I had no control over. My mother and others who knew no other way to explain my condition said I had "fits."

I had no clue what was wrong with me until I one day stumbled upon a copy of the Physician's Desk Reference book somewhere and was divinely led to look up my symptoms. When I read the description for petit mal epilepsy, I knew intuitively that was what I had.

I suffered for three years before one day the petit mal epilepsy disappeared as inexplicably as it had come. There was a two-year gap between eighth grade, when I was freed from the bondage of my alienating affliction, and the time of Upward Bound's salvation. It was Upward Bound that helped me regain my sense of well-being, confidence, and worth. Unlike Humpty Dumpty, the overall nurturance I received from faculty, staff, and students alike helped put me back together again.

Looking back, I can now see how Upward Bound invested fully in me. Assistant Director, Mr. Groff, who was old enough even then to be my grandfather, would sometimes invite me to his Gridley, California home to spend time with his loving wife and daughter. One of our many "family" outings included a trip to Sacramento to shop at Macy's Department Store. There, I saw a gorgeous yellow and white flowered chiffon spring dress with a white collar. I wanted it. The problem was I had no money to buy it. Sensing my want, Mr. Groff purchased the dress for me along with matching yellow patent leather sandals on *my* condition that I repay him.

Little by little, I paid off my debt.

Had it not been for meeting my mentor, Dr. J. Herman Blake from the University of California at Santa Cruz (UCSC), one Upward Bound summer in either 1966 or 1967, I probably would have followed Mr. Groff's daughter, Linda, to La Verne College in La Verne, California.

Due in great part to finding myself in Project Upward Bound, I began to excel at Oroville High School. Trying to make up for lost time, I was hungry to do as much as I could before I graduated. I earned membership in the National Honor Society (NHS), California Scholastic Federation (CSF), French Club, Service Club, became editor of the *Tiger Tales* school newspaper, was elected Senior Class Secretary, and was voted in as one of our three valedictorian speakers at our senior graduation. I competed statewide in public speaking competitions for the Lions Club. Thanks to Mr. Hughes, my French teacher who nominated me, I was also named *Girl of the Month* by the Soroptimist Club, an international service organization for women. Translated from Latin, the word *soroptimist* means "the best for women."

These accomplishments were no small feat in a rural high school with approximately fifty African American students out of a student body population of about 1,200. Clearly, I had become a high achiever in high school and received substantial recognition for my many scholastic accomplishments at school, in Upward Bound, and in my community.

Anything seemed possible.

I applied to UCSC despite the advice of my counselor, Mrs. Kunkel.

Looking over her bifocals, she questioned me using my birth name. "Lovey, don't you think Chico State might be a more realistic sight for you, instead of the University?"

I was stunned at what I heard.

I was set on going to UCSC, and applied only to that campus. I banked on getting accepted, and fortunately for me, I did.

Victory was mine when I was accepted into UCSC and proved Mrs. Kunkel wrong.

My birthplace of Oroville was a Northern California town that seemed to have been airlifted from the South and dropped in the Sacramento Valley. It was a small town of busybodies, rednecks, and a Black community that indeed raised each child. It was many years later before I made the connection between people I knew and observed as a child, and how they so greatly influenced me. My town folk strongly impacted my view of the world and my truth as an actor. I grew up around people who were as colorful as their names: Jinky Joe, Dan the Man, Poppa Skeeta, Tin Hat, Winky, Chilly Willie, Pimp Sam, Boots, Pootie, Dimple, Poncho, Bubble, Queen Esther, Cat, Chicken, Man, Joon Joon, and Spider.

I can still see old man Jinky Joe in his raggedy, unwashed green station wagon as he crept down our unpaved streets. Chilly Willy, Luther Tobias, Bubble Johnson, and Poncho Berry had so much style in their strides that it was like watching heated molasses unfold with each step. They were *just* that cool. On the other hand, Dan the Man was feared because of his dark energy. I kept my distance from him because he was mysterious, quiet, and he did not play.

Many in my community were "first-generation South," meaning those who were born in the South and had moved to California. Their rich speech echoed the cadences of our Southern ancestors.

I can still hear Aunt Ester emphatically saying things like, "I'm trying to tell you!", "You better know it!" and "Chile, honey hush!"

Though I left for college at eighteen, my ear never forgot the authenticity of that rich, earthy language. In my later portrayal of the likes of Sojourner Truth, Harriet Tubman, Mary McLeod Bethune, and others, I have come back time and again to the richness of that same language in its many cadences, shades, and rhythms.

The people I knew as a child would never describe themselves as storytellers, but they were. They thought they were just recounting memories, but they were people who could weave a story in such a way that you saw exactly the picture they were trying to paint for you. I often lingered on their every word. They created different voices for their characters, switched up rhythms, and knew how to throw in guttural laughter from time to time for good measure.

Looking back, those town-folk I watched and listened to in great detail gave me my earliest exposure to gifted storytellers and actors.

It's no wonder I learned how to tell a good story myself. My ear was trained from some of the best. Many lacked formal education, yet they were some of the most intelligent and educated people I have ever met. My brother Hollis often sat with the "winos" at "the barrel" around a fire listening to the wisdom of unlikely teachers.

In 2005, I learned something I never knew. At my brother's untimely funeral, my sister Norma recounted that many of those who sat around the barrel had gone to college only to find that jobs were not awaiting them. With unfulfilled dreams, many turned to the bottle to numb their feelings to cope with a life that held less than what they deserved.

The stories my brother heard both bothered and inspired him. Seeing the promise in my brother, many of the "winos" encouraged my brother to go on to college. The elders in my community wanted more for the youth than they may have had.

In truth, my entire village raised the young ones.

"Sense memory," or early memory that stems from the senses, has stayed with me and connects me emotionally in my work over and over again. When I want to experience a feeling of love between a mother and child, I conjure up the scent of Clorox. The "trigger" is the memory of my mother brushing and combing my hair for school. Every Wednesday she would stop her early morning wash to comb my hair. With the scent of Clorox still on her hands, I sat between my mother's warm, dark thighs on cold, worn linoleum floors while she groomed me for school. To this day, Clorox brings back the memory of my mother's loving hands. Whenever I now sit on the floor between a woman's legs to get my hair braided, the warmth of thighs takes me back to my childhood and my mother's loving touch.

That position between thighs is soothing to me.

Other strong childhood scents include cod liver oil, castor oil, and marigold flowers. My two younger brothers, Ellis and Edward, and I were forced to take those two oils to stay healthy. The thought of them still makes me want to vomit on the spot.

Marigolds, on the other hand, take me back to pleasant spring and summer memories of beautiful homes with lawns I passed walking up and down nearby streets like Burlington Avenue. Marigolds also soothe me.

They smell like home.

As an acting teacher, I sometimes use "sensory exercises" to trigger childhood memories. Whichever emotions we experience as adults, we first experienced as children. If an actor gets in touch with sense memory, he can enrich his work.

Former ACT Artistic Director Ed Hastings once pointed out to me "method acting," or systematic acting taught by master acting teachers, is only needed when actors are stuck and need something to jump-start them.

Otherwise, actors are continually making sensory and emotional connections subconsciously without even knowing it.

For me, the senses of smell and hearing are probably my most charged. Oldies songs immediately take me back to specific times, places and people. I can associate dances like "The Jerk" and "Four Corners" with a time, place and people. Clothing like bell-bottoms and miniskirts connect me to an era of music gone by. Music from the '60's—especially that of the Supremes, the Miracles, and the Temptations—is particularly rich for me. Some of my favorite songs that hold memories are songs like "Come See About Me" by the Supremes, "Really Got a Hold on Me" by the Miracles, "Stay in My Corner" by the Dells, and "My Girl" by the Temptations.

I can often tell you what was going on in my life at a given time by listening to a specific song.

In my youth, I was influenced by Black actors who would later become acting role models. One role model from childhood was Cicely Tyson. I remember her from the socially-conscious and highly controversial television series *East Side, West Side* with E.G. Marshall. The show premiered September of 1963 and only lasted one season. Cicely had the recurring role of secretary Jane Foster. She had a "natural" hairdo at the time. Afros were not fashionable then, so she made a huge personal statement by wearing one. Although embarrassed by her look at the time, I now respect her for her unconventional boldness.

In those days, seeing a Black face on television other than on the comedy series *Amos and Andy* was so rare that in Black homes across America, one was likely to hear someone yell out, "Everybody, come quick. There's somebody colored on TV!"

Whenever the announcement was made in my home, everyone stopped whatever they were doing to come get a good seat. We felt proud to see ourselves on television, and because it was so rare, we did not want to miss such an important moment.

The acting bug bit me as a teenager and over forty years later, I am *still* passionate about my work. I have been blessed to make a living by doing what I am trained to do. At the same time, I have chosen to fiercely guard my integrity both personally and professionally.

I have also maintained a quote from Ms. Tyson as my credo: "There are many times that I have been broke, but I have never been broken."

Without question, the most significant African American role model in those early days in the 1960's was actor Mr. Sidney Poitier. Each Sunday, I walked over a mile to our downtown movie theatre to sit in the plush State Theatre. On the rare occasions when I saw him on the screen, I sat straight up in my seat, transfixed. I most remember him in movies like *Lilies of the Field, To Sir, With Love,* and *Guess Who's Coming to Dinner.*

It was not uncommon for tears to roll down my cheeks during dramatic moments in Mr. Poitier's films. I took in his every eloquent word as I sat in the dark, eating my shoestring potato chips one by one.

Mr. Poitier was handsome, proud, and he looked just like me. He made me feel proud to be Black. Squinting my eyes on Sundays as I walked out of the movie theatre in the sunlight, I always felt a little taller after seeing him onscreen.

Little did I know I would eventually have the opportunity to meet Mr. Poitier in person. Initially, I had the pleasure of being in his company socially twice in Los Angeles but could not muster up the courage to approach him. I could not form words to speak. However, I promised myself that if there ever came a *third* time, I would force myself to walk up to him.

The third time came.

In 1993 at the National Black Theatre Festival I spotted him in the crowded lobby of the official hotel in Winston-Salem, North Carolina.

I probably would have passed up yet another opportunity to meet Mr. Poitier, had I not made that promise to myself.

When I finally got up enough nerve to approach Mr. Poitier, I began with something like, "Mr. Poitier, I was in your company twice before. I could not bring myself to walk up to you then but I promised myself that if a third time ever came, I would introduce myself. My name is Adilah Barnes."

He stopped.

He looked through me with his piercing eyes. I think he was struck most by my sincerity, because he gave me his full attention as I stood in front of him. During the short time we spent together in conversation, it was as if time had stopped and no one else existed in that crowded lobby. It was as if we were in an invisible and impenetrable bubble together.

Among other things, I remember blurting out something like, "You made me feel so proud as a child when I watched your movies in my little home town of Oroville, California. I just want to thank you for all that you have given to Black people, and for changing the way we were seen on the big screen. Thank you for opening the door wider for actors like me."

He listened.

I was surprised to hear Mr. Poitier say, "And you, my dear, will do greater things."

I said, "Oh, no, Mr. Poitier, I could not possibly do more than you have!"

There must have been something in our body language that stopped anyone from interrupting us, because no one approached us. Once we were done talking, Mr. Poitier hugged and kissed me on the cheek.

It was only when we began to move away from each other that fans began to yell out things like, "Mr. Poitier! Mr. Poitier! May I have an autograph?" or "Mr. Poitier, I love your work!"

I stood in that hotel doorway and watched Mr. Sidney Poitier move toward his black limo, graciously signing autographs along the way. He turned and gave me a smile with his final look as he stepped inside.

I had approached him humbly. I spoke from my heart. Because of that, I had no need to ask for his autograph.

As fate would have it, I met Mr. Sidney Poitier again a short while later at the 100th birthday celebration for the late Paul Robeson, given by Danny Glover's Robey Theatre Company in 1998.

I remember that evening in great detail. It was at the Actor's Gang Theatre, located at the time in Hollywood on Santa Monica Boulevard. Mr. Poitier had a front-row seat, along with the likes of the late Brock Peters and Mamie Hansberry, sister of the late playwright Lorraine Hansberry.

The place was packed.

Danny Glover, my longtime friend from California's Bay Area, was hosting the event. Danny spotted me from the stage at one point and acknowledged me with a smile. I smiled back. A short while later, Danny came offstage and headed towards me. He bent over me while someone on the program was still speaking onstage. He whispered, "I have a poem here by Pablo Neruda. Alfre Woodard was supposed to read it, but she can't make it tonight. I want you to read it." My heart began to palpitate as I asked Danny how long the poem was.

He simply said, "Three pages."

I gasped. "Three pages!"

He said, "Yeah, read it."

I agreed on one condition: "As long as you announce to the audience that this is my first time seeing this poem."

He agreed.

I read.

That evening I experienced one of my most fulfilling moments onstage. The icing on the cake was that I read in front of my childhood idol, Mr. Sidney Poiter. I again had his full attention. I almost melted in my seat as he complimented me onstage in front of over 200 people. He said something like, "I was asked to read that poem, but declined. I could not have brought more justice to that poem than the young lady you just heard."

Mr. Poitier had now seen me onstage and given me his nod.

Danny smiled afterwards as he jokingly said to the audience, "It's all in the casting." The audience responded with a spontaneous laugh.

That evening held a very important lesson for an actor.

Always be ready.

I have since run into Mr. Poitier on two other occasions. I saw him next in January of 2007 at Angela and John Witherspoon's 1st Anniversary celebration of the Artpeace Gallery, their beautiful art gallery in Burbank, California that primarily honors exhibits by African American visual artists. I stood next to Mr. Poitier as we appreciated artwork on display that evening. I reminded him of our prior meetings. Because he is so gracious, I am not sure he actually remembered me but he listened as I reminded him of the two other times we had shared a moment on our crossed paths.

As of this writing, our most recent exchange took place at Roscoe Lee Browne's memorial service at the Mark Taper Forum in Los Angeles on April 22, 2007. Upon walking inside the Mark Taper, I was surprised to find the theatre pitch black. A very moving retrospective montage of Roscoe's television and film work was being shown onscreen. The audience laughed wildly in recognition of some of Roscoe's most funny moments on camera that demonstrated his acerbic tongue.

It was next to impossible to get to a seat in that room of darkness.

I was finally urged to move aside by those so impatient to claim a seat they were willing to forge ahead in darkness. As I cautiously waited for enough light to make my way up the stairs of the nearby aisle, I heard a woman say, "There are two seats here." Although I was not seated in the center section that I preferred, I sat two seats over from her to allow another seat for a gentleman who was behind me. I sat and he almost landed in my lap as he quickly followed me. Like me, his eyes were not yet accustomed to the darkness. I guided him over to his seat as I whispered, "Your seat is here."

He whispered back, "Thank you."

Settled in, we both began to immerse ourselves in Roscoe's memorial service, hearing touching remembrances from the likes of Laurence Fishburne, Brenda Vaccaro, Anthony Yerbe, Gordon Davidson, Roscoe's niece and nephew, and Martin Sheen. Although I felt the man next to me, I never tried to look in his face. I felt him trying to see who was next to him at one point, but I never looked directly his way.

At one point, I felt an impulse to glance at him, but I never did. Although I did not, I could feel him as we laughed at some of the same moments, or when we responded individually to different moments in the program.

When Roscoe's partner of thirty-eight years, Anthony Zerbe, began to speak of Sir Sidney Poitier and how he could not make it, the gentleman next to me raised his hand and yelled out, "I am here." I was stunned as I looked next to me for the first time and saw Mr. Sidney Poitier.

I said to him, "I had *no* idea I was sitting next to you!"

He asked if he should go down and I said' "Absolutely!"

When asked from the podium by Anthony Zerbe if he wanted to speak, Mr. Poitier stood and further yelled out, "I do!"

He proudly made his way down to the stage, our moment together having come to a close. Being the prankster that Roscoe could be, I am sure he had something to do with that *seeming* coincidence. I thank Roscoe for placing Mr. Poitier and me unknowingly next to each other.

I am glad I followed my intuition to attend the service that day because I heard words I so needed to hear at that moment in my life. I was inspired by others who spoke, and I was reminded how blessed I am to have been given my gift as an actor. I was also reminded that we all have our inner struggles and demons. Although concealed behind his love and mastery of language, Roscoe owned his, too.

The day of Roscoe Lee Browne's memorial service made my fourth exchange with Mr. Sidney Poitier. The former three times we shared a brief conversation. This day we sat together silently in the dark sharing a heartfelt celebration for the irreplaceable Roscoe Lee Browne.

Chapter Two

Just Call Her a Woman of the Soil

I raised you to be a thoroughbred, so run your own race.
—Danny Thomas to daughter Marla

I t has been said that behind every great man there is a woman. Taking that saying a bit further, I believe that behind every accomplished child, there is usually an influential parent standing nearby.

And so it was with me.

In order to fully understand who I am, it is important to recognize the fabric I come from. My uncompromising sense of integrity, initiating spirit, and grit has everything to do with my mother, Mosea Lee Barnes. It is for this reason that I have included a chapter in this book that is centered around her.

She is worthy.

If I were to name the fabric of my mother, it would be burlap: earthy, practical, sturdy, and a little rough around the edges. My mother was born the eldest of twelve children in McComb, Mississippi, and was raised on a family farm. She was born December 12, 1912.

Twelve, twelve, twelve.

In fact, numbers are significant for other members of my family, as well. There is my son, Tariq, who has an uncanny relationship with the number seven. He was born on the seventh day, seventh month, seventy-seven. He was born the seventh hour, weighed seven pounds, and was his father's seventh child.

Seven, seven, seven.

Much to my mother's disappointment, she had to quit secondary school to help her family work their farmland. I thought, until the writing of this book, that my grandparents had a very small farm but my Uncle Herman set me straight. The Osby family actually owned 180 acres of land that had been left to my grandmother by her mother, Grandma Delia, daughter of Grandma Martha, a slave.

Speaking of Grandma Martha, my mother used to tell me stories about my great-great grandmother who was my mother's great-grandmother. My mother shared that Grandma Martha was a woman of very tall stature who always wore starched white aprons. She lived to be well over 100 years old and still remembered the institution of slavery in very vivid terms. My mother told me that sometimes Grandma Martha would go to faraway places in her mind as she recounted some of the horrific memories of slavery. She would say things like, "Massa, please don't let 'em beat him no 'mo. He's bleedin'."

Although Grandma Martha went blind in her last days, while she still had dimming eyesight, she would take my mother and other children out into the woods to look for hickory nuts. She could still see well enough to point out the nuts that my mother and the other children would pick up, as instructed. I was fascinated by stories of this strong woman who outlived slavery and whose blood runs through my family's veins. I could deeply feel the atrocities and emotional scars from Grandma Martha's recounted memories passed on to me from my mother.

Back to the story of my family's land in Mississippi. Of that acreage, 100 acres were used for farmland to raise cotton and vegetables to live off of and to provide income. Eighty acres of that land were used to pasture hogs, cows, horses, mules and chickens. Because my grandparents birthed twelve children, they had sufficient help and were able to profit well from their land.

When I asked my older sister Norma what she remembered of our family history, she said, "All I remember is that Granny and Grandpa Flowers had a lot of land. I thought they were rich."

My mother and father Edward Barnes, later sharecropped for a nearby Mr. Brock. He primarily owned pecan orchards that they tended. My Uncle Herman shared an interesting aside about that Mr. Brock. Apparently after my grandparents and most of the family had moved to Woodleaf, California, Mr. Brock decided he wanted to buy that 180 acres, but my family would not sell. He wanted the land because Highway 55 was coming and would cut right through the acreage. He wanted to profit by buying the land and then turn around to sell it for the building of the highway.

He knew that as long as anyone lived on the property, my grandmother would not sell. Mr. Brock finally convinced someone the family knew, to burn down the house to force my family to sell. My Uncle Thado, along with our cousins Fred and Ethyl Everett, had houses they were living in on the property, but they were forced to move after the burning.

My grandparents did sell the acreage, but they were also shrewd business people. They negotiated well by keeping half the mineral rights that still belong to the Osby family today. My sister Norma still remembers the time when my grandmother received a handsome check from oil on the property. My sister recounts that my grandmother divided the money with all of her many children.

This family story is only one of many where African Americans were forced to give up land in the South through racism, coercion, physical force and the use of intimidation.

Although my mother loved school, she only got as far as the eighth grade. A woman in a child's body, she told me she began to learn to cook at three years old.

Judging by her extraordinary talents in the kitchen, I believe her.

My mother learned two very important lessons from her humble beginnings: to value the earth and to value a formal education—something she did not have.

Given her love of education, my mother took great pride in my brother Hollis, who became the first college graduate in my immediate family. He received a Master's Degree in Social Welfare from the University of California at Los Angeles in the mid '60s.

Hollis made our mother very proud. He also inspired the rest of our family to think bigger. He proved to all of us that a college education was attainable. My cousin, Tobie Burton Marsh, followed his lead and graduated from Cal State, Long Beach. I became the third person in our immediate family to become a college graduate, graduating from the University of California at Santa Cruz in 1972. Others in our family including Derrie Osby, Christine Burton, Theresa Moore Colvin, and Venita Jacobson have since earned their college and law degrees.

Had my mother lived a few years longer, my brother would have made her even more proud when he went back to school after retiring from his civilian post with the U.S. Army. During his professional career for the army, he headed social service programs for the military throughout the world. Like many, he looked forward to retiring.

Also like many, my brother had not seriously thought about life beyond retirement. In his early days of retirement, he busied himself as a volunteer by preparing taxes for seniors. He also obtained a real estate license, but neither post-retirement endeavor seemed to fully satisfy and challenge him. He wanted to do more than just keep busy. He wanted his life to still have valuable meaning, and to keep his mind sharp.

Hollis took on perhaps the biggest challenge of his work career when he decided to become an attorney. Tears rolled down my face as I witnessed him walking across the stage at the University of Oregon to receive his law degree in 2000. My family watched as he sat in his seat surrounded by other graduates who were young enough to be his children. He was the oldest law graduate in his class.

Hollis earned his law degree just shy of his 59th birthday. He also passed the Oregon bar on his first attempt. Until his sudden death on August 11, 2005, caused by a tragic auto accident, my brother was a practicing attorney in Klamath Falls, Oregon.

Having a second career after retirement, he was living proof that you are never too old to start a new career.

Like myself, Hollis comes from that same burlap cloth, Mosea Lee Barnes. Coming from a very humble beginning, he and I sometimes beat seemingly insurmountable odds.

In many ways, my mother was a self-taught woman. She never stopped learning. Possessing a curious mind, she loved to read and write. I never knew my mother to be without a subscription to our small-town newspaper, then called the *Oroville Mercury*. With black-rimmed bifocal reading glasses, she daily read our newspaper from front to back. On Wednesdays, "sale paper day," she also mapped out which stores had the best buys on meats, produce, and staples. She would drive from Currier Bros. Market to Wentz Supermarket to Barnes Market just to save a few pennies on groceries.

My mother also read passages from the Bible nightly before going to bed. She enjoyed spending her time at the end of each day in silence. Living alone in later years, much to my surprise, my mother traded her nighttime silence for a bedroom radio that she left playing all night long. Living alone by then, the radio seemed to keep her company.

Although one who believed in the Bible, my mother was fascinated by what some might call "the occult." She privately relished reading her dog-eared astrology and dream books. Like her, I used her tattered dream books to interpret my dreams.

My mother also knew more superstitions than I could ever memorize. I have forgotten many of them, but I remember my mother saying things like, "Watch that broom, girl. You know if you sweep somebody's feet, they goin' to jail. That's why Bluford runs every time he sees somebody sweepin'." She would also say, "Girl, I know I'm a git me some money, cause my right palm is itchin'." When she heard a howling dog in the night, she would say, "Somebody is gon' die." Dropping a comb with hair in it meant a man would be visiting soon. Saying a person's name when you meant to say another person's name meant the mistaken person was talking about you. Many a time I would hear my mother say, "So-and-so must be talkin' 'bout me." You could remove seven years of bad luck from a broken mirror by running cold water over it. It was bad luck if your left eye jumped, good luck if the right.

My mother also made sure that during thunderstorms, we turned the television, radio, or record player off. Many a day we would sit in silence as we waited for a storm to pass. We were told to sit without speaking until God silenced the skies. It was in those moments of quiet that I felt the awesome power of God. We were taught to honor God's presence through thunder and lightning.

Although she was limited to letter-writing, my mother used her pen to stay in touch with faraway loved ones. She also made sure she sent Christmas cards out every December in her distinctive handwriting. In letters written to me, she always ended formally with, "Your mother, Mosea Lee Barnes."

My mother was a consummate homemaker. She prepared our meals from scratch, had piping-hot meals ready for us when we returned home from school each day, canned fresh fruit and vegetables for our long, cold winters, sewed many of our clothes on her shiny black Singer sewing machine, raised a garden each year, caught more fish at the creek than many men, raised chickens, and did not hesitate to wring the necks of those same chickens for our Sunday dinners.

We, too, felt guiltless as we ate her succulent fried chicken or her mouth-watering chicken smothered in onions and gravy. I have not yet met anyone who could outfry or cut up a whole chicken into more pieces than my mother. We would purchase many of our chickens as tiny "biddies," but they were raised to be eaten, not for pets.

It never dawned on me that my mother may have wanted to do something else with her life until I took a writing class where we began to discuss our mothers. When our instructor, Nancy Agabian, asked about our mothers' dreams, I realized I did not know that side of my mother. I knew her as a homemaker. I never thought seriously about her any other way.

I could not wait to get home that night to call her. She was one who could talk on the telephone for hours, so it was no surprise she was already on the phone when I called. A time before call waiting, I had to wait for her to clear her phone line.

When I finally reached her, I said, "Mom, if you could have been anything you wanted, what would you have been?"

I was met by silence.

And more silence.

When I gently asked the question a second time, she finally spoke. "I don't know," she mumbled. After my third try, I could hardly hear her soft voice as she said, "I used to like teaching Sunday School."

A teacher.

In that moment, I understood fully why Mom encouraged me to become an English teacher. Although I had become an acting teacher, I was a teacher nonetheless. After that conversation, I was especially glad I was.

What became very clear to me in that conversation was the importance of actualizing our dreams.

I now understand my mother may have settled for less than she wanted. I also realize it may have been so long since she had allowed herself to dream that she had to take her time to remember.

As a child, I would periodically hear her say, "I didn't want to have any chaps, but now that you are all here, I love you."

Coming along during a time before birth control, my mother had had children out of circumstance, not choice. After our conversation that night, I also realized how much she had sacrificed for all seven of us. Oddly enough, my mother was twenty-three years old when she gave birth to my oldest sister, Dorothy.

In 1936, that was relatively old to be having a first child.

My Vietnamese manicurist talked to me once about her life. She talked about how she works seven days a week in her shop to make ends meet. She talked about how tired she is from working, and how she does not want to live a long life.

Shocked, I said, "You don't?"

She said, "No, not my life."

In that moment, I was reminded that many people do work because it is "a job." As a teacher, I encourage my acting students to follow their passion rather than settle for something they do not want to do. To lessen any apprehensions they may harbor about being able to support themselves by their craft, I ask them to release their fears of making it in the business. I remind them they are being guided by what they love, and that is sufficient.

However, my mother came along at a different time. She came along when women were expected to find success only in the home as a good wife, homemaker, and mother. Although my mother was not a formal teacher, she taught many with her wisdom.

The smart ones listened.

She possessed a knowing that was both respected and made use of by some in our community, both young and old. She was also, without doubt, one of the most perceptive people I have ever known. My mother's piercing eyes rarely missed anything when reading people. Watching her, I could always tell by looking in her eyes how she felt about someone by what that person had said. In a framed photo I have of her, I can feel those same knowing eyes as they seem to speak directly to me.

For the most part, my mother liked people. She "never met a stranger."

A principled woman, my mother had little tolerance for anyone who lied *unnecessarily*. She would say, "If you'll lie, you'll steal, and if you'll steal, you'll kill." As a result, my punishment for lying was always meted out more severely. To this day, no matter what the consequence, I always try to tell the truth. If necessary, I will skate around a lie by carefully choosing my words.

My mother had everything to do with my strong work ethic. Even if it was no more than working around the house, my mother was always working. At the very least, she was cooking, washing, grocery shopping, or minding her garden.

My family was reared on welfare. It was only after becoming an adult that I have been able to talk about growing up on aid. I always attached a feeling of shame to being a "have not." Although my mother was married to my father, Edward Barnes, they separated when I was young. He did contribute to our family, and he remained in my life until he died. However, for as far back as I can remember, he did not live in the same house with us.

I do have fond memories, though. One memory that has forever been etched for me is of my mother lovingly removing ingrown hairs from his cheeks as he would lay across her bed. It was a very tender moment they shared on more than one occasion.

One story that speaks to my father's determination and humility, is the one I have heard from my older sister Norma. She shared with me that my older siblings taught my father how to sign his name. Having gotten only as far as the third grade, he did not know how to write his name in cursive until they taught him.

My father eventually moved to Gary, Indiana, where I visited him several times before he passed. The first visit was when I was sixteen and took a Greyhound bus cross country alone from California to spend time with him. I always enjoyed his company, because he was playful, a prankster, and had a warm sense of humor. He was also a dapper lady's man who loved flashy cars, nice hats, suits and his Stacy Adams shoes.

My last memory of Daddy was speaking to him when he was in the hospital dying of liver cancer. It was the first time I faced death with someone close to me. His last words over the telephone in a very weakened voice were, "Daddy is leaving, so you are going to be on your own now."

Being a single parent, my mother was creative in her non-taxable ways. She would moonlight as a hairdresser, clean pheasants during hunting season for a hunter each year, do light housework for a senior citizen, taxi people around town, and load us children in our Chevy each summer to pick prunes to help pay for our school clothes.

Having my own money was extremely important to me. Being a have not, I always wanted more. I can clearly remember the day I did not have my nickel to put into the girl's Christian group that was headed by my neighbor, Mrs. Phoebe Officer. My mother made it plain to me that she did not have a nickel that day, and that I was going to go to the meeting without one.

I wailed and wailed, because I did not want to go without my dues.

Mrs. Officer felt so sorry for me that she said, "Baby, it's all right. I will put your nickel in for you."

To make sure I had my own money, I became an "entrepreneur" at age eleven by selling cinnamon suckers to my classmates. I was in the fifth grade, and bussed to Byrd Street School, a closed campus across town where most students did not look like me. I knew I was "different," but I did not mind being bussed. I enjoyed the ride across town, in the yellow school bus that was always full of chattering children who *did* look just like me. I was able to think and give vision to my dreams as I looked out the window and watched how the neighborhoods changed along the way.

I enjoyed cinnamon suckers, and often brought them with me to school. Other children eventually asked where I got them. It finally came to me one day that I could make money by selling cinnamon suckers during lunchtime. Initially, the suckers were for my own pleasure. Once I found others wanted them, too, I came up with a business plan.

Since no one could leave campus, I decided to supply cinnamon suckers to those who wanted them at lunchtime. I loaded up my purse with store-bought suckers from Mr. Johnson's corner store before boarding my early-morning bus. Mr. Johnson was our only Black storeowner, and, coincidentally, our only Black fireman.

By lunchtime each day, there was a high demand for the suckers I was selling. I arrived at school with an out-of-place, bulging white Easter Sunday purse. It had an unmistakable fragrance of cinnamon. I returned home each day without suckers, but with the jingling sound of coins in my otherwise empty plastic purse. I bought suckers two for a nickel and sold them for a nickel a piece. I doubled my money.

That experience taught me the business concept of "supply and demand."

My lucrative business fared well until word got back to the unimpressed administration. To this day, I do not know who told them, but the school immediately put a screeching halt to my growing business. I was able to console myself over the loss of my business by taking some of my profits and buying a wonderful collection of clothes for my doll.

My entrepreneurial spirit was only temporarily dampened.

The following year, I moved on to babysitting for my sister Dorothy and family friend Dora for fifty cents an hour. Eventually,

I began to offer babysitting services to others in my neighborhood. With each hour that passed, I counted my money as I watched babies, television, and the clock.

One of the earliest jobs I remember having was picking prunes in the dusty fields of Marysville, twenty-six miles from Oroville. I absolutely detested those fields. They once again reminded me we were part of the have nots. I played more than I worked, but those early days in the fields helped define my work ethic.

At sixteen, I landed my first "legitimate" job as a page at the Butte County Library. My $1.65 an hour validated me as a real employee because I was paid with a check. I distinctly remember my first check. It was long, and it had my name typed on it. Because my mother did not have a checking account when I was growing up, a check was both foreign and a very big thing to me. Needing to cash a check forced me to open up a checking account for my "real" job.

I had the distinction of being the second Black girl in our town to hold the coveted position of Library Page at the Butte County Library. Ruthie Clark was the first, and Sandra O'Quinn followed me.

My mother would proudly drop me off after school at the front door and pick me up on time at the library's closing. From the moment I entered that library door, aisles and aisles of books and sacred silence surrounded me. I began to acquaint myself with literature of many genres. There were science-fiction books by Isaac Asimov, novels by writers like Louisa Mae Alcott, and classical playwrights led by William Shakespeare.

Based on my love of language and literature, it is no wonder that in 1994, I co-founded *Circle of Sisters: A Reading Circle*. Our African American literary group shifted in membership over about seven years. We ritualistically met the last Monday of each month over dinner, rotating homes as we critiqued our literary choices. The love of books brought us together, but it was a kinship of spirits that kept us together.

During the latter part of 2005, co-founder Michelle Harrell and I met at a commercial audition. We acknowledged how much we missed our *Circle of Sisters* and decided to revamp the group. The following January, the *Circle* began again. We are now grounded with a new set of women that includes loyal members Alice La Touche, Joyce Lee, Smeralda, as well as longtime returning member Jeanette Vines.

My mother was also an initiator.

She was a doer.

In 1959, she decided to build a house at 3330 Fallbrook Avenue in Oroville. My mother just barely scraped together enough money to buy the $200 vacant lot at the corner of Fallbrook and B Street. Always resourceful, she eyed an empty house that had been ravaged by a fire, and approached the Anglo stranger who owned the charred property. By the end of their conversation, that kind gentleman agreed to give my mother anything she could salvage.

That is how we got our bathtub. Each nick in it reminded us of where it came from.

My Uncle Thado, who had first built his own home in Oroville, headed the project. Word traveled quickly throughout Southside, our part of town. "Chile, Mosea Lee's buildin' herself a house!"

Men stopped in front of the cement foundation as they walked, bicycled, or drove past.

They'd yell, "Mosea Lee, you need some help today?"

My mother would yell back, "Yeah!"

She was also known to roll up her sleeves and work right along beside them.

My mother never turned help away.

Once given the nod, men would hammer their identity nail by nail into that three-bedroom frame. Hammers and saws rhythmically punctuated the silence at the corner of Fallbrook and B. Musty ebony men glistened in sweat-drenched cotton shirts as they worked until sunset to make my mother's home a reality.

Little by little, everybody on Southside saw that frame become a home.

In exchange for work, my mother's deft hands prepared different combinations of hot meals that might include fried chicken, rice and gravy, cornbread, black-eyed peas, and collard greens with okra. She baked pies or cakes that ranged from sweet potato to egg custard, and three-layered chocolate or coconut cakes.

All were prepared from scratch with pride.

Men huddled on our cement foundation to eat. They seemed to enjoy those home-cooked meals as if they had been paid in cash. In between mouthfuls of my mother's food, they would throw their heads back to laugh loudly, dream, and lie about all the women they had.

Many men within the Black community of Oroville, California helped build our modest home.

Building our home was a personal feat, but my mother also served others in our community. Unsatisfied with reading only the *Oroville Mercury,* my mother was responsible for bringing Black news to our small community. Having been raised in the South, she was used to Black newspapers. Given that, she took it upon herself to subscribe to the *Pittsburgh Courier,* one of the oldest Black newspapers in America.

Along with my younger brothers, Ellis and Edward, We took orders for the weekly salmon-colored newspaper. Once we had our customers, we began to receive bundled newspapers each week by mail. I loved the ritualistic moment of opening each new batch of *Pittsburgh Courier* newspapers.

We drove from house to house to deliver each one. My mother enjoyed knowing that it was solely because of her efforts that we could read about ourselves each week. The *Oroville Mercury* oftentimes had stories about the darker side of who we were. The *Pittsburgh Courier* made us feel proud.

Like my mother, I have never been one to wait for things to happen. I fully understand that it is possible to *make* things happen.

I believe anyone can achieve what they will. My mother certainly did.

At the time of this writing, as much as I am dreading it emotionally, I am considering tearing down our family home. It is now boarded up and I need to make a decision about what I will do with it. It was not built solidly enough to withstand the test of time and is in need of repairs beyond what may be wise to invest.

Still, the house that was built at 3330 Fallbrook Avenue in Oroville, California in 1959 is living proof that anything is possible.

Chapter Three

Crossing Over

There is no learning without controversy.
—Andrew Young,
Cleric/Politician/Political Activist

I knew I was about to enter a world far removed from my agricultural community of Oroville as I watched my mother, sister Dorothy, and her husband Marvin pull away in their white Chevy station wagon.

At the University of California at Santa Cruz, I had now crossed over into a world of privilege, filled with wealthy and well-educated students. I was entering a place where I knew I would now be measured chiefly by my scholastic performance.

Left behind were the dusty roads and prune fields I worked in each summer to earn my school clothes. I was now a student at UCSC, the newest of the UC campuses with an enrollment of only 2,400 students. Its unique teaching style boasted no letter grades—only a pass/fail and narrative evaluation grading system. Small classes allowed us to get to know our professors personally, *and* we could declare independent majors.

Nestled in a redwood forest setting with the backdrop of the Pacific Ocean, we had little to distract us from learning. At that time, UCSC did not allow fraternities and sororities, nor did the campus participate in inter-collegiate sports. Without these distractions, and if you applied yourself, you could basically write your own ticket.

At the foot of our "city on a hill" campus was the Santa Cruz boardwalk, known for its hair-raising roller-coaster rides. A coastal town, it survives in great part because of its summer tourism.

As foreign as my new environment was, even more alienating was leaving behind my familiar world of the have nots.

I felt very much out of my element.

It would be years before I would realize I made friends with community folk in the town of Santa Cruz so easily because many reminded me of those I knew from my past. The locals mirrored me. Many were also have nots. For the most part, the Black youth who came to visit on campus were not welcomed. Many had an edgy street quality and did not look like they "belonged" there.

A part of me felt I did not belong there, either.

It was true I prepared myself academically for college during my last two years at Oroville High and I still had my ambition of becoming an English teacher, but there was no mistaking my awkwardness in my new environment.

The year was 1968.

I could not have experienced a more volatile time for my personal coming of age. I was one of twenty-eight Black students influenced by the Black Power Movement. As our historic backdrop, we had the Civil Rights Era, which included the rise of the Black Panther Party in 1966, formed by Huey P. Newton to combat police brutality in Oakland, California. Like other campuses across the country, UCSC students rebelled against the controversial war in Vietnam. The counter-culture of San Francisco's Haight-Ashbury District took psychedelic drugs and countered the war in Viet Nam by living the slogan, "Make Love, Not War." The term "flower children" grew from the 1967 "Summer of Love" gathering in San Francisco where hippies wore flowers in their hair to symbolize "love, not war."

At UCSC, we had musty, unshaven "long-hairs" who walked around campus barefoot and shirtless, high on acid, mescaline, and marijuana. Juxtaposed were the "health food" students on campus who ate only from our macrobiotics line in the cafeteria.

Amidst the Civil Rights Movement of the 1960's, assassinations of our public figures became commonplace. The killings were led by President John F. Kennedy's assassination in 1963, followed by Malcolm X in 1965, and both Dr. Martin Luther King, Jr. and Robert F. Kennedy in 1968.

Santa Cruz was not untouched by the volatile times.

It had its own racial incidents that sparked tensions, including the night a young Black man was assaulted in town by the Hell's Angels. This incident caused both community fear and solidarity.

The "Free the Soledad Brothers" Movement was fully underway in 1970 to free political prisoners George Jackson, Fleeta Drumgo, and John Clutchette. The three were accused of killing a prison guard at California's Soledad Prison following the murders of three other political activist prisoners there.

Ultimately, Angela Davis would be listed on the FBI's 10 Most Wanted list in 1970 for fleeing charges of murder, kidnapping, and conspiracy for her alleged role in the 1970 bloody shootout at the Marin County Courthouse that left 17-year-old Jonathan Jackson, brother of George Jackson, and Judge Harold Haley dead.

One of my roommates came to be a regular San Quentin visitor of Soledad Brother John Clutchette. Once, while I sat in the waiting room with her young daughter, John Clutchette was taunted by guards in the visiting room in front of her. Within seconds, while defending his honor, he tore apart a wooden chair to arm himself against his perpetrators.

I knew something was terribly wrong when I heard scuffling and screams coming from the visiting room. My friend came running out of the visiting room in tears.

I nervously asked, "What happened?"

She panted something like, "The guards provoked John and he fought back. Let's get out of here!"

On the tense trip home to Santa Cruz, we were almost run off the road by an unknown car. It was made clear to us that night as we were followed by headlights that we were in way over our Santa Cruz heads.

On another occasion, the FBI showed up at our apartment door to question us about James Carr, a released political prisoner turned UCSC student. I came to know James after he was released, and although I knew political things were going on around me, I still subleased my apartment to him while I was away on a Mississippi exchange program in 1970. Upon my return, I asked no questions about the mattress that appeared to have a bullet hole in it.

James, who authored the book *BAD: The Autobiography of James Carr,* is quoted in his book, "When I was nine years old, I burned down my school." Later, he linked up with prisoner George Jackson in Folsom where they led the notorious "Wolf Pack."

Amidst the political climate of the times, I had the opportunity to meet Panther leader Huey P. Newton in an Oakland apartment.

Huey was surrounded by his "no-nonsense" bodyguards but I stole quick glances at him whenever I could. I was struck by his slender, yet muscular build, high-pitched voice, and commanding presence. I was in awe of how handsome he was, and there was no question who the leader in the room was.

Huey's security was heavy. I had somehow wound up in Oakland with other Santa Cruz students who were experimenting with the Black Panther Party Movement and had made the drive to Oakland. Aware of the danger that surrounded me, I tried to hide my fear.

After I graduated, Huey came to be enrolled as a student at UCSC. He received a degree in 1974 as an independent major in Philosophy/Religious Studies, and he subsequently earned his Ph.D in the History of Consciousness Graduate Program in 1980. Coincidentally, that is the same Graduate Program Angela Davis now teaches in. Huey's dissertation focused on the repression of the Black Panther Party. He always wanted to teach at a community college but that never happened. He was gunned down in Oakland, California in 1989.

There is much speculation as to who killed Huey and why. The assassination theory can be supported one way in the lyrics of the political rap duo Dead Prez's song "Propaganda" in which the enigmatic words pointed the finger, "They killed Huey cause they knew he had the answer."

The times, they were a-changing.

Like most other Theatre Departments around the country, ours was Eurocentric in scope, and Black students at UCSC rebelled. We wanted acting roles that reflected who we were and spoke to the political climate of the day. Our burning desire to be heard on our own terms gave rise to Black Magic Theatre. It was formed by Eugene

Calhoun, Sandra Mills Scott, Gracie Gatson, Peter Fitzsimmons, and me. We were the only Black theatre majors on campus, but we were joined by Linda Hornbeak, Debra Walton, and every other Black student on campus willing to become a part of our theatre troupe.

We had something to say, and we were intent on being heard.

Our first project represented "guerilla theatre," a political form of theatre that can be performed without notice, anywhere and any time. Our piece was based on the highly publicized 1969 gag-order trial of Bobby Seale, the Black Panther accused of advocating a violent response to police brutality in a speech delivered outside the 1968 Democratic Convention. He was charged with violation of the 1968 Anti-Riot Act along with the Chicago Seven, who were charged with conspiracy to create a riot.

One day, without warning, Black Magic Theatre actors walked into the UCSC Cowell College dining room in white face.

Eugene Calhoun yelled out, "Court is now in session!"

Anglo students, caught by surprise over their meals, were coerced to stand as Eugene continued, "Here comes the judge!"

Bobby Seale's real-life case, at this point, had been separated from the Chicago Seven defendants. In protest, we created our mock trial for Bobby Seale. Our political intent to address the injustice of Bobby Seale's trial was clearly understood by the time we left that dining room.

We also performed scripted plays that toured locally in Santa Cruz and Monterey Counties, and as far away as the San Joaquin Valley agricultural town of Modesto. We performed plays and scenes from social and political writers of the day, that included Ed Bullins, Sonia Sanchez, Ben Caldwell, LeRoi Jones, (who later became known as Amiri Baraka), Wanda Coleman, the late Ron Milner, and Marvin

X. Their tongues were on fire, and we gave voice to what they were saying. Plays like LeRoi Jones' *Dutchman* met racism head on.

Although older and conservative in her viewpoint, Dr. Ann Reed later joined our UCSC campus as our first African American Theatre Arts instructor. An eloquent and pearl-wearing chain smoker, I can still see Ann, cigarette in hand. Her political stance was not ours, but she did look like us. We saw her as representing the Black bourgeoisie, but having a Black theatre professor was still a victory for us.

To our favor, we also had two "liberal" theatre instructors. Jeans-wearing John Hellweg's gentle, youthful, and open spirit welcomed us into the Theatre Department. Short and full-bodied in stature, Sheldon Feldner possessed a very quirky and funny Jewish sensibility that made me like and trust him immediately. Interestingly enough, many years later, he and my son shot a commercial together as actors for the San Francisco Giants. It turned out to be a very odd and touching coincidence.

It was Sheldon who also wrote the play *Justifiable Homicide*, based on the real-life police brutality shooting of a Black man in San Francisco's Hunter's Point. I remember well the two-hour drive the cast took to do our research at the scene of the crime. The most moving moment for me in that haunting, dark San Francisco alley was when I unknowingly met the woman I was to portray. She was a short, slight, dark-skinned woman. In another setting, she might easily have gone unnoticed.

After asking us who we were and what we were doing there, she relived what she had witnessed at the scene of the murder. She spoke of the policeman who had unjustifiably pulled the trigger on a Black man. After she made her presence known that day, she recounted her run-in with the guilty police officer.

She told us, "He called me a nigger bitch, and I called him a honkie."

She took her time for emphasis as she continued, "I told *him*, 'I want *you* to go on up to heaven and ask God why he made *me* a nigger bitch and *you* a honkie. Then I want *you* to come back down here and tell *me* what he said!'"

We added her funny, yet poignant quote to my courtroom scene. That speech always triggered laughter from our packed houses. I could not have been more honored to speak for my real-life character.

Her real-life voice spoke for the oppressed.

The next play that helped shape my decision to become a theatre major was world-renowned Spanish playwright Fernando Arrabal's *And They Put Handcuffs on the Flowers*. Theatre majors competed heavily at auditions to work with Fernando on his highly controversial and political play. He was invited to campus to direct the production and many wanted the opportunity to work with him. Because I had never heard of him, I thought I was just auditioning for another play.

At the time, Arrabal was in exile in France, due to his inflammatory political writings. His work was influenced by the unrest in Spain during the Civil War from 1936-39 when his father, an army officer, was sentenced to death for his opposition to the right wing military coup led by Generalissimo Francisco Franco. His father's sentence was commuted to life imprisonment but he somehow escaped in 1941 and vanished.

Arrabal's work sprang from the genre "theatre of pain," where physical pain can be utilized as part of the theatre experience. Much to our audience members' surprise, they were physically assaulted in the dark as they entered the foyer of the Barn Theatre on campus. Our cast became mock perpetrators who inflicted pain on our innocent theatergoers. Moans and groans could be heard as we roughed up our paying audiences while they tried to use their arms and hands to protect themselves. This sensory introduction to Arrabal's play was shocking, and it was meant to be. From that first moment in the foyer, no one knew what to expect next.

What audiences *did* know was they were about to have a theatre experience like never before.

Our highly-charged play drew media attention far beyond Santa Cruz. In the Bay Area, we received coverage from the *San Francisco Chronicle*. I had never heard of Arrabal before his arrival, but it became quite clear early on that he was a writer of great prominence, and one to be reckoned with.

Short, but sturdy in stature, Arrabal spoke very little English. I communicated intimately with him by looking behind his wire-rimmed glasses and into his sparkling, light brown, laughing eyes. When needed, his French female assistant was always standing nearby to interpret what our bodies could not.

For some reason, I seemed to amuse Arrabal. I could always get a heartfelt laugh and warm smile from his bearded face during our exchanges, both in and out of rehearsal.

At that point in my theatre training, I had never been engaged in work that was so surreal, so demanding, and so cutting-edge. Our play even had a moment of nudity. One of our male actors shed his clothing at the end of the play. Audiences were stunned as they looked at his genitals.

I absolutely loved this challenging piece of theatre. It had something political to say, and I wanted to be a part of its political statement.

In the process, this play made me stretch and grow as a human being.

My only apprehension was a scene in which my theatre instructor and I were required to kiss. As directed, I stood over him for our kiss as he sat on a stool in his tutu looking up at me. I was directed to flutter my arms like a bird while we kissed. It was not the kiss that made me uncomfortable. It was his choice to make the kiss a French kiss. I never expressed my discomfort because he was one of my teachers. I was too shy to insist that we could get the same effect without our tongues meeting. It was apparent he wanted to totally go where his character went, but I was not as uninhibited as him.

I did not know then how to say no, but I do now.

One feature I appreciated about UC Santa Cruz was the opportunity to do field studies, both abroad and in other parts of the country. My student mentor Claudia Krich lived on a kibbutz in Israel during her junior year. Cheryl Smith, a Black student from San Francisco's Fillmore District, majored in Italian and lived in Florence, Italy for a year. Many other students gained practical experience by taking at least a semester away to study.

Dr. J. Herman Blake established community programs that took multicultural students to places that included the Neighborhood House in North Richmond, California, and to the "primitive" Daufuskie Island off the coast of South Carolina. Only male students including Sabra Slaughter, John Rickford, Khalid Muhadji, Bill Downey and Glenwood Mapp were allowed placement on Daufuskie Island. Females who wanted to participate in that particular field study were delegated to do work on the mainland in nearby Buford County health clinics because the land was still very much undeveloped.

Ironically, over forty years later, Daufuskie Island has now become a tourist resort complete with oceanfront hotel villas, championship golf, spa services, and an equestrian center. It no longer resembles the Daufuskie Island remembered from the '60s.

I made another field study choice.

I chose to participate in an exchange program in Mississippi at an all-Black private school. Tougaloo College is located in Tougaloo, near the state capitol of Jackson. My best friend, Jacki Scott, who was not about to let me have the Southern experience without her, accompanied me. At the last minute, Eugene Calhoun decided to join us. It was that dangerous time of the Civil Rights Movement and Eugene felt we needed a male to go with us. Not a popular UCSC campus placement, we were surprised when curly-haired Jewish student Phil Freshman decided to take the sojourn down South with the three of us.

None of us had ever been to the South. All we knew were the stereotypical images fed us—photos of Black men hanging from trees, Dr. Martin Luther King Jr.'s marches punctuated by vicious dogs and sprinklers, racist rednecks, and the well-known segregated schools, restrooms, and drinking fountains.

Our pictures were not pretty.

We held some degree of fear, but our curiosity outweighed our fears. To our amazement, we were oftentimes met with middle class, educated Blacks enjoying lifestyles that were much more affluent than our own. We found Black entrepreneurs who owned their own businesses, loving Black families still intact, and we witnessed Blacks and whites co-existing in the complex way they have, dating back to slavery.

It was not our intent to get involved in Mississippi politics. We went to Tougaloo for a Southern experience at a Black college. However, activist Fannie Lou Hamer came to Tougaloo College to speak that spring. It would not be until much later that I would understand the significance of who Fannie Lou really was.

She was known nationally for her Civil Rights advocacy, most notably for her fight for the Black vote in Mississippi. She was one of the organizers of the Mississippi Freedom Party, and before the Student Nonviolent Coordinating Committee (SNCC) came to Mississippi, she did not even know Blacks had a legal right *to* vote. She also spoke at the 1964 Democratic National Convention in Atlantic City, New Jersey. Partly as a result, President Lyndon B. Johnson signed the 1965 Voting Rights Act, and the Democratic Party vowed never to have an all-white delegation again.

In 1963, Fannie Lou Hamer was beaten by two Black Mississippi prisoners forced to beat her by a state trooper while she was in jail for her Civil Rights advocacy. She recounted that she was forced to lie face down while one prisoner "beat her until he was tired." As a result, she received a blood clot in one eye and permanent kidney damage, but neither was enough to quell her calling.

We had hardly been on campus six weeks when she enlisted students for a "peaceful" demonstration for equal jobs in nearby Mindin Hall, Mississippi. We agreed to participate. Once we decided to rally for civil rights, we soon learned we were no longer just "those four California students."

We had now crossed the line.

There were three vans of us who agreed to go to Mindin Hall. The march began peacefully enough as we prayed, interlocked hands, walked, and sang freedom-fighter songs that included, "We Shall Overcome." I had demonstrated for equal jobs in my hometown of Oroville as a child, and remembered singing that song as we picketed for jobs at Barnes Supermarket. However, the stakes in Mississippi were far greater than I could have imagined.

We were stopped in our tracks when we saw something that brought fear to each of us. Facing us were state troopers with outstretched guns. We had never been the target of guns, nor had I ever seen such racial hatred in anyone's eyes as I witnessed that particular spring day in 1970.

Later that night, those of us who had made it back to Tougaloo learned that Phil Freshman and Eugene Calhoun's van had been pulled over on the way back to campus. Theirs was the last van to leave Mindin Hall so we did not miss them. Doug Hummer was told by troopers he was being stopped for reckless driving. When we later learned of the charge, we knew better. We believed the van was pulled over because the driver was a long-haired outsider; a Northern white boy who had overstepped Southern boundaries.

Those in the van were taken to jail and held overnight. The NAACP's Black lawyer's attempt to get them released that evening was fruitless. Ironically, it was the Anglo president of Tougaloo College who was eventually successful in getting his students safely back to campus.

While at Tougaloo, we balanced our political activism by using our creative energies to act in the Theatre Department. Eugene, Jacki, and I were all cast in Ed Bullins' play, *Goin' a Buffalo.* We had no female Anglo students to play the role of "Mama Too Tight," so I was cast. Had one not known the role was written to be played otherwise, one would not have known.

The casting brought a different racial tone to the role, but it still worked.

The casting was again a testament to how we can color the roles we play based on what we bring to the role.

Jim Barnhill, a native Mississippian on sabbatical from Rhode Island's Brown University for the year, was our director. He, along with a Black student from Brown University named Gene, and we California students were all considered to be outsiders. It was no wonder we all bonded.

Tougaloo was a learning place for me on many levels. It was the reason I was called to the South for the first time. It was also the first and only time I had ever been enrolled in an all-Black college. Although I was Black, Tougaloo was actually a culture shock for me. There were many intellectuals and a social life that included Black sororities and fraternities, students who played cards daily in the student union, and there were many wild parties on campus. There were also more Black male students than I ever imagined seeing on my UCSC campus. On the down side, there was strong female competition, peer pressure, and the isolation of being seen as "different."

Again, I felt out of my element.

Interestingly enough, Tougaloo was located on the site of an old plantation. Our administrative offices were housed in a three-story building that was the original "big house" during slavery. Years later, San Francisco psychic London Wildwind would ask me if I knew someone by the name of Wesley. I told him I knew two. London decided it must be John Wesley, a student I knew at Tougaloo College. He said that in another lifetime, we lived during slavery, and our love was unrequited. I was the daughter of a plantation owner in that lifetime, and he was a slave.

Needless to say, our love was not allowed.

In this lifetime, John and I were both students on the site of an old plantation. In the Ed Bullins play, *Goin' a Buffalo,* John played my pimp. As characters, I loved him, but he did not love me in return. In real life, I was very attracted to John, but he already had a girlfriend he was serious about.

One rainy night the following year in 1971, John and I ran into each other in Boston, Massachusetts. I noticed him immediately as I exited the Beacon Hill subway stop near Emerson College. John caught my eye because we were the only people walking in that block. The street was dark and perfectly still. I also noticed him because he had a camera around his neck. Although protected by a leather camera case, I wondered who was carrying a camera in such rain.

At closer glance, my heart skipped a beat. I shrieked, "John, what are you doing here?"

In his cool way, he replied, "I am now working for Prudential. What are you doing here?"

I inquired, "John, whatever happened to that girl you were dating?"

John answered simply, "We got married, but she hasn't moved up here yet."

John invited me to dinner at his place, as we caught up on what had been happening in our lives over the last year. We shared a delicious home-cooked meal together, but neither of us made contact again after that night.

Again, in this lifetime, unrequited love.

What brought me to Boston that year was an opportunity to do a field study at Emerson College, a fine arts school. Former UC Santa Cruz professor Sheldon Feldner was then teaching at Emerson. We had stayed in touch after he left Santa Cruz. I told him I wanted to join him in Boston to do a field study in theatre. He worked things out on his end, and I did the same at Santa Cruz. As I expected, Emerson opened the door to an entirely new world for me. All the students were artists of some sort. At that point, I had never been in such a richly creative environment before.

At the same time, 1971 was during the Black Power Movement, and racial lines were clearly drawn at Emerson College. Blacks sat on one side of the dining room and Anglos on the other. Since I had a friend who was Jewish, I straddled the uncomfortable fence by sitting on both sides. However, that decision to defy group pressure was not without its consequences.

Off campus at the Elma Lewis Center in Roxbury, I was immediately cast in Ed Bullins' play *In The Wine Time.* I replaced another actor in the snooty "walk on" role of Beatrice. I had only a moment onstage, but I was so excited to be in a play by Ed Bullins at Emerson College, I did not care. Our cast was led by a fine actor by the name of Brent Jennings. Little did I know that many years later, Brent and I would again cross paths.

Fast forward to 1989 in Los Angeles.

Brent's wife Juanita and I performed simultaneously in two different plays at the Los Angeles Theatre Center. I played the role of Martha Pentecost in a production of August Wilson's *Joe Turner's Come and Gone,* and she played a role in a production of Steve Carter's *Eden.* We shared space in the dressing rooms downstairs. In conversation one day, we realized I had performed many years before in Boston with her husband. Brent was one of the leading Black actors at Emerson College. Admiring his talent then, it was no surprise to me to learn he was still acting and had moved to Los Angeles to further his career.

Santa Cruz served me in many, many ways. It moved me beyond Oroville. It was the place of my "coming of age." It helped me navigate into the world of the "haves." It was where I got in touch with my newfound definition of "blackness," and it also taught me how to think analytically. Furthermore, it gave me my academic training as an actor.

I now had the academic tools I needed to test the practical waters of acting.

Chapter Four

Training Ground

If you learn to think big, nothing on earth will keep you from being successful in whatever you choose to do.

—Benjamin Carson, Physician

Six months after graduating from UC Santa Cruz, I made my acting debut in my first full-length play in the Bay Area. Little did I know then, I was about to be cast in one of my most memorable and acclaimed roles in my seventeen-year stint in the Bay Area.

The city was San Francisco.

I auditioned for and was cast in the "pistol-packin" role of Norma Faye in J. E. Franklin's moving play, *Black Girl*.

Although Norma Faye's long-lost father jokingly described her as "pistol-packin," we never actually saw evidence of that claim. However she did whip out a knife onstage. Without doubt, Norma Faye was one of the "baddest" sisters I've ever played. A bully, Norma Faye could cut you down to size with only a glare.

I loved the writing of the play.

Although entertaining, *Black Girl* had a message. The play also had nice ensemble roles, and playing Norma Faye allowed me to shine. This leading role introduced me to my new acting community. We had a long run and inevitable cast changes along the way. Even though some evolutions of the play were uneven, I still loved my much talked-about role in it.

Prior to *Black Girl,* I had dabbled in Bay Area theatre with UC Berkeley's Walter Dallas and his stable of Bay Area actors. However, it was being in *Black Girl* with Stanford University director John Cochran and co-founder Dr. Sandra Richards that allowed me to cut my teeth as a newcomer to Bay Area theatre in 1972. *Black Girl* was the most successful and longest-running play produced by the West Coast Black Repertory, and I was proud to be in that number of actors that John and Sandi had pulled together.

One story that stands out for me was the night my college buddy, Eugene Calhoun, brought his mother and one of the hairdressers in his mother's shop, the late LeOna Harris, to see the play. Eugene introduced LeOna to me following that night's performance. In meeting her, it became immediately clear to me that although LeOna had no acting experience to speak of, she was very serious about becoming an actor. I saw the excitement in her body language. I saw it in her eyes. I unmistakably heard it in her voice. All she wanted was a chance.

She asked me to introduce her to our director. I did. John later chided me for introducing him to a "would-be actor." Her experience at 40 years old amounted to little more than church productions in Kansas City, Missouri. To boot, she had no photos, and she had no resumé.

However, LeOna wanted to act.

She got the last laugh, because amidst all the cast changes in our production, the day finally came when we needed to replace our "Ma

Deah." I remembered my meeting with LeOna and let her know the role was up for grabs. She jumped at the opportunity to audition. She was hungry to act and she wanted that role. She came *so* prepared that she blew John away with her audition.

She got the part.

The universal lesson in that instance is to never make the assumption that because a "would-be actor" has no experience to speak of, that the actor cannot act.

LeOna's extensive career would go on to include countless plays in the Bay Area, as well as locally shot national commercials and film roles. Until she passed in 2007, LeOna told the story of how seeing *Black Girl* inspired her to actualize her dream of becoming an actor.

I do have John Cochran to thank for such an enjoyable, long-running, and well-received production. To this very day, I am still reminded of my work in *Black Girl* from those who fondly remember my work as "Norma Faye."

I would come to perform many roles in the Bay Area, but "Norma Faye" was one of my most-loved, both by audiences and by me. This signature role gave me permission to be down-and-dirty, bad, and intimidating.

And funny.

In 1973, I became one of the founding members of the Oakland Ensemble Theatre (OET). Ron Stacker Thompson, then a theatre professor at Merritt College in Oakland, California, was our enthusiastic and ambitious visionary. His wife, Cle, an actor and dancer in her own right, was right there at his side, supporting his dream step by step. Many a night we rehearsed in their beautiful Oakland home.

Ron secured an old, forgotten, Victorian brick building on 13th Street in West Oakland. With the help of those who believed in his vision, he converted that abandoned property into a beautiful, thriving theatre home. I remember well all the elbow grease and love that went into that building. We, along with our coerced friends, rolled up our sleeves and painted those dingy walls, cleaned those filthy toilets, and generally transformed that unlikely space into a professional theatre.

At the time, OET became the first and only Black theatre in town that was an Actor's Equity Association (AEA) professional theatre house. It became one of the nicest resident Equity theatres in the Bay Area. I joined the first cast in our maiden production of *No Place to Be Somebody* by Charles Gordone. In it, I played the prostitute role of "Evie."

This was the second of three prostitute roles I came to play.

The success of our maiden production was only the first of many vibrant and well-received productions to grace our stage on 13th Street. OET came to be known for quality, professional Black theatre in the Bay Area. Most of the actors were Black, but OET also had a sizeable number of members who were not.

As politics would dictate, there were circumstances that created an artistic divide. I left after the first production, but it still warms my heart to know I was one of the founding members of OET who helped make Ron Stacker Thompson's vision a reality.

In 1977, I was accepted into the American Conservatory Theater's (ACT) Black Actor's Workshop. This new program was the talk of the Black theatre community. Any actor worth his salt who was serious about becoming a professional actor wanted in.

I was no different.

I probably would have gotten into the program in 1976 when the Black Actor's Workshop first began, but I had a serious auto accident on the Bay Bridge. Ironically, I was rushing to my ACT audition for that same program when I had the accident. I am blessed to be able to talk about it now.

That night, it was pouring down rain. I could hardly see beyond the beads of raindrops that swiftly rolled down my windshield. I was driving much too fast in such adverse weather. Running late, I was trying to beat the clock.

The car in front of me began to brake. I tried to stop. I could see the red car lights in front of me braking, but I did not have enough time to stop. Against my will, my car skidded out of control. I hit the car in front of me, and my car turned sideways on the bridge.

I could only brace myself as I saw a car coming directly at me. A time before required seat belts, I was not wearing one. I knew I was about to be hit. There was nothing I could do but cling to my steering wheel with all my might. I sat looking at the oncoming car lights as I waited for the inevitable. My car was hit on my passenger side, causing it to be tossed around in a circle. It finally came to a screeching halt, resting on the safety bracing of the bridge.

The water was below me.

In a state of shock, I jumped out of my car sporting a huge hickey on my forehead as I yelled uncontrollably, "What time is it? I have an audition I have to get to."

Other drivers looked at me in disbelief. One man quietly said, "Ma'am, I do not think you will be making that audition tonight."

Looking at myself in my rearview mirror, I was forced to agree.

It was not my time to die in that accident, and it was also not my time to be in ACT's first year of the Black Actor's Workshop. Had I made it to my audition that night, I probably would have joined

Danny Glover's acting class. The following year, I *was* accepted into the program and joined his then-wife Asake's class. She was still an actor at the time.

During my days from 1977 through 1979 in the Black Actor's Workshop, Bennet Guillory ran the workshop. One was likely to see other ACT students in the halls. ACT former Advanced Training Program students include the likes of Denzel Washington, Delroy Lindo, and Annette Bening. None of them could possibly have known the fame that awaited each of them.

They were only focused on strengthening their chops and immersing themselves in theatre.

ACT was a significant place for me as I continued to train as an actor. It fine-tuned my "instrument" through acting, voice, and movement classes. I would become very close friends with other Black actors during that time including Delroy Lindo. I distinctly remember the day Delroy and I started to become close friends. I was alone in a dance studio, surrounded by windows overlooking Geary Street. I was in a down mood about something, and he listened.

Delroy is one of the most attentive listeners I know.

I also got exposure in ACT's student production of *To Be Young, Gifted and Black* by Lorraine Hansberry. That production was largely responsible for landing me theatrical representation at the Brebner Agency, the then most prestigious Bay Area talent agency.

I had previously submitted my photo and resumé on several occasions to Brebner's, only to be sent the same rejection letter time and again. After my last submission, I decided I would not put myself through the rejection process with the Brebner Agency again.

And I did not.

However, unbeknownst to me, sitting in the audience at ACT one night as I performed *To Be Young Gifted and Black* was Ms. Ann

Brebner herself. I did not know what she looked like and had no idea she was watching our production.

Directly following our performance, fellow actor Susan Brown yelled, "Guess who was here tonight?"

As some of us looked at her waiting for the answer, she blurted, "*Ann Brebner!*"

Susan Brown is daughter of Willie Brown, former Speaker of the House for the State of California. He, along with his family, were sitting in that same audience. I warmly remember eyeing him inconspicuously as he enjoyed his ice cream bar, while he patiently waited in his seat for the show to begin.

I was both elated and terrified to learn that Ms. Brebner was in the audience that night. I felt my performance was good, but what would *she* think? Would she now want to represent me at the Brebner Agency? Would she still *not* want me?

I got my answer the following day when one of her female staff called me and said, "Miss Brebner would like to meet with you."

Just like that.

Here I had repeatedly submitted over and over again to the most powerful San Francisco agency. It had been like hitting a brick wall. However, in one night, Ms. Brebner saw my work and was now interested in *me*.

This was an example of how an actor's career can literally change overnight.

I immediately made my appointment to meet with Ms. Brebner. I felt nervous and excited at the same time. I waited in the lobby to be summoned by the most well-respected and powerful San Francisco agent in the 1970s.

I waited.

I was finally led into Ms. Brebner's subdued office of darkly painted walls that held a dimly lit lamp on her desk. I adjusted my eyes from the bright outer offices. I sat across from the very proper woman from New Zealand. She had a very clipped accent and a no-nonsense business manner. Her distinguished demeanor was underscored by her conservative attire, coiffed gray French roll, and piercing eyes. She represented wealth and power to me.

We sat.

I thanked Ms. Brebner for inviting me in, and reminded her of the many times I had submitted to her agency. Out of curiosity, and because I wanted to broach the subject of my previous rejections, I asked her why she decided she wanted to finally meet me. She stated simply that she enjoyed my work at ACT and wanted to meet me in person.

She continued with, "When I get photos and resumés, I place them in three piles: the *yes, maybe* and *no* piles. I remember yours very well. I would go back and forth with yours from the *maybe* to the *no* piles."

I asked why.

"Your photo did not look like you were ready for success," she flatly said.

I felt stung but I never forgot that.

Whether it was true or not in my case, it is true that photos are quite telling. Much can be learned about an actor by their photos. It is in the eyes, the posture, the level of confidence, the grooming, and the composure.

Who we are cannot be hidden in a headshot.

I don't think I ever booked any jobs with Brebner, but they *did* represent me. At that time, Bay Area actors did not have to be exclusive with one agency. To try to beat the odds, I was registered with more than one agency. It did not matter to me if I worked through Brebner's or not. What mattered most to me was that I had *finally* succeeded in getting through the door of the most sought-after San Francisco agency.

I finally felt accepted.

My days completed at ACT, I moved on to another role that would put me on the Bay Area theatre map. It was the title role of Ed Bullins' *Jo Anne!*, based on the life of the real Joann Little.

It was 1981, and I was well aware that auditions were being held at the Julian Theatre in San Francisco by long-time and well-respected Bay Area director, John Henry Doyle.

Yet I opted not to go.

I heard the title role would require the re-enacted rape scene of Joann Little, the historical figure who killed her Beaufort, North Carolina prison jailer with his own ice pick in 1975 when he tried to rape her.

My absence noted, John Doyle called me directly following the auditions that evening. He seemed to take my noticeable absence personally. He asked me why I had not read for the highly coveted role. I told him I understood the role required nudity, and I was uncomfortable with nudity. I further told him I had no interest in the role.

We talked at length, and John ended our conversation by saying, "I'm telling you, Adilah. If you do this role, it will put you on the map in the Bay Area."

I was more concerned, however, about the partial nudity.

John assured me that the "Rashomon effect" rape scene, re-told differently by each person recounting it, would be re-enacted three times and done "tastefully" with subdued lighting and a velcro dress and bra that would be easy to rip off. He also gave his word that full nudity would not be required.

At the same time, John also felt we needed to make the audience feel the brutality of rape.

He invited me to the callbacks uttering his well-known line, "Trust me."

I cautiously agreed to go, although I was hoping John would not cast me. As fate would have it and much to my disappointment, I got the part.

Although I had my concerns, much to my surprise and delight, renowned playwright Ed Bullins arrived to the Bay Area to become a part of our rehearsal process for his controversial play. I perked up when I heard he would be present at our rehearsals.

I will never forget the day I first met Ed Bullins.

I approached the Potrero Hill Neighborhood House in San Francisco where Richard Reineccius' Julian Theatre was housed. I noticed Ed sitting outside the theatre on a bus stop bench. I recognized him immediately from the many photos I had seen. Here was the legendary Ed Bullins himself, sitting right in front of me.

I immediately walked up to introduce myself to one of my favorite playwrights of the day. Although Ed looked like his photos, I was taken aback by the fact that he was short in physical stature and so very, very quiet. Like playwright August Wilson, Ed's demeanor seemed to contradict the overpowering voice that flowed through his pen.

I was at once elated and intimidated by the fact that *the* Ed Bullins would be sitting in the Julian Theatre, night after night, watching me breathe life into the title role of *Jo Anne!* During rehearsals, I could feel Ed taking notes, whispering with my director, and studying me as I shaded in the character based on

Joann Little. Our playwright's presence made me feel extremely self-conscious. I constantly wondered what he was whispering to John.

I never knew.

Once we began the rehearsal process, I realized how much playing Joann Little would require of me. She was a historical figure who was very much still alive. At age twenty, she had made history. She used her assailant's ice pick to kill him, fled the jail, and was returned for her trial. Her brave act of self-defense was adopted as a symbol of defiance by the Women's Movement. Due to their rallying, Joann Little became an unlikely media celebrity. She received so much national attention that the singing group Sweet Honey In The Rock even released a song in her name.

Some felt Joann became a pawn for the Women's Movement's own selfish gains. Many saw their interest in Joann as just another cause of the day. Joann herself was not known to be political, nor had she expected such widely-covered support from the Movement. For her, the murder was an act of survival. The truth was, she *did* have a record. She had previously been in trouble with the law and some still saw her as little more than a common criminal.

There was much controversy around this volatile play, which begged the question of who the real criminal was.

Jo Anne! worked.

We received tremendous coverage and critical acclaim throughout the Bay Area. We extended the show twice to sold-out, multicultural audiences. It was, without a doubt, an exciting run for me. It was also a powerful piece of theatre that made an important social statement.

In the courtroom scene when I was on the witness stand, I cried freely onstage as I gave Joann's account of what happened to her. I was able to bring tears up effortlessly, which does not always happen for me but because I felt her predicament so deeply in that theatrical moment, tears flowed honestly night after night.

We invited and urged Joann to see our production. She never made the journey from New York to see herself onstage, but she was well aware of our play in her honor.

Joann did not come, but there were many who did, including San Francisco native Danny Glover, who came to our closing night performance with his daughter Mandisa. He and his then young daughter, hung out with us late into the night as we celebrated the closure of our long, successful run. His career had not blown up yet, but Danny was clearly on his way. We were touched that Danny still made time for his fellow Bay Area theatre comrades.

One thing was certain. John was right. *Jo Anne!* did make me a Bay Area crossover actor.

I received a *DramaLogue Award* for Outstanding Achievement in Theatre in 1981 for *Jo Anne!* Although DramaLogue was based in Los Angeles, it also acknowledged and awarded Bay Area theatre productions. I also received a Bay Area Critics Circle nomination for *JoAnne!* The Bullins play was written in a surreal and stylized fashion, but there was no mistaking the edginess and power of the piece.

The rehearsal process of *Jo Anne!* was a particularly grueling one for me. I worked full-time during the day and rehearsed at night. At the time, I held the position of Assistant Volunteer Coordinator at the University of California Medical Center in San Francisco. My "day job" was just as demanding as my play. The process was rigorous, and I never seemed to be able to satisfy John. He continually pushed me. As a director, it seemed he always wanted more. I told him I was giving him all I had, but he never accepted my limitations. I often left rehearsal feeling spent and near tears.

John has directed me in theatre more than any one director. Having an athletic background, he directs actors like he is coaching a football team. He demands a sense of ensemble, yet it is not beneath him to instill competition in his actors as a way to make them strive for excellence.

At one rehearsal, he warned me, "If you don't watch out, other actors are going to steal this show away from you."

What he said made me angry, but it also made me produce.

John's "psychological tactics" often worked. However, it would be easier if the constructive criticism were balanced with praise. Still, John is one of the best directors I have ever worked with, and I trust him. I have been pleased with my work with him, and I believe, in the long run, I have always delivered for him. Occasionally, he has intimated praise, and that has been good enough.

Whenever I have received a compliment from John, it has been left-handed. I was in San Francisco to sit on a panel for the International African Women's Film Festival in 2002. A longtime theatre friend, the late Brandi Swanson said from the audience, "John's very proud of you. He talks about you all the time."

I was shocked.

Although I did not receive my compliment directly from John, I got it. It touched my heart to know he could speak favorably of my work to others. He has never told me directly he is proud of me because that is not his way, but Brandi's comment confirmed what I felt was so.

Although we still spar regularly, that is our dance.

I publicly want to say I love John and respect and appreciate his heavy influence on my career.

Later, John directed me at the Julian Theatre in another Bullins' play, *Daddy*. It earned me a second Bay Area Critics Circle nomination. John also directed me in the Western Addition Cultural Center's (WACC) run of a third play by Bullins, *The Taking of Miss Janie*. Over the years, I have been in at least five Ed Bullins plays, more plays than for any one playwright.

The young blonde in the title role of "Janie" was not a seasoned actor, but she was forced to give her best, playing opposite our lead Shabaka Henley. Like Danny, Shabaka is a San Francisco native, and has gone on to a very successful career in Hollywood.

The Bullins' plays I have acted in have always had strong social messages. *The Taking of Miss Janie* centered around a love/hate interracial relationship between a Black man and Anglo woman. In that play, I played a bisexual prostitute. I had to kiss fellow female actor Valeri Parker Ross, who played opposite me. It was an interesting challenge for me as an actor, because I had never had a role that required that kind of intimacy with another woman before.

I rose to the occasion by doing what I often ask my students to do: justify, not judge, the character.

This was my third and last role as a prostitute.

I remember well the WACC venue for two of my Bullins productions. It was then a funky community theatre space. The Center has since changed its name to the African American Art and Culture Complex. With its new name came a facelift. When I stepped into the space in the early 2000s, I could not believe it was the same building. Deservedly, it is now a very beautiful and well-kept center.

A memory I always associate with the Western Addition was the day I arrived at the theatre for a rehearsal and found out that then resident playwright Buriel Clay had been killed in an auto accident. He and his girlfriend were hit at a San Francisco intersection while riding in his tiny sports car.

It was a senseless auto accident caused by a teen driver who ran a red light.

I clearly remember fellow actor/acting teacher Gloria Weinstock's reaction of hysteria upon hearing the news as we drove up. She wailed the word, "*No!*" as I have never heard uttered before.

Buriel was her friend.

The irony was that I had *just* met Buriel Clay. He came with John Doyle to see me in *To Be Young, Gifted and Black* at ACT.

I immediately took a liking to Buriel.

He had a beautiful smile that showed off the gap between his front teeth, and he had dancing eyes that hid behind his glasses. He had a warm spirit, and I was secretly intrigued by and attracted to him. He was a fine human being and a good writer. I wanted to know him better but I only got the opportunity to cross his path that one time. I felt gypped when I realized he was gone.

I could not make sense of it. His career had just begun to take off. How could that tragedy have happened?

The Bay Area Black theatre community mourned Buriel's death. In honor of him, WACC renamed its resident theatre the Buriel Clay Theatre, to make sure he would always be remembered. Those of us who knew him, no matter how briefly, *have* remembered Buriel.

Jo Anne!, *Daddy*, and *Black Girl* have all garnered me some degree of critical and audience favor in the Bay Area. Still another play that served me well was Moliére's *Tartuffe*. Playing Dorine, I was able to try my hand at the classics. The classics have never been my passion, and perhaps that is why they have never come easy for me. Dorine was no exception. To try to get past my difficulty, I even went to see a hypnotist because I wanted to relax into the role. Hypnotism did *not* work for me but once I stopped forcing the work and allowed myself to enjoy playing the character, I found a place of truth that allowed me to embrace Dorine.

I achieved a great measure of self-satisfaction once I began to own the role.

In 1985, I was interviewed with four other African American women for an article in the *San Francisco Examiner* entitled "Black Actresses in White Theatre," written by journalist Nancy Scott. Those who shared that interview with me were Deborah Asante, the late Dr. Camille Howard, the late Jacquii Marshall, and Gloria Weinstock, the only one of us who still lives, acts, and teaches in the Bay Area.

Nancy Scott's interest in a story on us was sparked by our need to collectively go public with our casting frustrations. What triggered our solidarity was an open company-call audition at a highly respected resident theatre in the Bay Area. Black female actors had especially been wooed to the auditions. Seven of us showed up.

None of us were cast.

Perhaps that, in and of itself, would not have been noteworthy, had it not been for the fact that we had all individually been sought out and invited to audition. Many considered us to be representative of the leading Black female actors in the Bay Area at the time. We were known to be talented and well-trained, and our collective credits were impressive. The majority of us were also card-carrying Actor's Equity Association union actors. It was widely felt that you could not cast any better.

The message seemed to be the "best of the best" were not good enough.

One of us had been told at the auditions that she was not "suitable" to play a traditionally-cast Anglo type who was described as "brittle." To add insult to injury, this same actor was told, "As a race, you Black people are so warm."

This was said in the midst of the theatre company's self-professed "non-traditional" casting.

She was crushed.

We were all subjected to varying degrees of painfully stereotypic characterizations in that particular audition process. We also cited in our interview other recent auditioning woes. Then Stanford University's professor, the late Camille Howard, gave an account of an audition for a Shakespearean production.

"They read everybody but me," she uttered painfully. "I was called there to be ignored."

Camille's stinging quote, "I see apartheid in Bay Area theatre," was the comment that horrified Bay Area Anglo companies most as they read the article in defense and shame.

That 1985 *San Francisco Examiner* article rocked the Bay Area theatre world.

African American theatre spokespersons voiced their concerns. Oakland Ensemble Theatre's then Artistic Director Benny Ambush said, "It's a myth out there that we don't have skills." Lorraine Hansberry Theatre's co-founder Stanley Williams said, "If the companies were hiring, my sense is that the trained talent would come out." Speaking to the dearth of work, actor Shabaka Henley said, "All those training at ACT are from somewhere else and they're going somewhere else."

Prominent resident theatres, feeling backed against the wall, came out in defense of their theatres in varying degrees. That article gave them their day in court. Spokespersons at the American Conservatory Theater, Berkeley Repertory Theatre, Eureka Theatre, Berkeley Shakespeare Festival, One Act Theatre and Magic Theatre were all quoted in the article.

Some put their feet further in their mouths in printed quotes attributed to them. One spokesperson was actually quoted as saying, "The kind of stuff we do requires a certain professional proficiency—you can hire more Blacks when you're doing realism."

To their credit, some theatre companies had made notable headway in non-traditional casting. The previous year, I was cast Japanese in Berkeley Repertory's *Kabuki Medea*, the production that was responsible for me earning my Actor's Equity Association union card.

The article also gave high marks to the Julian Theatre, San Francisco Mime Troupe, and San Francisco Repertory for their notable gains in multicultural casting. Other theatres began some serious soul-searching. Some even began more non-traditional casting after that 1985 article that became known as "the wake-up call" of the day.

The following season, I was invited to join the prestigious American Conservatory Theater's Advanced Training Program. It is my understanding my hire made me the very first full-time African American instructor to teach in its highly competitive Advanced Training Program.

Our collective stand in that Bay Area theatre article seemed to make a difference.

Chapter Five

Juggling

You must always give something to get something . . . In other words, sacrifice is a basic concept of our universe.

—Traditional Afro-Cuban Rite

Something had gone terribly wrong that day.

We drove up to Thornhill Elementary School and found my six-year-old son sitting alone in the dark at the bus stop. He knew he was to wait there to be picked up each day. This day, wires had been crossed. The person who was to pick Tariq up after school had not.

I was in grueling daytime rehearsals for Berkeley Repertory's *Kabuki Medea*. It was a professional play that required our cast to rehearse throughout the day. I thought the arrangements I had made for Tariq that day were made clear. It was when I called to make sure he had been picked up that I got the news he had not been and would not be. I dashed out of rehearsal to get him.

This time, rehearsal would just have to wait.

I was without a car at the time, so fellow actor Pamela Minet offered to take me. We were excused from rehearsal, and sped in her white convertible Alfa Romero by freeway to get my son. I prayed all the way. I asked the Lord to protect my child until I could get to him. Finding him untouched, I grabbed my son and placed him in my waiting arms.

I yelled, "Tariq! I am so sorry!"

In his quiet, he appeared unaffected.

Waiting.

Tariq knew my demanding life as an actor. He also knew someone would eventually come to pick him up. He truly demonstrated an act of faith as he sat obediently in the dark.

I got chills as I looked around and realized there was not another person in sight at the school that evening. The school was secluded amongst trees in the suburban Montclair Hills of Oakland, California, and only occasional lights from passing vehicles pierced the darkness. We three squeezed into the sports car as I took my son home to safety.

I am ashamed to admit my child was the last person to leave his school that day.

In 1984, children were not an "endangered species" as we have come to know them today. Child molestation, abductions, and child abuse were virtually untalked about during the '80s. Children usually seemed loved and safe with their parents, other family members, and adults, in general. That was another time in history, and seems so very, very removed from the horrific stories we know of today.

I shudder to think what might have happened to my son had he been left there in the world we now live in.

This chapter was, without doubt, the most difficult one for me to write. I had to look myself squarely in the mirror, with all my imperfections. I first began to write this book shielded behind my intellect. When I re-read what I had written in this chapter, I knew I could not hide. I knew I had to start again and speak nakedly from my heart. I had to speak from my frailties, not just my successes.

I know there are female actors out there who are trying to have a career, a relationship with a significant other, and who are, in some cases also trying to be a mother. Perhaps, by standing naked, I may spare someone some measure of grief by sharing a part of myself that is not part of my public self.

In my mind's eye, every time I see my son sitting on that bench in the dark, I am again overcome with feelings of guilt and thanksgiving. I am also reminded of how many times I placed my career before my son.

I did not see what I was doing then. I rationalized that I was trying to make a living for us, and if I worked hard enough, things would be better for both of us. I told myself by doing what I loved, it would make me a better person.

I never saw myself as selfish.

Knowing what I know now, if given the chance again, I would do parenting *completely* differently. Perhaps I would have adopted the ideals of Bette Davis and chosen not to become a parent at all. She firmly believed a woman could not effectively be both a mother and actor. Maybe I would still have chosen to become a mother, but would have taken more time out from my demanding career to stay home longer with my young son. Maybe I would have waited longer to become a mother. There are a host of "maybes."

But then hindsight is always 20/20.

Periodically, when something triggers my guilt, I again ask for my son's forgiveness for not having been a better mother. He always seems uncomfortable talking about the time-worn subject, but always allows me to express my feelings yet again. When I told him I wanted to embrace this painful subject in my book, he tried to soothe me as best he could when he voiced his exasperation.

"Mom, it was hard for us in the early days. But I guess in the end it was all worth it."

The jury is still out on that one.

As scary as that day at Thornhill Elementary School in the dark was, my most frightening day as a parent was the day Tariq was struck by a car in front of his first elementary school. He was within the crosswalk, but the driver said the sun blinded her and she could not see him. Tariq was thrown seventy feet from where he stood. One of his shoes had actually been knocked off from impact and was found further down the street.

Medics cut his colorful new green jacket off at the scene of the accident, and rushed him to nearby Children's Hospital in Oakland. Thank God the hospital was only walking distance from the scene of the accident and our home.

The principal came to my door to deliver the news. I knew something was very wrong when he approached my front door. We rushed together to the hospital. Without my own car, I rode with him for a five-minute drive that seemed forever. I realized how bad my judgment had been when I finally gave in to my son and allowed him to walk to school with another child. Instead of walking with her, he had run ahead of her on his own.

We finally arrived at the hospital. In the emergency room, I stood over Tariq, holding his hand. He was in so much pain lying on the emergency room table that he could not even cry. Only the tiniest, almost inaudible moan occasionally came from his tiny lips.

As I paced outside my son's emergency room, I, too, could only moan. I felt a fear and powerlessness I hope never, ever to feel again.

Tariq went into a coma and was not conscious of any of us gathered around him, even after he was moved to ICU. After many tests, we learned the accident left him with a contusion on the left side of his brain, a collapsed lung, and paralysis on his left side. The initial prognosis was questionable. The doctors tried to keep the injury in perspective by reminding Tariq's father Faruq and me that Tariq was very lucky to still be alive.

They were right, but we wanted our son back *exactly* the way he was before the accident.

We prayed for a full recovery. Faruq, Tariq's godmother Jacki, and I all took turns massaging him daily with medicinal oils as we visualized and prayed over him. We talked to him in his comatose state. His father placed a bronze pyramid under his mattress in visualization of a full healing. Jacki's girlfriend Geri brought in a group of prayer warriors who marched in and prayed "in tongues" over him without ceasing. Many others we knew, and those we did not know, all galvanized in prayer around the country as we asked the Lord to save my baby.

We claimed a miracle for my young child.

It was certainly no coincidence that a nurse just "happened" to be at the scene of the accident and cared for my son until the ambulance arrived. To this day, I do not know who that woman was. I never met or saw her. She disappeared as quickly as she appeared.

I believe she was Tariq's guardian angel.

More times than one, Tariq's birth date has proved to be in his favor. The day of that accident was no exception. As I mentioned in a previous chapter, Tariq was born seven, seven, seventy-seven.

His numbers are also no coincidence.

I remember how Tariq's wonderful European doctor at Children's Hospital came in each day to talk with him as she assessed his progress.

Cheery and patient, she tried to lighten us all up with her warm sense of humor.

Daily she asked Tariq if he could move his left arm and leg. Tariq refused to accept defeat, and answered his doctor by using his right arm to move his paralyzed left side.

Yes, he could move his left side.

We all rejoiced the day Tariq moved his left leg on his own. His doctor promised him candy if he could move his left leg unassisted. When he said he could move his left leg, we expected him to again move his left leg with his right arm. He surprised all of us by miraculously moving his left leg up in the air without the help of his right arm.

He got the candy.

Eventually, all paralysis on Tariq's left side was gone. Many times when I now see a person with a disability, I again thank God for sparing my son. Aside from a very slight limp and minimal atrophy, he was spared to live a normal life.

I do not believe in luck. I believe my family was blessed.

This story is one of my greatest testimonials to the possibility of miracles and the power of prayer.

My challenge as a parent was made greater, because although Tariq's father and I were still together in his formative years, we did not live together. Ours was a complex and non-traditional relationship, with its own set of challenges.

Most of my immediate family, including my mother, lived in the Sacramento Valley, and I lived in the Bay Area. I learned parenting mainly by trial and error. I did have the support of Tariq's father in the early days, but he was not always available.

I needed more help.

Like many mothers in the business living away from immediate family, I tried to juggle motherhood creatively. I called upon other family, friends, neighbors, and my babysitting co-op. When I really got in a childcare crunch, I used the services of teens I interviewed from bulletin board listings and Cal Berkeley college students who were registered to work off campus.

I juggled as best as I could.

My cousin Derrie Osby and his family also lived in Oakland. They were a huge support to me. Margaret, Derrie's wife, and their three daughters Ershla, Octavia, and Ariel, comprised my extended family in the Bay Area. I especially felt secure when I left Tariq with them, because I knew Derrie was a positive male role model and would also keep Tariq in check.

A house full of females, the girls seemed to enjoy having a little boy around.

During the summers, I got help from my family by taking Tariq to Oroville to spend a couple of weeks with my mother, my younger brother Edward, and his family. Tariq was exposed to the country, while he also established his own relationship with my immediate family. At Edward's home, Tariq was again in a house with three girl cousins: Malika, Ebony, and Aminah. His aunt Vickie took to him and seemed to enjoy having a boy around.

Trying to be a consistently health-conscious mother, I took home-cooked split pea soup and other nutritious foods to Oroville with us. I asked that my foods be frozen until used. I was horrified to later hear rumors that Tariq was taken straight to McDonald's as soon as I was out of sight!

I did the best I could as a mother based on what I knew at the time. Yet the cost was far greater than any child should ever have to pay. I was always "fitting" my son in around my hectic schedule when it worked best for me. As a result of not having his needs met, he often acted out at school. How out of touch I was.

I love my son and I gave him what I felt I could. I may not have spent as much time with him as he needed, but I was consistent about some things. We attended church regularly together to establish a religious foundation for him. Education was important to me so I made sure I checked his homework daily. To nurture his imagination and to encourage his love of books, I read him bedtime stories at night.

Tariq always looked forward to his annual birthday bash, because I chose different surprise locations each year and made special honor of him on his day. I also planned special outings for him, and his older brother and sister on his father's side, Nizam and Aminah. I tried to expose the three of them to cultural and educational things I thought they might enjoy and also learn from.

I was not one of the best parents, but I also was not one of the worst.

I recognized early my son's gift as a visual artist, and made sure he always had art classes and supplies to express his talent. Fortunately, Faruq passed on his gift as an artist to our son.

Tariq always seemed to find peace in his drawings, painting, and sculpturing. He seemed to go into a meditative state at his bedroom desk each evening as he quietly expressed himself through his artwork before going to bed. I believe Tariq's artwork also got him through a testy childhood. Growing up in our home as an only child, he learned how to occupy himself alone. I often watched him in fascination as he daily created beautiful artwork that we hung on his bedroom walls.

Despite our many challenges, somehow Tariq and I made it through the early days. We had our battle wounds along the way, especially when he was an adolescent, but we made it through the war. We are still not without our issues, but underneath our baggage, there is unconditional love and we are still working toward mending old wounds.

I would like to think I learned from my costly lessons as a mother. I have been given a reprieve as a grandmother. Malik Isaiah, my grandson, has given me another chance to mother, yet in a different role. Although I now spend far less time with my grandson than I want to, I give him as much love as I can when we are together.

I say to all women reading this book who are trying to mother, and have a career in the business too, learn from me.

Place your child first.

The career will always be there. An impressionable, growing child will not. Children need us more than any career possibly can. We can be replaced on a job, but we cannot be replaced as a natural parent. The cost of putting one's career first is not worth the cost to our children. It is no wonder our children are expressing varying degrees of rage and insecurity. They are crying out to be heard and loved. They need our love and time more than they will ever need the materialistic substitutes we sometimes try to give in our place.

If you are a mother with a young child, please learn from me.

In hindsight, I can see now that being a good parent is infinitely more important than being a good performer. I look at some of my friends like Amy and Ron Reed, Eugene and Amy Calhoun, and Liz Benoit and her husband, who are some of the most loving and wonderful parents I have witnessed. In the early days of their children's development, they invested the time and reaped the rewards.

Being a good parent is my real measure of success.

Not only did I juggle as a mother, I also juggled many day jobs with my career as a professional actor. I lived in the East Bay but often worked and performed in San Francisco. I sometimes had to have someone pick Tariq up from daycare so I could stay in San Francisco for rehearsals. I always regretted the days I had to work and perform late because it affected our homework and bedtime story time together.

Although Faruq contributed as a father, it was not an easy life for the three of us.

I think back now on some of the exhausting schedules I juggled. I worked at UC Med Center during the day as I rehearsed *Jo Anne!* at night. To make it through the day, I went to the restroom near my office to lie on the cold leather cot for breaks and lunch. The day I got dizzy and saw stars, I knew my body was overloaded. Something had to give.

Due to the success of *Jo Anne!*, my growing fatigue, and an escalating conflict with my supervisor, I eventually quit my highly-coveted position at UC Med Center and began temping instead. The commute and the commitments of a career-track position, as well as having a superior I ultimately did not get along with, exhausted me. I thought the success of *Jo Anne!* was my ticket to finally "making it" as an actor without having to work a day job anymore.

I was naïve.

Jo Anne! was not my ticket to leaving the traditional work world. It was simply a moment in time where I was part of a very well-received play. When I realized I needed to keep working, I decided to do work as a receptionist. Being a receptionist afforded me the opportunity to do a lot of my personal work at the receptionist desk in privacy. I learned my lines for plays, made personal calls, handled my bills, and everything else I could juggle at the front desk. Even with all my personal work in front of me, I did not skip a beat answering calls and greeting the public. I enjoyed being a receptionist, and was actually very skilled at it because I was good with the public and with answering telephones.

Oddly, I have never waited tables like many actors I know. In that regard, I feel I have not fully "paid my dues" with day jobs. However, it is probably best that customers did not find me at their tables to take their orders.

During the early days of my career, I worked many jobs out of necessity. I refused to give up my career, yet I had to work. Fortunately for me, I found some degree of satisfaction at most of the places I worked. In some cases, I actually enjoyed the challenges of my work, especially in the fields of hospital volunteerism and mental health counseling.

I learned later that it was also possible to create my own work.

I say to others who are serious about being an actor: try to figure out a way to create your own work or develop another talent. That way, if necessary, you can work your schedule around your career, and your family. This is a very demanding business. The more we can create our own vehicles, the more we can control our lives.

Creating my solo show, *I Am That I Am:* Woman, *Black,* has certainly allowed me to empower myself as an entrepreneur. I made my down payment on my home in North Hollywood in 1995 from earnings that came *exclusively* from bookings of my one-woman show.

Now, to embrace the subject of juggling a love relationship.

First of all, I love Black men. I have been blessed with some good men in my life whom I believe loved me. One of the earliest was Samuel Archer Lee, whom I was engaged to when I was only eighteen, before I left home for college. His love came to me at a young age, and I did not know how to fully accept it. Sam demonstrated his love for me more passionately than any man who has followed him, but I was too young and inexperienced to fully appreciate him. Although we had a very strong attraction to each other on many levels, we were also very different. I was still a teenager and he was a twenty-one-year-old young Air Force man. I came from have nots and he came from a middle-class Black family. I was a country bumpkin and he was from the city of Baltimore, Maryland. He wanted a wife and I wanted college and a career.

Had we married, I am certain I would not be telling this same life story.

The man who most influenced my life was my son's father Faruq. I met him one day in 1975 as I pulled up to my Oakland apartment building to park my white Volkswagen bug. He noticed me before I saw him crossing the street toward me. Once I did notice him, what caught my eye was his physical presence. He was very tall, dark, and quite handsome. Dressed impeccably in a dark suit, I could tell by his demeanor he was a Muslim brother selling his bean pies. His initial look attracted me that day, but his mind sustained my interest.

Faruq exposed me to higher consciousness in ways that included religion, spirituality, metaphysics, diet, meditation, astrology and numerology. I had never been exposed to many of the things he taught me. Fascinated by him, I was open to learn all that he wanted to share.

In part, it was because of him that in 1977 I chose to release my birth name of "Lovey," and took on the Arabic name of "Adilah," which means "one who deals justly."

Although we separated after six years together, I still loved him deeply. Today, we are still connected because of our son and grandson.

Faruq's impact on me in terms of my higher consciousness is unquestionable.

Because my career has been a driving force in my life, I have never been in a relationship with any man who has asked me to choose between him and my career. I believe each of the significant men in my life admired my talent. They certainly supported my work. They seemed to take pleasure in seeing me onstage as I continued to develop my craft. Although it was never discussed in words, it was always understood I was not going to give up my career. Some of the men in my life were artists themselves and understood well both the joys and demands of the creative process.

Marriage.

When I am asked if I am married and I reply "No," invariably a common follow-up question is, "Have you ever been married?" My second "no" usually opens the floodgates of surprised looks and a number of questions. Since I am a single parent, the question always boils down to "Why?"

I liken the continual inquiry of marriage to that of women who have chosen not to have children. In either case, an explanation always seems to be in order.

The subject of marriage has always been a sore one with me.

It is not that I have never been asked to be married. In fact, I have been proposed to five times in my life. It has been I who has *chosen* not to marry.

I have rationalized in many ways why I have not chosen to marry. I have told myself I might marry the wrong person and end up getting a divorce. I might get suffocated. I might grow tired of marriage. In my younger years, as a single mother, I did not want to have another man over my child. In any case, I now believe that underneath it all, I feared I might fail at marriage.

There has also been the matter of my career.

The truth is, as a young woman, I barely had enough time and energy to give to both my son and my career. I have been in several very significant long-term love relationships where we have lived under the same roof, but it has always been the finality of the "I do" stage that has made me feel uneasy.

I am *finally* beginning to embrace the possibility of marriage.

I have a relatively full life, but the one thing I am missing is intimacy. What I want in a marriage at my age is companionship with a man who is whole within himself, and who is spiritually evolved. I want to share intimacy with someone I love, doing things we both enjoy. I want someone whom I trust and who is willing to accept me as I am.

I want a man who can express his love through a look or a fleeting touch. I want someone who can be both my best friend and my intellectual equal. I find intelligence very attractive, even sexy. I want a man who is playful, who can laugh, and who can make me laugh. I know I may not get all that I want, but I believe I can get *most* of what I want.

To those in the business who are wrestling with the notion of a love relationship, it might not be a bad idea to consider someone who is not in the business.

My experience has been I can rarely leave work when I am with someone in the business. I remember once dating another writer/actor who decorated his bedroom like a stage, and black was the dominating color!

Focusing on the industry all the time can take up too much space in a relationship.

Unless both persons are unusually centered and secure within themselves, being with someone in the business can also lay the groundwork for competition. It is likely both will eventually begin to measure who works more and who makes more money. I know firsthand of the jealousies, especially if the woman earns more and is termed "more successful."

It is hard sometimes for actors to maintain perspective. Many of us value our worth by whether or not we are working. I know many actors who are miserable unless they are working.

I say, get a life.

I am finally beginning to find more balance in my own life. I am coming to appreciate things that have nothing to do with the business, because they sustain me when I am not working. I especially love being outside with nature. I enjoy developing my spiritual side, spending more time with my family and friends, walking, reading, and writing more. I am also trying not to work on weekends, unless it is work *I* want to do.

Acting is what I do, not who I am.

To that end, I try to maintain a spiritual ritual that grounds and relaxes me. On days that I am successful in disciplining myself, I begin my day by writing three "morning pages" from Julia Cameron's book *The Artist's Way*. It is a stream of consciousness daily writing exercise. I try to keep my hand on the page writing thought after thought without stopping and without editing. Sometimes I even resort to sentences like "I do not feel like writing today. I do not have anything else I want to write but I will keep writing. Yes, I am still writing but I do not want to write right now," as I try to pad what I write to successfully make it to the third page.

I follow my morning pages by opening my Bible to a random page to read whatever passage I am led to. I also read the "thought for the day" from Iyanla Van Zant's *Acts of Faith*. I pull an "angelic card" from a set of inspirational cards I found at a spiritual bookstore in Sedona, Arizona, during a Thanksgiving holiday trip with Tariq and my friend Vesper Osborne. I might pull a card on the subject of "potential" or "change" or "introspection." It is uncanny how I always seem to be drawn to the card that says exactly what I need to hear that day.

There are also my morning yoga and transcendental meditation that support my daily tightrope walk. I occasionally choose a day for a "talking fast," where I may not utter one word aloud for twenty-four hours or more.

I am still trying to balance my juggling act by exercising more and by eating a healthier diet. At the time of this writing, I am now a vegan. Although I have not eaten red meat in thirty-two years and my diet is a relatively healthy one, I can still do better. I do not want to admit it, but sweets are my "drug." I do not drink, smoke, or do "drug-drugs," but I do sweets, even though they may be vegan pastries.

Yes, sweets.

As I sit down on December 31ˢᵗ of each year for my year-end ritual that includes candles, incense, and soothing smooth jazz music, I review my goals I set the previous year. I check off all the goals I successfully accomplished. It is amazing to see how many of my goals have come into fruition during each year. It is also a wonderful feeling to check completed goals off one by one.

I make sure I list my major blessings received for the year during my ritual. It is important to me to take the time to name my blessings as a way of acknowledgment. I also write my new goals for the coming year at each year's end.

Being a visual person, there is something about seeing my life defined on paper.

I try to write six goals each day and check completed goals throughout the day. I also like to acknowledge in writing one miracle each day. Not only does this ritual keep me focused on my priorities, it also allows me to see my blessings unfold on a daily basis. Some are small and some are huge. I will try harder to do this ritual more often.

Since I have always been a person who multi-tasks and who wears several hats at any given moment, I need organization in my life to accomplish the many things I do. I am an actor, teacher, producer, writer, and writing retreat owner—*far* too many hats for any one person to wear.

I especially give thanks to my personal assistants I have had over the years who have helped me keep some semblance of order in my life including Ranier Kenny, Janora McDuffie, Ricie Frazier, Shamika Frankin, Chaka Ra, Phoebe Holston, Karimah Westbrook, Teri Akpovi, and my cousin Christine Burton. They have each helped me find balance with my juggling act. They have also seen me at my very worst and very best. To each of them, I offer a very public thank you.

When interviewed several years ago by actor Marla Gibbs, host of the Los Angeles Women's Theatre Festival's cable show *Los Angeles Women's Theatre Festival: On The Air!*, it seemed the interview would never end.

I kept asking between takes, "When are we going to be done?"

Marla smiled and said, "If you didn't do so much, we wouldn't have so much to talk about."

Chapter Six

From English to Acting

I haven't done too much of anything that did not fit me.
—Dexter King, politician

S he looked me in the eyes and said, "I'm a director. I'd like to work with you one day."

I was a mental health counselor at a Walnut Creek sub-acute facility and it was not uncommon to hear patients speak in delusional states. I had been prepped to work at this mental health facility, having previously worked at a halfway house in nearby Concord, California. In both facilities, I was exposed to a diverse group of colorful patients who were diagnosed as what was then termed psychotic. On many occasions, I heard some speak of their fantasy worlds as if they were real.

Indeed, they were real to them.

Without judgment or commitment, I replied to this patient, "I would love to know your work as a director."

Like many I came to know in my four years as a mental health counselor, thanks to my friend Khalil Muhadji who introduced me to the world of mental health counseling, this Jewish patient was exceedingly bright, articulate, and sensitive. She was actually one of my favorite patients at the hospital, because we shared a love and passion for theatre, and our conversations often centered around the arts.

At the same time, I knew she was medicated because she was not well. I also knew that more likely than not, she was not a director and we would never work together.

Imagine my surprise several years later when our paths crossed again. By this time, she had been named Director of the East Bay Center for the Performing Arts. Not only did she appear well, she was also in a position to cast me in an upcoming play she was about to direct. She was also in a position to hire me as one of the Center's acting teachers.

The tables had turned.

She straightforwardly said, "I'd like to hire you to teach acting in our after-school program, both here and in the Berkeley public schools."

I thanked her for the offer, but declined. I explained to her that I had not *really* taught acting before and did not feel qualified to teach.

She smiled as she assured me, "I think you would make a very good teacher."

I will forever be grateful to this woman who believed in me and opened the door for me to become an acting teacher. Prior to her offer, I had only taught acting at Upward Bound at Chico State, and that had been the summer following my freshman year in college. Looking back, I believe I was mainly hired to come back as a role model for other Upward Bound students, and to keep me in the womb of Upward Bound for one more summer.

After some coaxing, I accepted her offer to teach. Although reluctant, I began teaching elementary students in the Center's after-school program. On the one hand, it was a non-threatening way to begin as a teacher, because the children were so young they had little to compare our acting class. On the other hand, the kids were quick to let me know through their disruptive behavior when they were bored.

Young students of acting need to be stimulated in a very different way.

In my early classes where I trained as a teacher, I taught those from the very gifted to those who were only enrolled because their parents needed coverage until they were able to pick them up after work.

Some were attentive and others were not.

In the beginning, I relied on acting exercises I learned from my acting teachers at UC Santa Cruz and Upward Bound. I also used acting books that gave me still other exercises and technique choices. Although I learned to teach by trial and error in those formative days, I also got better at it and more confident as time went on.

I learned that different keys needed to be used to open up creativity in young children. In truth, that principle works for students of any age.

Each student must be met where he or she is and approached in a way that unlocks their creativity. That is the starting place.

Most of my early elementary students seemed to enjoy many of the Viola Spolin theatre games, improvisation, and class-created skits I prepared. What worked in class, I learned to build on. I learned with children the importance of making acting feel like play, while at the same time teaching principles of the craft.

And so began the next twist on my career path.

As I said earlier, from childhood I always wanted to become an English teacher. I *love* language. I love the manipulation, sound, and rhythm of language. I also love its power. I always want to share what knowledge I have, and feel comfortable in front of others. I also want others to be the best they can be.

I did not consciously understand it then, but knowledge is power.

There was never a doubt in my mind that I would actualize my ambition of becoming an English teacher until I began taking acting classes at UC Santa Cruz. There I began to shift my attention from a major in English to Theatre Arts. At that crossroad, acting won out over my lifelong desire to major in English.

So it was fitting that I would become an acting teacher. During those early years, I taught at a number of Berkeley Elementary Schools in the East Bay Center's after-school program. I navigated the city of Berkeley by teaching in both the inner city flatlands and quaint residential areas of the Berkeley Hills.

In the flatlands, some of my students I already knew, including my son's brother and sister, Nizam and Aminah. There was also my young cousin Ershla Osby. Having family in class provided comfort, but also created a special challenge. They knew me personally, and it sometimes required extra work to get them to see me as a teacher, not just a relative.

Zorana Edun was one of my first students at the East Bay Center's Saturday program. A precocious and beautiful five-year-old, Zorana was already a very poised and professional union card-carrying actor. She also had a traditional "showbiz mom," Merriam, who was always by her side.

Zorana is a very special former student of mine, because I have witnessed her growth from a small child to a young woman. In August of 1993, I attended her unusual wedding at a castle in the Los Angeles Hills. I was very moved as I saw her cross over fully into womanhood as a young wife.

After all these years, Zorana and I are still connected. She literally lives in my North Hollywood neighborhood and is a part of my Los Angeles Women's Theatre Festival. It has been a pleasure to see her unfold from a small child actor to a young woman who is still following her passion in the business.

My former mental health patient also cast me in one of my favorite plays, *A Raisin in the Sun* by Lorraine Hansberry. This acclaimed writer was the first Black playwright to be produced on Broadway. In her production, I played the daughter Beneatha, in this highly charged and well-crafted play. Also in the cast were the likes of DeBorah Pryor and the late LeOna Harris, who became lifelong friends of mine.

My former mental health patient did *exactly* what she said she wanted to do. She cast me in a play and directed me. She turned out to be a good director, and we worked well together.

She also believed in me enough to give me my first *real* teaching job.

I forged ahead and expanded my knowledge and experience by teaching children in other Bay Area schools. I taught at Shelton's Primary Education Center and Green Door. These were private schools my son attended, and where I bartered teaching as a creative way to offset the cost of his tuition. By teaching children in all these different settings, I continued to sharpen my skills as an acting teacher.

Teaching youth proved to be a very safe and challenging way to hone my skills as a teacher.

My teaching later took me to other Bay Area institutions, such as the now defunct San Francisco School of Dramatic Arts, where Whoopi Goldberg and I taught. I moved on to the prestigious American Conservatory Theater in San Francisco. After my move to Los Angeles, I taught at both Marla Gibbs' Crossroads Arts Academy and the Los Angeles Theatre Center before I finally chose to teach classes privately in Hollywood and North Hollywood. I still continue to teach classes privately from time to time, although I now prefer coaching actors one-on-one.

I have taught actors from those who had never taken an acting class to those who are a household name. In the early days, I had no idea I would move to Los Angeles and work with celebrities. Some, like Benjamin Bratt, Kym Whitley, and Lauren Lane, I had the pleasure of working with before their careers took off. I have also worked with some celebrities such as Chris Brown, Joe Torry and Earthquake for a fleeting moment. In either case, I try to leave something lasting with each person I coach.

Some celebrities come to me as crossover actors, especially those who are comedians or singers. Some, like Jada Pinkett-Smith, whom I coached when she was about to shoot *Set It Off,* get private coaching when they know they will have to "carry" a film. Some actors, as in the case of Toni Braxton, have received moment-by-moment feedback from a trained eye while shooting projects on location on film and television sets.

In addition to my high-profile clientele, I have worked with students over the years who are not "known" actors but who are just as good, hard-working, and committed to their craft as any well-known actors.

The only real difference is some have "made it" and some are on their way.

Although I did not become an English teacher as I dreamed, I did become a teacher nonetheless. I feel very blessed to have become what I always wanted to become. I understood my calling at a young age, and thirty years later, I still love teaching. My teaching time is now limited, so when I do teach workshops, I combine students of all levels in my classes. It makes for a very interesting dynamic, because the "beginners" are forced to move at a more accelerated pace, and the "advanced" students have the distinction of being at the "top of the class."

I began this chapter with the story about my mental health patient, and I would also like to end with that same story. She reminded me that you never know who your angels will be. You also never know who will one day be in a position to open doors for you.

I have learned that our gifts may come from the most unlikely of places.

Chapter Seven

Cowboy Boots

No earthly power can break you . . . An unbroken spirit is the only thing you cannot live without.

—Paula Giddings, educator/writer

E very time I looked down the row and saw cowboy boots, I was reminded of my place.

Friday mornings were the highlight of the Advanced Training Program at the American Conservatory Theater (ACT) because first year students presented their scene work for critiques. An unmistakable excitement filled the air as acting students nervously prepared to strut their stuff in hopes of praise and favor from faculty in front of an in-house Conservatory audience. Most had plans to become "company journeymen" on the mainstage of the Geary Theater their third year, and this was the first step.

The packed audiences for scene presentations usually included second year students, Conservatory instructors, and professional actors from the ACT Company. Staff members who were able to get away from their work schedules would also sit in. First year student scene presentations were an exciting communal event at the Conservatory.

Friday mornings usually held some degree of anxiety for me because I felt the pressure of having to critique the work of first year students. I would like to think it was only because I was the "new kid on the block" I was usually called on last to give my student critiques. In any case, there was an unstated hierarchy of faculty critiques. Once I realized this hierarchy, I became more and more uneasy about my placement. Usually called on last to speak, I feared it would be perceived by everyone in the room that what I had to say held less value.

Like my peers, I wanted to earn respect from my students. However, I felt the critique structure, whether intentional or not, might make me appear to be "less than."

Nonetheless, Friday morning scene critiques were where my teaching chops and survival skills were forced to kick in. Out of my need to be taken seriously, and in my fight for respect, I found a way to contribute meaningfully. I began to develop a sharper eye for detail as I identified less obvious things that my peers either missed or chose not to comment on.

Sometimes my colleagues acknowledged my critique comments. Sometimes they did not. Whether I got my props from them or not, I praised myself for the keen eye I was being groomed to develop more fully.

Being a "first" is never easy.

The year was 1986. At that time, it was not uncommon for some 1,000 applicants to compete annually for only twenty-four full time Advanced Training Program slots that would last for two years.

ACT's former Artistic Director Ed Hastings invited me into the fold of ACT "trainers." His unilateral decision brought me aboard. He knew my work as an actor from my days in ACT's Black Actor's

Workshop, and must have known I had gone on to teach acting at other institutions in the Bay Area.

In either case, Ed had not forgotten me.

My heart began to pound with excitement and trepidation with Ed's initial telephone call to my Richmond, California home. It was not as though I had applied for a teaching position or even been asked to interview at ACT. I had unconditionally been invited on the team as an acting instructor. Ed asked only that I meet with him in his office to discuss the offer in more detail.

It appeared to be just that easy.

The fact that the invitation came only from Ed became glaringly clear early on. Not everyone on the teaching staff welcomed me with the same open arms. It was apparent to me who wanted me there and who did not. It also became apparent to me that I had crossed over into a teaching staff dominated by men.

Mainly driven by my need to succeed, coupled with the old adage that "if you are Black, you have to be twice as good," I felt a need to prove I deserved to be in the Good Ole Boy's Club. I felt like I was in uncharted waters and would have to navigate myself on my own if I was to make it safely to shore.

I could not fail.

Inherently Eurocentric in curriculum, ACT's Conservatory was not unlike many of the other "league" schools around the country, in that it had very few students of color in its full-time program. Visibly noticeable and few in number, students of color always stood out. As the only full-time African American trainer, I also stood out. My look further contrasted with that of my jeans-and-cowboy-boots-wearing counterparts. My "uniform" consisted daily of colorful sweat suits and berets. The solid-colored sweats were comfortable and became my trademark.

This was not the first time I had entered a world of Eurocentric theatre. The same was true as a UC Santa Cruz student. After college, my mainstream credits included the likes of John Guare's *Snow Angel*; *Kabuki Medea,* based on Euripides' classic play; and Moliére's *Tartuffe*. However, my favorite writers were Black and included the likes of Lorraine Hansberry, Ed Bullins, J.E. Franklin, and newcomer August Wilson.

Nonetheless, I had once again entered a world that favored Eurocentric classics. From where I stood at ACT, a lot was at stake. I wanted to do well. To that end, every week when scene selections for first-year students were posted for the following week's presentations, I would check the bulletin board to see which acting students were paired with whom and which plays had been assigned them. More importantly, I made note of which plays I did not know.

Thus began my homework as a teacher.

I went to great lengths to prepare myself for Friday critiques. I spent each week voraciously reading any unfamiliar plays on the weekly lists. Some plays I already knew, but there were many I did not. Because there were twelve scenes presented each week, sometimes I had to quickly read all the unknown plays. I made it a habit to read them in time, because I refused to critique any plays I was unfamiliar with.

For me, it was not enough to critique scenes based on what was presented before me. I wanted to know the world of the characters. I wanted to know the depth of their relationships, as well as the past, present, and future circumstances surrounding each of the characters. That is why I took the time to meticulously read the plays unfamiliar to me. I needed to know everything I possibly could before Friday scene critiques. I also wanted to come fully prepared.

Similarly, in my acting classes, I require my students to select scenes and monologues from actual plays so that they may fully enter the world of their characters. I believe an actor creates uninformed work when characters are created from scene and monologue books that are not from plays. With limited information, the work can lack believability and depth.

In my mind, it makes much more sense to choose monologues and scenes from plays, because there simply is more information available from the text of an entire play to draw from.

My story of being a "first" is not unique. Truth be told, there are other "firsts" and some "not firsts" who have stories like mine—in other Conservatory training programs and also in academia. In environments such as the one I placed myself in, there is an insidious need to be liked, respected, included, and advanced. For some, approval and acceptance can sometimes outweigh principle.

I was especially aware and protective of *my* students at ACT because I could relate to what some of them were going through. I was battling to earn my respect and acceptance, while holding firm to my integrity. Some of them were waging a similar fight.

In general, ACT students were trying to make the inevitable cut that awaited most of them after their second year of training. Yet most of them still had their eyes set on becoming full-time, third-year journeymen in the acting company. Many with an undergraduate degree planned to complete their Master's Degree while at ACT. The wise ones earned theirs.

Getting a Master's Degree at ACT actually had better odds than getting chosen for the few third-year journeymen slots in the company. It was always painful for me to witness the ones cut that I personally felt deserved to make it to the third year. Because students of all ethnicities had initially been embraced into the ACT "family," it was shattering for some to be "ousted" from their kin. I imagine this process is little different than at other "league" acting schools, and it can be brutally devastating to the ego.

I could read the questions in some of their faces after they found out they did not make the cut: "Why didn't I get selected?" "Am I not as good as the other actors chosen?" "What did I do wrong?" "Didn't they like me?" "What will happen to me now?" "Where will I go?"

This juncture was always a turning point because most were weaned from the safety and security net of the Conservatory. They were forced to take the inevitable next step in their careers.

Most students had been stripped of their acting techniques when they entered, only to be replaced with Uta Hagen's acting technique. Most had actually become better actors after their two years of training, but some became less sure of themselves and their instincts during the process.

Those who were not chosen for the third year got their first sobering taste of the real world of professional acting. Competition and rejection have always been part and parcel to this business. For most, after their two years, they experienced this reality up close.

Competition and rejection simply come with the territory.

As an actor, there are times when I want a role but may not get it. When that happens, I remind myself that the role has someone else's name on it. Just as a role may not be mine, surely there will be other roles that *will* have my name. Understanding this helps soften the rejection process and keeps in perspective that I will get the roles meant for me.

I *will* continue to work.

Some ACT students I taught during the late 1980s went on to successful careers after ACT. Some went on to regional theatres in cities like New York, Chicago, Los Angeles, and Denver. Some, like Benjamin Bratt and Lauren Lane, met with fame and crossed over into television and film. Some left the business altogether. Some, like Allen Taylor and Keeley Stanley, became college professors who have taught acting at Marin College and Central Michigan University, respectively.

Being an actor can look very easy and glamorous from afar.

Unless you have experienced it firsthand, though, it is impossible to know the stresses of rejection, the toll of not working for long periods of time, and the commitment needed to build a successful career.

In 2002, I mentored New Jersey teen Sasha Pemberton. She "shadowed" me in my home for three and a half weeks as part of *The Signature Experience* at the prestigious Peddie School's high school summer placement project. As Sasha followed me around daily, she witnessed an unexpected and realistic glimpse of the world of acting.

She accompanied me on a seventeen-hour shoot for an episode of Lifetime's *For the People*. It was far more grueling than she or I anticipated. We were both absolutely spent by the time we left the set.

Sasha said to me once during that summer, "I'm not sure I still want to be an actor. It's a lot of work!"

Indeed, being an actor is not as easy as it looks, and one needs to be in it for the long haul to have a sustained career. Even then, there are no guarantees. There have been many twists and turns on my particular roller-coaster ride. However, for the most part, my journey has been a more fulfilling and easier one than for some.

ACT introduced me to Uta Hagen's technique of acting. Her *Respect for Acting* book was our bible. My style of teaching today has been heavily influenced by her approach. Her "method" involves given circumstances, relationship to other characters and objects, object exercises, personalizations, sensory and emotional recall, and, in a word, creating truth onstage by making use of a number of practical principles.

The Conservatory prided itself in non-traditional casting of student projects. Sometimes this approach brought opportunities to play roles that student actors probably would never have been cast in the real world.

However, sometimes the non-traditional ACT casting approach could present its own set of challenges. For example, I remember the time I directed a student production of the play *Homeland* by my South African friend Selaelo Maredi. The play, written during the time of apartheid, placed race at the centerpiece of the theme. Since we could *request* which actors we wanted to cast, I took care to ask for the students I wanted for my show. I wanted Black students to play Black characters and Anglo students to play Anglo characters.

Because of ACT's non-traditional casting, most of my choices for this play were not given to me. I was given an Asian female actor to play a South African Black maid, an Anglo female actor to play an American Black maid, and so on and so forth. I knew if color was not honored, the play would not have the stinging bite it deserved. My production would become completely diluted and would look and feel silly. I chose to direct this play, and I wanted to make it a powerful and believable piece of theatre.

This is another instance where my creativity kicked in.

I decided that since I had to work with the actors given me, I *could* achieve the presence of color through costumes. All my actors who were playing Blacks *wore* black, and all my actors who were playing white *wore* white. By making that one adjustment, I found a visual way to constantly remind the audience of color and race.

Although I had found a way to get around racial color, I still had to get my actors to own who they were racially. There were cultural orientations that had to be addressed.

I remember the day my female lead actor Mary Jo Bradley walked up to me in her frustration and said something like, "I am having a very hard time playing a Black maid. I have never been Black, I have never been a maid, and I have never been the object of racism."

I knew she had once been a nurse, so I asked her if she remembered the oppression she sometimes felt from doctors.

Her body reacted strongly as she said, "Yes!"

I had found a visceral "personalization" (a personal experience) that she could use as a "substitution" (a replacement that triggers the same emotion).

I said, "Use it."

That personalization allowed Mary Jo to go exactly where she needed to with the Black character. She ultimately opened herself up as a person *and* actor, while she created an honest portrayal.

Although challenging on a number of levels, I was pleased with the results of my student production. Actors were forced to see through the eyes of those who looked nothing like them, and we maintained the strength and integrity of the play. It was an important learning experience for all of us. Most of my actors had walked a mile in the shoes of those culturally different from themselves and were exposed to roles they were very unlikely to be cast in the real world of acting.

Although my experience as a teacher in ACT's Advanced Training Program had its many challenges, fortunately, I also taught in two other ACT programs that were more comfortable for me. I taught in the full-time Summer Training Congress (STC), where admission was far less stringent. I also taught in the Extension Program, which is now called Studio A.C.T. The latter provided both evening and weekend classes for those in the community.

What I enjoyed most about those two programs was that I was able to teach freely and independently. The Summer Training Congress was a ten-week intensive program that in some ways was a condensed version of the highly touted Advanced Training Program. Students attended class full-time and also received training, utilizing their entire instrument through acting, voice, and movement classes. Essentially, it was a mini Advanced Training Program. At the same time, it was not as competitive to get in.

Many of the students in STC who were enrolled were from all over the country, and even beyond. Students were often young, vibrant, and passionate about developing their chops as actors. Some of the more ambitious ones had their eyes on the Advanced Training Program and hoped that the Summer Training Congress would be their side door entrance.

Coincidentally, Laura Kollar, a former student I taught in the Summer Training Congress, I saw again in her home state of Virginia during the fall of 2002. I had come to Richmond to shoot the award-winning HBO film *Iron-Jawed Angels* with award-winning Hilary Swank. I also spent time with a former Advanced Training Program student, Cameron Allen. Neither of them were able to join me on the set, but I appreciated spending time with each of them in their home state after so many years. The twists and turns they experienced in their lives after ACT fascinated me.

Interestingly enough, neither is still an actor.

I have maintained contact with some of my other former ACT students. Some call and visit me from time to time. Some I run into at auditions and other places that happen to bring us together. It is always heartwarming to see them again and to see where their life paths have taken them. It is also challenging to be up for the same roles as some of my former students!

Some students left me with mementoes that remind me of them. For example, in my kitchen is the crystal cake dish that my Advanced Training Program cast gave me at the closing of the play *Bus Stop*. Because the play takes place in a diner, the cake dish was given with a very special meaning. Although the cake dish cover got chipped while moving once, I still have it.

Perhaps my most memorable gift was from a class of Summer Training Congress students who presented me with an unusual, white, hardback journal with dried leaves on the cover. Everyone signed a sheet of paper they left inside. They said the book was for "when I was ready to write my acting book."

Writing an acting book seemed very unlikely then. However, those students planted the seeds for this book. When I began performing my solo show, *I Am That I Am:* Woman*, Black,* I decided to use that same book they gave me as a prop for my Mary McLeod Bethune portrayal. It is onstage with me every single time I perform my show in its entirety.

I hope every one of those students who signed that book will come in contact with this book. I want them to know the seed they planted many years ago finally came into fruition.

In the Extension Program, a part-time student had a huge impact on my career. Sterling Anderson was a young aspiring actor who was also a very astute businessman. At the time, he was the then only African American running a winery in the state of California.

Sterling took my evening classes and guided me to my first theatrical agency in Los Angeles. Sterling was a commercial client of the very powerful and well-respected bi-coastal Triad Agency.

Sterling suggested that I send my photo and resumé to the only African American agent in either of their offices. He began to rattle off some of the names of their bigger clients at the time that included Roseanne, Victoria Principal, Shari Belafonte and others. It became immediately clear to me that Triad Agency was a major player in the world of Los Angeles agencies.

At the time, I was still a Bay Area actor and had not yet seriously entertained the thought of moving to Los Angeles. I had considered it occasionally, but Los Angeles seemed way off my radar, both in terms of distance and possibility. It seemed so very far away.

Out of politeness, I thanked Sterling for the contact, but unbeknownst to him, I had no real intention of following through on his lead. Not only was Los Angeles not in my consciousness, I was also extremely intimidated by the thought of approaching that powerful agency. At that point in my career, my thought was, "Why in the world would they be interested in little me?" I *was* a big fish in the Bay Area, but then again, that was the Bay Area.

After giving me the agent's name, address, and phone number at Triad, Sterling asked me each week if I had sent my photo and resumé yet. I would brush aside his promptings with vague and quick answers.

Finally, unwilling to be dismissed further, Sterling asked me why I had not yet contacted her.

I replied, "I need to get my photos duplicated."

Sterling looked me squarely in the eyes and said, "Give me your photo. I'll get copies made."

With dread, I gave Sterling my photo for duplication the following week.

The next class, Sterling walked in with a white cardboard box. He met me with his smiling face and dancing eyes as he handed me a box containing 50 black and white photos.

He said, "*Now* what is your excuse?"

From the mouths of students.

By the time I was finally ready to do my mailer, I coincidentally was planning a trip to Los Angeles to see ACT's production of August Wilson's *Ma Rainey's Black Bottom.* I had understudied the role of Dussie Mae at ACT, and the production was now enjoying a successful run at the Los Angeles Theatre Center in downtown Los Angeles. I wanted to go see it.

I mentioned in my cover letter to the agent the dates I would be coming to Los Angeles. I told her I would welcome the opportunity to meet with her while in town. I stuck the stamp on that manila envelope, dropped it in the mailbox, and gave a big exhalation. I could now tell Sterling that I had followed up on his lead, and release the matter.

I had done what I told Sterling I would do, and I did not give another thought to meeting with the agency. I went back to my familiar Bay Area world of acting and teaching without looking back.

Imagine how stunned and terrified I was when only days later, I got a call from Robin, the female assistant at Triad, stating "Jenny got your letter and would love to meet with you while you are in Los Angeles."

Never let them see you sweat.

I casually talked dates and times. Once we scheduled my appointment, I hung up and looked at the telephone. I had a panic attack. Somebody in Los Angeles wanted to see *me.*

Now what to do?

I did not know the city of Los Angeles, and I did not have the slightest idea what to expect in my meeting. However, I *did* know Triad was a big agency, and this appointment held the potential to change my life. Depending on the outcome of the interview, the door would either be cracked open or slammed shut in my face.

My friend Earl Franklin offered to share his studio apartment in Hollywood, so I did not have to worry about a place to stay. What I needed next was to get to someone who knew the inner workings of the business, and I needed to do it quickly.

Danny Glover.

I called Danny's San Francisco Haight Ashbury home and got his answering machine.

In desperation, I left an urgent message that went something like, "Danny, I have an appointment in LA to meet with a big agency. Please call me as soon as you can. I need to talk to you!"

I gave the date and time I would be flying out and then waited for Danny's return call. His career had taken off, but I also prayed he would understand the importance of the trip and squeeze in a call to me.

I waited for Danny's call.

And I waited.

Finally, at about 11:00 p.m., the night before I was to fly out, my phone rang.

I picked up my phone and said, "Yes?"

I heard that familiar, raspy, quiet voice on the other end of the telephone.

He said, "What's happenin'?"

I shrieked, "Danny!"

Without taking a breath, I went on to explain the details of my impending journey. When I gave the name of the agency, Danny's response went something like, "That's a good agency. I know some people with them."

Danny eventually became a client himself.

Danny further went on to say, "I'll tell you what's going to happen. They're going to have you meet some of the agents there. They'll put a few calls out to casting directors to meet with you. Then the casting directors are going to let Triad know what they think about you."

Finally, Danny said, *"Just remember two things. One, your stage background is your calling card, and two, people respond to sincerity."*

I remembered Danny's words time and again during that LA sojourn. It became my mantra. Earl Franklin was kind enough to drive me to the agency. Together, we took the elevator to the 12th floor of the Century City high rise that housed the agency. Triad actually occupied the entire floor and also had offices on still another floor directly above.

The building smelled of million-dollar deals and possibilities to me. When Shari Belafonte sailed past me in the elegant wood-paneled lobby to see her agent, it became very clear to me that I was in a place where dreams really could come true.

As Sterling suggested, I wore a blue silk dress with pearls, and my shoulder-length hair down. Looking back now, I realize I was *way* overdressed, but I do think I exuded the well-groomed image Sterling was going after.

I waited.

Finally, I was summoned by Robin to come through the lobby door that led me to my future.

I entered.

As I walked into the office area beyond the lobby, I was struck by the number of outer desks where all the agents' assistants sat. They appeared to be positioned as both guards and servants. There were countless assistants and just as many agents. Phones were ringing off the hook, and there was frenetic movement all around me. There was an energy of excitement and stress. I knew there were mega deals being made in my midst at that very moment.

I entered Jenny's office and was met with a smiling face and awesome windows that took in a breathtaking view of Century City, facing Santa Monica Boulevard. Inside were a number of personal framed photos placed neatly around her office. It looked like an office that was well lived in. I would come to know that my agent spent many, many hours in that office.

Don Spradlin, her later assistant who went on to become an agent himself, proudly referred to Jenny as a "booking machine," because she made phenomenal deals for her clients. In time, she would also make deals for me.

Jenny and I talked a while, and she eventually invited in several other agents who came in to meet me and look me over. Their demeanors were polite, and at the same time, they definitely had an air of business in their upscale attire. One agent, after looking at my resumé, commented favorably on my stage background.

The manicured grey-haired agent said something like, "She has a strong stage background. That's good."

Danny was *right*. My stage background *did* matter.

The agents spoke with me briefly, and as they huddled, they quietly discussed me in third person. I heard comments like, "She has a good look." The truth was, in addition to being a person, I would learn I was also considered to be "talent."

Danny was right *again*. Agents were brought in to meet me.

I spoke from my heart when I voiced that Los Angeles was new to me. I admitted that being from the Bay Area, I did not know how things worked in LA.

I remember saying something like, "I am from the Bay Area. Things are very different there. I don't know much about Los Angeles."

My vulnerability was met, surprisingly, with nurturance. By sincerely owning my naïveté, I was met warmly and positively.

I was reminded of Danny's words, *"People respond to sincerity."*

Jenny placed a few casting director calls on my behalf. "General meetings" were scheduled with them as I watched and listened. I was not sent out to audition, only to be met.

The conversations from my agent went something like, "Hi. I have an actress here from the Bay Area. Her name is Adilah Barnes. I'd like you to meet her."

Danny was *still* right.

The first casting director on the list was Reuben Cannon, the African American agent at the time who arguably had been around as a casting director in Los Angeles longer than most other Black casting directors.

At the time, Reuben had an office at Universal Studios. When I first laid eyes on him, I was struck by how much he reminded me of my brother Hollis, both in look and demeanor.

I said, "You remind me of my older brother."

I remember him smiling over his glasses in return.

Again, people responded to sincerity.

Reuben looked over my photo and resumé and spoke honestly. "I think you would do well here, but you need to be in LA. Let me hear from you when you move down here."

He had given voice to what I knew inside. I would eventually have to make the move.

I next went to my appointment at the Los Angeles Theatre Center where I met with their casting director. I got my first real taste of what it is like to wait to be seen, because I waited and waited. Finally, I met briefly in the casting director's cubicle in between her many phone calls. Hers was a very different kind of general interview than the one I had just had with Reuben. It sobered me. Our meeting seemed more perfunctory. She was clearly busy, and it seemed I was being seen solely as a courtesy.

My third and final general audition fared much better. I met with Eileen Knight, an African American casting director who was then based on KTLA's television studio lot in Hollywood. We met in her intimate studio office. I periodically gazed at the photos on her wall. There were 8 x 10 photos of actors I was not familiar with. At one point, I stood in front of the photos, and Eileen came from around her desk and joined me.

As she looked at the photos with me, she said, "That is the cast of a new show I am casting for."

I looked at the name of the show and said, "*A Different World*. I have never heard of that show."

The rest is history. I chuckle silently every time I remember that day.

Due to my appointments, I ended up staying in Los Angeles longer than I had expected. While in town, I also had an agency audition for a number of "theatrical" agents at Triad. The room was packed. Sterling flew down to LA to do a scene with me from *Separate Tables,* the British play by Terrance Rattigan that I directed in ACT's Conservatory. I also gave the agents a contrasting monologue from Athol Fugard's play, *Boesman and Lena*, a three character play with only one female. I played the character "Lena."

Looking back, I think my audition went well, but they must have thought it strange that I dressed so formally in the red silk dress I had changed into for my character in *Separate Tables*. For the monologue, because I had no time to change clothing, I remember tying a bandana on my head to separate the two characters.

I was so green.

I suppose the feedback from the casting directors must have been promising, and the agents felt I had potential from the audition I gave, because they took me on as a "side pocket." That meant I would be represented, but without a signed contract. From that point on, Triad looked out for me and I occasionally flew to LA to audition for major film roles.

I first flew down and read for a project at Twentieth Century Fox. The casting director took one look at me and asked me to try to "dress down" a bit by making some adjustments in my clothing and jewelry. The casting director seemed to like me, and she made me feel comfortable. We discussed the work of August Wilson. I had come to know him a bit because of his presence at rehearsals of his two ACT productions that I was a part of. Coincidentally, she also knew him very well personally.

August Wilson was our connection.

She asked me to hang around to meet with the producers. I did. As I waited around for the "producer's session," I remember well the feeling I had as I sat on a bench at the Twentieth Century Fox lot. I looked around at all the studio sound stages, the studio logo everywhere. I watched pages weaving around the lot driving their off-white carts, making deliveries from building to building. I thought, "I am actually here at Twentieth Century Fox!"

I felt like I had indeed arrived.

Incidentally, it was actor Tina Lifford who was kind enough to give me a ride back to the home of a former student, Michelle, whom I was staying with in Santa Monica. Tina had never laid eyes on me before, and we were competing for the same role, but she felt compassion for me. I needed a ride and she had a car.

I have never forgotten her graciousness to a stranger.

So I owe landing my first LA agent to Sterling Anderson. He saw more in my career possibilities at that juncture than I did.

ACT had its perks. Getting an LA agent was one of them. At the same time, my ACT contract allowed me to teach in the three programs I have mentioned, and to join the acting company. What brought me great satisfaction was being able to perform on the Geary Theater stage.

Onstage, I felt my work spoke for itself.

I was a cast member in the "studio" production of Anna Deavere Smith's play *Piano*, directed by Dave Meier. *Piano* is a period piece in which I played a supporting role as a wise Caribbean slave mother who was being separated from her daughter. The interesting thing about that intense scene between a mother and daughter was that it was a purely non-verbal scene. Every emotion between us as we were being separated had to be relayed through our bodies, particularly the eyes. Anna seemed very pleased with our production, and, as a gesture of appreciation, gave a beautiful pair of earrings to each of the women in the cast.

I came to know Anna as a writer through her play. I had already come to know her as a teacher, since she also taught at ACT in the Summer Training Congress. She and I also came to be fellow actors in the ACT mainstage production, *Joe Turner's Come and Gone.*

Because the spaces were smaller, studio productions at ACT were more intimate. Plays were also sometimes more risky than across the street at ACT's mainstage Geary Theater.

I loved the Geary Theater. It was a professional regional theatre with a history that dates back to 1910. Its illustrious performers include Paul Robeson, Sarah Bernhardt, Basil Rathbone, Ethel Waters, Clark Gable, Ethel Barrymore, Edward G. Robinson, Mae West, and Sammy Davis Jr. When it reopened in 1996 following the 1989 earthquake, it was renamed the American Conservatory Theater.

At the Geary I had the freedom to come fully alive as an ACT actor. It was where I received my theatrical exposure. Before gracing the stage, however, I had to pay my dues. I understudied the role of Dussie Mae in August Wilson's play *Ma Rainey's Black Bottom*. It was humbling to understudy a role bestowed upon a third-year student. To Kimberley LaMarque's credit, she did a fine job in the role. Even though I was an understudy, that production allowed me to come to work peripherally with actor Charles "Roc" Dutton, director Claude Purdy, and most of all, playwright August Wilson.

However, it was in ACT's repertory production of Charles Dickens' *A Christmas Carol* that I was first given the opportunity to shine on the Geary stage. It seemed I had come full circle in terms of non-traditional casting because, like in my first play as a teen in the production of *The Ugly Duckling*, I again played a mother with a rainbow family. This time, however, I not only had an Anglo husband and daughter, but a tribe of children who represented the color spectrum even more. We were Black, white, yellow, and brown in color.

My ACT days from 1986-1989 were bittersweet. In hindsight, when I weigh it all, I can see the many gifts I was given. I became a much better teacher and director while there. I also established some meaningful lifelong relationships and performed in the company.

I can now see that one big payoff of three roller-coaster seasons at ACT was my ticket to Los Angeles in an ACT production. Had I not taught and performed at ACT, I may never have moved to Los Angeles. For that, I am very thankful.

It is now a new day at ACT.

It is a different place than I remember in the 1970's and 1980's. Today's ACT has new leadership. At the helm is Carey Perloff, whom I have never met because she came aboard in 1992 after my 1989 departure. Now located on Grant Street, the Conservatory is physically in an entirely different space than I knew it. Many who worked with me are now gone. They left with the changing of the guards after Artistic Director Ed Hastings resigned.

I trust that with ACT's replaced leadership in 1992 and new blood since that time, it has become a more welcoming, equitable, and healthy place than I remember. In 1992, the year Carey Perloff began her tenure, a multicultural committee was established, and in 1997, the Diversity Council was formed. I understand at the time of this writing that it is chaired by Priscilla Regalado, whom I remember well as a movement instructor during my stint at ACT. I understand the Council addresses diversity in terms of play selection, casting, and curriculum for the MFA program. Hopefully, the Council has addressed some of the diversity issues prevalent during my ACT days.

I am sure ACT still maintains the vibrancy of talented students walking the halls excitedly, and creating magic in the studios as they explore their craft in classes and onstage. I imagine that ACT continues to present beautifully produced professional productions at the old Geary Theater that also include meaningful plays by playwrights of color.

My tenure completed at the American Conservatory Theater in 1989, my next stop was Los Angeles.

As Whoopi Goldberg said to me on the set of *Kiss Shot* when I told her I was about to finally make the move to Los Angeles, "We'll be waiting for you."

Chapter Eight

Moving On

Learn to recognize your God-given talents (and we all have them). Develop these talents and use them in the career you choose.

—Benjamin Carson, Physician

In 1989, the late August Wilson's much-talked-about play *Joe Turner's Come and Gone* broke box office records at ACT. I was both surprised and thrilled, because the play was penned by an African American playwright, and ACT was not a Black theatre. I was also excited about being a part of such a stellar cast headed by the late veteran actor Roscoe Lee Browne. Other cast members included such able actors as Anna Deavere Smith, Steven Anthony Jones, Delores Mitchell, Ty Granderson Jones, and Kimberley LaMarque.

ACT bought the set and costumes of the original touring production. I inherited both Angela Bassett's role of Martha Pentecost and her turn-of-the-century, long-skirted, navy blue and white costume. It was accented by my ACT corset that tightly cinched me in each performance.

I was concerned I would not be able to fit Angela's costume because she was a bit smaller than me. I prayed we could make it fit because I wanted with a passion to wear the same costume I had previously seen her in during the Old Globe Theatre run in San Diego. At the invitation of my ACT friend Delroy Lindo, I had flown with my friend Alta Butler from the Bay Area to see the San Diego production. There I saw Angela Bassett onstage in that same skirt, blouse, hat, purse, and shoes. Fortunately, our costumers were able to make the wardrobe work by letting the outfit out some. I could feel Angela's spirit every time I wore her costume onstage.

Neither Angela nor Delroy had become a household name yet, but both were clearly on their way to stardom. Now they both have become widely acknowledged for their fine on-camera work. They have also come to know their individual measures of success. Both began onstage and both seriously trained as actors at "league" schools. Delroy trained at ACT during my time there, and Angela at Yale School of Drama with the late Lloyd Richards.

When word first spread throughout our San Francisco cast that Bill Bushnell's Los Angeles Theatre Center (LATC) was interested in bringing our production of *Joe Turner's Come and Gone* to Los Angeles, my body trembled with glee. This could *finally* be the ticket to take me to Los Angeles. I believed that going to Los Angeles with an already successful August Wilson play would be the safest and most opportune way for me to test the new waters that seemed to be summoning me.

The timing seemed right.

I already had side pocket agency representation in Los Angeles at the then Triad Agency. The pending 1989 run would afford me the opportunity to go out regularly to audition for television and film roles. I would also gain theatrical exposure in the number one film and television market in the country. Being seen favorably by casting directors could potentially support me in getting more auditions, and ultimately more work.

It was a win-win situation.

Finally, the formal offer from the Los Angeles Theatre Center came. Our ACT production was a "union production" because ACT was a "union house," and we fell under the auspices of Actor's Equity Association (AEA), the union for professional stage performers and technicians.

By union regulation, we had to be offered two lodging choices. When Roscoe Lee Browne heard what our two choices were, he spoke with the powers that were. The next thing we knew, we had a third accommodation choice; the then very spacious and nicely laid out Oakwood Apartments in the Mid-Wilshire district of Los Angeles. We were close enough to get to our nearby downtown theatre quickly, and yet far enough away to avoid the pervasive homelessness and nearby stench of the city's underbelly that our theatre was in the heart of.

Most of us jumped at our third lodging choice. I personally liked living at the Oakwood because it was a community within itself. We had our own dry cleaners, two conference rooms, a golf practicing room, two pools, two exercise rooms with saunas, two jacuzzis, a full-sized outdoor basketball court, a tennis court, a huge lounge with a bar, and a big screen TV. Our lounge doubled as a social space for programs, activities, and a place to eat on Sundays when it was transformed into our complimentary Sunday brunch space.

Until I got situated, my son who was then eleven years old, stayed in Oakland with my longtime friend, the late LeOna Harris. Tariq had never been separated from me other than to visit my family in

Oroville. He made it known in no uncertain terms that he wanted to join me in Los Angeles. As a result, he soon came down from the Bay Area to be with me. Tariq quickly found his own place at the Los Angeles Theatre Center by earning money as an usher and by helping out in the lobby. Although mischievous, the theatre staff embraced him and he found a way to both occupy himself and make money while I worked. He could be seen in the lobby wearing his LATC apron just like the rest of the paid staff.

Our *Joe Turner* production had broken box office records at ACT, and did the same at LATC. People came to see our successful show for many reasons. Some came because Roscoe was our headliner. He knew *everybody*. Many celebrities, including Diahann Carroll, attended at his invitation. Others came because they were devout August Wilson followers and wanted to see his much-talked-about latest work. There were those who came because of our sterling reviews. Industry folk came to scout new talent, and there were those who occupied seats because our show was part of their season subscription.

Whatever the motivation, audiences packed the theatre, night after night. We had a wonderfully diverse audience throughout our extended run. What began as something like a two-month commitment became three.

Our run was magical on many levels.

I met or saw from afar many well-known actors. Those who came to see our show included Denzel Washington, Robert Guillaume, the late Lou Rawls, Brenda Vaccaro, Clifton Davis, and many, many more.

Our cast checked our actors' bulletin board expectantly upon arrival each day. It was not uncommon to find messages from casting directors inviting us in for "general interviews" or auditions. We compared notes to see who got calls and from whom.

Everybody in the cast heard from somebody.

Each day held exciting new possibilities for our cast. In my case, I landed three film roles in the three months I was in Los Angeles. I got edited out of *Gross Anatomy* but I made it on the screen in *Cast the First Stone* and *The Image*. It may have taken me three years to get those same "day player" roles had I still been in the Bay Area. The signs pointing south were all around me.

I knew my days in the Bay Area were numbered.

Even so, Los Angeles was a bit unsettling because I had never lived in a city that large. It is the second largest city in the country and its size made me a bit apprehensive.

However, my fears were quickly erased as I began to navigate my way through the city by car. I learned right away that LA was laid out geographically like a grid. If you knew your directions, you could get wherever you needed to go with relative ease. If you also knew the major streets and which direction they ran, you had it made, because the major streets run for miles and miles.

One of our union regulations stipulated transportation. To that end, another female actor and I shared a rental car that was provided for us. It was from the Ugly Duckling car rental. It was indeed ugly, dingy and old. However, we cleaned the car up as best we could and made it our own. The car was reliable and got us to and from the theatre, and anywhere else we needed to go locally.

There was only one problem.

The female actor and I, though previously "friends" while at ACT, fell out once we went to LA. I still cannot say exactly what happened between us. I only know that whatever the reason was, our relationship became lethal.

It got to the point where we only spoke to each other professionally and only when we *absolutely* had to. This boiled down to pretty much only talking to make arrangements to ride together to and from the theatre. Our only other contact took place while we performed together onstage. In the car, we rode both directions in total silence. Having my son in the car with us made the ride all the more unbearable. Although we never discussed it, he must have felt the tension in the car between us each day.

She did not like me, and I came to not like her.

Since we shared the rental car, we agreed we would alternate who had priority use of the car each week. Things eventually got so bad that I once hid the car away from our subterranean parking lot to make sure she would not take it.

She found the car!

The irony to this anecdote is that in the play, our characters had not seen each other in many years and were very happy to see each other. When my character stepped onstage, we were required to hug, smile, and lovingly reunite. Offstage, we tried our best to ignore each other.

Looking back, it seems that all we needed to do was talk about what we were feeling, but neither of us took the lead to make that happen. I now regret that I did not take the opportunity to take the high road and work through such a silly and unnecessary situation.

Despite our personal differences, we were first and foremost professional actors. Although we had unresolved issues with each other in real life, it was impossible for the audience to detect our offstage relationship. For the sake of the show and due to our level of professionalism, we could not afford to allow our personal challenges to seep into our work onstage.

And it did not.

We sometimes hear of celebrities who have worked together under similar circumstances. At the same time, as with us, the public never detected their offstage tensions in their work. An audience ought never be privy to such things.

Audiences are there to be entertained, not to be a part of any real-life drama.

My exceptional mother Mosea Lee Barnes and me posing for
a newspaper article on me for the *Oroville Mercury Register*.
(Courtesy of Oroville Mercury Register)

Photo of my father and me, Theoplis Dennis. We celebrated
his 99th birthday together in 2008 in Oroville, California.
*(Photo of my daddy Edward Barnes was unavailable for publishing
but I also acknowledge my deep love for him here.)*

A photo of my beloved son Tariq and me together.
Like his father Faruq, he is a very gifted visual artist.
(Barnes Family Archives)

My son Tariq and grandson Malik Isaiah at
Universal Studios, one of their favorite places.
(Barnes Family Archives)

A smiling photo of my grandson Malik Isaiah, who is a very loving and agile child. He is the apple of my eye.

My talented godson Sterling Ardrey, who has become an established young working actor of television and film.
(Courtesy of Robert Kazandjian)

A childhood photo with my siblings before baby Edward was born.
Top row left to right: Norma and Hollis, center: Dorothy,
and bottom row left to right: Ora, myself and Ellis.
(Barnes Family Archives)

My family reunion at Camanche Lake, California in 2003.
Left to right: Norma, Hollis, Ora, myself, Ellis, and Edward.
(Barnes Family Archives)

My extraordinary brother Hollis following his graduation
from the University of Oregon Law School in 2000.
(Barnes Family Archives)

My grandmother Lillian Osby's 65th birthday party in 1959
surrounded by her many children and grandchildren.
(Osby Family Archives)

Long time friends, Ted Lange, Danny Glover and me
backstage at the Los Angeles Women's Theatre Festival.
(Courtesy of Los Angeles Women's Theatre Festival)

Actor Loretta Devine and dancer/choreographer Lula Washington
of the legendary Lula Washington Dance Theatre.
(Courtesy of Ian Foxx Photography)

This 1981 photo is of me in the title role of the historical and
controversial figure Joann Little. This award-winning play *JoAnne!*
extended twice at the Julian Theatre in San Francisco. I received
both a *DramaLogue Award* for Outstanding Achievement in Theatre
and a Bay Area Critics Circle nomination for this career-elevating
role. Directed by John Henry Doyle.
(Courtesy of Pat Goudvis Photography)

With chorus cast members in Berkeley Repertory Theatre's 1984
production of *Kabuki Medea*. Left to right are Kathryn Roszak,
Robin Karfo, myself and seated Pamela Minet. Directed by Shozo Sato.
(Photo by Ken Friedman. Photo courtesy Berkeley Repertory Theatre.)

Ed Hodson and myself in the 1988 American Conservatory Theater production of *A Christmas Carol. (Photo by Harry Wade. Photo courtesy American Conservatory Theater.)*

An action shot from the 1989 Los Angeles Theatre Center production of *Joe Turner's Come and Gone.* Left to right above me is Kimberley LaMarque, Roscoe Lee Browne and James Craven. Directed by Claude Purdy. *(Courtesy of photographer Chris Gulker)*

Angela Davis and me in 2005 on a panel at the University
of California at Santa Cruz. *(Courtesy of photographer Jim
MacKenzie and the University of California, Santa Cruz)*

My portrayal of activist Angela Davis in my internationally-toured
one woman show, *I Am That I Am:* Woman, *Black*
that has toured close to 40 states and the continents of
North America, Africa and Europe. Directed by Lewis Tucker and
Philip Walker. *(Courtesy of Asilee Parkinson)*

On tour with *I Am That I Am:* Woman, *Black*
at Seattle Community College in Washington.
(Adilah Barnes Productions)

A night out at the theatre in Hollywood with some of my acting
students following the play *Medal of Honor Rag*, directed by Delroy
Lindo. Top row (left to right) Steffan Ganske, Gregory Abbott, Jr.,
actor/director Delroy Lindo. Bottom row (left to right)
award-winning vocalist Freda Payne, myself, Tyesha Anthony,
Scott Bratcher, and Marla LaBerge.

Myself with dear college buddy from UC Santa Cruz,
Jacquelyn Scott, a longtime friend of 40 years.
(Photo by Patrice Jenkins)

With friends Kwakiutl Dreher, myself and childhood
friends Brenda Jackson Stovall and Mararice Davis at my
1st annual HOTLANTA summer party in 2007.
(Courtesy of photographer Freddy Stovall)

Marcia V. Ellis and Muhjah Shakir walk the grounds of
The Writer's Well in 2007, my literary retreat for women
writers in the Atlanta, Georgia area. *(Courtesy of photographer
Freddy Stovall)*

Posing at BOB-TV Marketplace in Abuja, Nigeria in 2006.
Left to right: myself, a participant, and Amaka Igwe, one of
Nigeria's foremost filmmakers. *(Courtesy of Amaka Igwe)*

A 2007 photo with Mr. Sidney Poitier and me in conversation
at the Artpeace Gallery in Burbank, California owned by
my former acting student Angela Robinson and
her husband actor/comedian John Witherspoon.
(Courtesy of Ian Foxx Photography)

Chapter Nine

Stepping Out on Faith

If you have a purpose in which you believe, there's no end to the amount of things you can accomplish.
—Marion Anderson, Singer

I had opted to make the drive back to Los Angeles from Oakland in my old, funky, navy blue, square-back Volkswagen. This I decided rather than compromise myself by giving in to the ultimatum of an old boyfriend who offered to take my son and me.

He agreed to take us on one condition.

Here I was in my Richmond home, musty and exhausted from packing while I moved frantically around the house. I was trying to beat the clock. I was trying to uproot from my home for the last two years. I was already overwhelmed with the finality of leaving behind seventeen years of my life in the Bay Area. I was moving from one part of the state to another and leaving behind many close relationships that had nurtured me over those seventeen years.

And this man looked at me and thought what he thought.

Although I was not surprised there were strings attached with his offer, I *was* surprised he tried to negotiate sex with me on the very day of the move.

I looked him squarely in the eyes and told him, "That's okay. I'll find another way for Tariq and me to get to LA."

He thought he had me over a barrel.

Yes, I had counted on him renting a truck and driving us to LA with my car on a flatbed. And yes, I had given my landlord my move-out date. Yes, I also needed his financial support to make the move.

But no, the move was not going to go down that way.

My mind was on my future and his mind was on control.

I politely escorted him to the door as my mind began to race to Plan B. I called my close friend Jacki and told her of the proposition I had just declined. She listened in disbelief. After she got her voice back, she said she would ask her mechanic husband Tam if he would check my car to make sure it was drivable for that 350-mile-plus trek to Los Angeles.

He agreed.

Since it was impossible to take everything in my VW, I decided to send by Greyhound the boxes I could not load in my car. A monkey wrench was thrown in my way, but I had come too far in my decision to turn around.

I had no intention of beginning my new life in Los Angeles by selling out.

I arranged with my landlord to stay in my house a few days longer. Once my car had been checked out and our boxes sent ahead of us, Tariq and I loaded up our worn car and began our six-hour drive to Los Angeles. He was my co-pilot as we made our way south in a car that had no air conditioning. The outside heat was almost unbearable, but we did not mind. We were on our way to meet our future. We paced our drive as we listened to lively music on cassette tapes along the way. We watched the sign posts to Los Angeles as the miles posted got smaller and smaller in number.

The sweltering ride was both scary and exhilarating. I knew my car was unsafe for the long, hot ride, but I also knew something exciting awaited me. I could not turn back. Our car may have been smoking from burning oil, overheating, and choking from clogged fuel injectors by the time we arrived, but we made it.

More importantly, we made it on my own terms.

I had passed my first rite of passage to Los Angeles.

When my son and I pulled up to the Oakwood Apartments to make it our permanent home this time, I was quickly met with a rude awakening.

Things had changed.

Joe Turner's Come and Gone had successfully run from March until June of 1989 to sold-out houses at LATC. It had attracted celebrities, agents, casting directors, producers, other actors, and loyal theatergoers. The play had been one of the most successful and talked-about Los Angeles runs during that spring. It had been one of my most enjoyable theatrical experiences onstage. Naively, I expected the carpet ride to continue upon my return later that summer as I made Los Angeles my permanent home.

However, the carpet ride was over.

I had no show to return to, no day job to go to, and I had exactly enough money to guarantee a roof over my family's head for our first month. Coincidentally, at my Bay Area going-away party at ACT that summer, my "money jar" totaled the very same uneven amount for my first month's rent of $603.

I may not have had money, but what I did have was faith.

I believed in 1989 that Los Angeles was where I was meant to be. I trusted that the uncanny amount of $603 in gifts equaling my first month's rent to the dollar was confirmation that I was doing the right thing.

My going-away party was both surreal and heartwarming. I had arranged to have my going-away party at ACT, but the Black theatre community and personal friends dominated the guest list. In my going-away speech, I said, "Every time one of us from the Bay Area goes to LA and makes it, it is a feather in the cap for the Bay Area." My guests roared with applause.

I meant what I said.

The success of the likes of former Bay Area theatre artists such as Danny Glover, Ted Lange, Carl Lumbly, Shabaka Henley, Delroy Lindo, Art Evans, Ron Stacker Thompson, Esther Scott, Tony Haney, and Montrose Hagins speaks volumes to the theatrical talent that has come out of the Bay Area.

Not all of those I have named were born and raised there, but we each lived there long enough to claim the Bay Area as our home. Even Whoopi Goldberg claimed the Bay Area during her short stint there. A native New Yorker, she came directly to the Bay Area from San Diego. She took the Bay Area by surprise just before she crossed over into stardom. She subsequently brought significant commerce to the area by choosing the Bay Area as location for some of her most memorable films. I had clearly earned my stripes in the Bay Area and fondly saw it as my home, too.

Once Tariq and I were settled in LA, I did something I had never done before.

To make ends meet, I humbled myself by taking a job working at a hotel. In fact, I eventually worked at two downtown hotels on Grand Avenue, directly across the street from each other. I worked full time at the newly built five-star then named Checkers Hotel, and part time at the legendary and opulent Biltmore Hotel. The two jobs gave me more security than my temp work and they also allowed me to answer phones, something I could do with great ease.

I was now a Los Angeles resident, but I was no longer in a hit play.

I was now just another actor in LA trying to make it. Earlier that year, I came to LA in one of the safest and most visible ways possible. Now I was hitting the pavement like most everyone else. My return was far more humbling than I expected.

I would now be tested to see what mettle I was made of.

Thanks to my friend Charli and her late husband Malcolm Smith, I returned to live at the secure Oakwood Apartments. As much as I have always dreaded asking anyone for anything, I put my pride aside and asked for help. Fortunately, Charli and Malcolm knew me well enough to put their credit on the line for me. I will forever be thankful to them because they stood in the gap so my son and I could have the kind of roof over our heads that I wanted.

Although I had no permanent employment in the beginning, we did have the familiarity and safety of living at the Oakwood. At the time, the rent was somewhat pricey for us, so we again squeezed into a studio as we had during the run of *Joe Turner*. By union regulation and as a touring cast member, I only had to pay ten percent of my rent during the show's previous run. Now I was responsible for coughing up the entire amount of $603 each month.

I was still a side pocket client at Triad Agency, so I did have LA representation. Although I was virtually penniless, my representation kept me hopeful. I knew that anything was possible. I also knew that work would come.

I oftentimes needed to write grocery checks at Vons supermarket for purchases that included "cash back" money to tie me over as I tried to beat the checks to the bank. I initially got paid weekly from my temp assignments, so I usually did beat the checks to the bank. However, I occasionally got caught with insufficient funds in the checking account game I was forced to play.

Temping made me learn the city, because I had assignments that took me all over Los Angeles. It also made me feel I belonged. Work came sporadically, but I was setting a schedule for myself, and meeting people.Making money was a juggling act, but somehow my son and I made it through those rough times.

One of my long-term assignments at that time was as a receptionist at HBO in Century City. From its 42nd floor, HBO overlooks Century City's breathtaking views. Its stupendous views reminded me of Triad's nearby upscale offices that were also in Century City. I loved looking out the windows at both places, because the views were so awesome.

Working as a receptionist at HBO allowed me to greet visitors as they came and went. My most memorable experience was the day Lou Gossett Jr. walked through HBO's doors. His smiling bigger-than-life presence lit up the room.

I could not believe it. Momentarily, I had Lou Gossett Jr. to myself.

What I remember most as Lou Gossett waited to be seen was his warm and jovial demeanor. He had an infectious smile and hearty laugh. Much to my surprise, he offered me his business card.

Unfortunately, I did not follow up quickly enough, and we never spoke again. As time passed, I am sure our meeting became, at best, a very blurry memory. By the time I did muster up enough courage to call, I was no longer able to reach him at that number.

I learned that you must move quickly on an offering or you may miss your opportunity.

Interesting to note, I saw Lou Gossett again in 2006 from the stage of the African Academy Movie Awards (AAMA) in Yenogoa, Nigeria. Onstage, he was far more formal, and his energy felt much more serious. Although eloquent, he also spoke in a much more no-nonsense tone than I remembered.

I was glad I had once had him all to myself for a few moments and saw his lighter, more playful side.

Working at HBO was a very surreal experience for me. I was close enough to the industry to have an up close view of some of the inner workings of HBO, but too far away, I thought, to parlay my position into anything for myself as an actor. It was painful to watch casting directors passing my desk daily as they called in actors for roles I hungered for but had no shot at.

Instead of seeing HBO as an opportunity to introduce and promote myself as an actor, I retreated. Working there as a receptionist, I did not think I would be taken seriously as an actor so I kept my identity as an actor unknown.

Looking back now, it may have been that the universe granted me an opportunity that I could not see. After all, I had earlier that spring booked a role in an HBO film, *The Image*. In my mind, my role in *The Image* had been a small one and I did not think it substantial enough to mention.

However, as the saying goes, "There are no small roles, only actors, who think them so." The truth was, I *did* have a recent HBO credit in *The Image* that I may have been able to use as some kind of entrée.

In 1989, I worked with Albert Finney on *The Image*. I remember well how gracious he was the day I worked on the film. He introduced himself to me outside my trailer.

In his beautiful British accent, he said, "I'm sorry we did not have more time together in this film. Maybe we will next time."

I smiled back.

Little did either of us know that "the next time" would eventually come. In 2000, Albert Finney and I worked together on location in a much more substantial way in Universal's award-winning *Erin Brockovich.* I reminded him of our first time working together in *The Image*. Still gracious, I doubt he *really* remembered us working together that first time.

But I did.

The lesson in that meeting was you never know who you will work with again. The other lesson is to always work with someone in a way that your next meeting may be a positive one.

Perhaps, had I been confident and aggressive enough, the HBO temp story may have had a different ending, but I was unsure of myself then. I did not know how to speak up for myself. I also did not want to jeopardize my livelihood.

I did contact one HBO casting director after I left that job, but the timing was all wrong by then. I never heard back from her.

Again, I learned the importance of timing.

For me, I wanted to be known as an actor at HBO, not as a receptionist. I liken my set of circumstances to that of actors who are doing extra work and who do not let it be known that they are also legitimate actors. In both cases, the chances of being taken seriously as actors are slim.

I decided to bide my time. I preferred to meet HBO "brass" in the same way I saw other actors coming in and out of HBO's doors.

In the early 1990s, I waited for my number to come up.

I say to any actors who are new to the field or new to LA, be patient as you work toward your goal. Keep your eyes on the prize as you maintain your belief in yourself and your trust in the universe. Strategize, create a plan of action, and continue to build relationships with those you like. You never know who will one day be in a position to act as a vessel in your career. At the same time, continue to hone your skills in classes.

Although I had the security of full-time work at Checkers Hotel early on, it was not enough for me. I was not working in my field. It was a day job for me. Probably the best thing that happened for me there was I met a lifelong friend, Tammie Delaney. She is not in the business, but is still one of my biggest cheerleaders.

Working at Checkers Hotel, I learned that you never know who will go on to do greater things. There were a number of other actors who worked at the hotel with me. Two hotel employees went on to become agents. One of them I ran into much later and was very surprised to learn he had become an agent with Gersh Agency, one of the most respected "boutique" (smaller and quaint) agencies in town.

Ironically, he said he tried to find me when he first began agenting, but could not.

The lesson in that incident is to make sure your contact information is kept current at the Screen Actor's Guild and continue to be listed in the Academy of Motion Picture's Player's Directory.

Although William has now moved on to yet another agency, it is comforting to know that I may have an agent available to me, should I need one in the future.

During my Checkers days, I wanted to do more than work at their beautiful five-star hotel. If I could not work regularly as an actor, I at least wanted to teach acting.

One school I heard of soon after arriving in LA was Marla Gibbs' Crossroads Arts Academy. I thought perhaps I might be able to land a teaching position there because of my substantial teaching background and also because I, too, was African American.

I called Crossroads.

I was surprised to find the late Whitman Mayo working there in the capacity of Artistic Director. Many will remember him for his unforgettable role as Grady on *Sanford and Son* with Redd Foxx.

Whitman doubled his role at Crossroads as an acting teacher. He was very cordial, but he also made it quite clear on the telephone that Crossroads was not accepting any new teachers at the time.

However, having the heart I came to know he had, he said, "But send me your resumé. I'll put it on file."

I quickly responded, "Thank you. I will."

I immediately sent Whitman my cover letter and resumé, and was pleasantly surprised to receive an immediate telephone call from him. He invited me in to interview with him in person at the Crenshaw District location.

I jumped at the opportunity.

Although Whitman could be said to have "curmudgeon" energy on the outside, he was warm and generous on the inside. He also had a sense of humor all his own, and he could always make me laugh.

One of the unique things about Whitman's style of teaching was he did not allow female students to wear *any* make-up in class. He said he wanted them to come to class "unmasked." There were those who were uncomfortable coming to class without their made-up faces, but because they wanted to study with Whitman, they obeyed his mandate.

At the time I came aboard in 1990, Crossroads was housed in an office building on Crenshaw Boulevard. It took up three tiny upstairs office spaces. I interviewed with Whitman in the administrative office. By the time we completed my interview, I had been invited by Whitman to come aboard as a teacher. I was absolutely thrilled. The door had been opened for me to begin teaching again. I will forever be grateful to Whitman for opening the door for me to teach in LA.

The lesson in that instance was to never take no for an answer.

I joined the ranks of other Crossroads teachers who at that time included the legendary and late Edmund Cambridge, Deirdre Weston, Michele Lamar Richards, and Sharon Newman.

Deirdre eventually went on to establish Faith Acting Studios, one of the most successful and longest-running children's acting schools in Los Angeles. Faith Acting Studios opened in 1992 and thrived for ten years. Deirdre developed many young actors who went on to meet their fame. Actor Wendy Raquel Robinson later came to teach at Crossroads when I hired her after our move to Leimert Park. It was by way of having hired Wendy as a dance instructor in Crossroads' summer youth program that Wendy came to meet and work closely with Deirdre. It was during that time I also hired actor/dancer Candy

ON MY OWN TERMS *One Actor's Journey*

Brown to teach dance at Crossroads. By that point, I had also become an administrator at Crossroads myself. We were all using our many talents to give back to inner city youth.

Wendy went on to work with Deirdre at Faith Acting Studios before branching off to found her own acting school for children, Amazing Grace Conservatory.

Although none of us knew it then, Wendy would later come to be known as a household name. In 1996 she landed the regular role of "Regina Grier" on WB's *The Steve Harvey Show*. When I first interviewed Wendy, I intuitively knew she was on her way in the industry. She exuded confidence, beauty, talent, and had a very likeable and energetic personality. She was also very funny. At the time of this writing, she is now a regular on CW's television series *The Game*.

I have had that same intuitive feeling of approaching stardom with students of mine, including Kym Whitley. She studied acting with me in Hollywood and I knew it was just a matter of time before her career would take off. She too is likeable and funny and has always been able to put people at ease with her uninhibited sense of humor.

Personality goes a long way in show business.

When Crossroads went on hiatus with its teaching programs in 1991, some students frantically asked me where they would go to study. The continual question made me decide quickly to offer my own acting classes in Hollywood. Fortunately for me, eighteen of my students followed me. They made up my first private class. I coined the name "Character Development Workshop" for my classes, because my focus has always been to bring out depth and truth in the work of my students.

Crossroads began attracting more students than its tiny two-office spaces could hold and began to burst at the seams on Crenshaw Boulevard.

Ironically, the office spaces that housed us later succumbed to the ravages of fire during the civil unrest in 1992 following the "not guilty" verdict of Anglo officers in the Rodney King case. Fortunately, we had made our move long before fire ravaged that Crenshaw office building.

In its heyday, Crossroads became a bustling Leimert Park facility on the Afro-centric and highly artsy Degnan Boulevard. I was proud to be on the team. Our spacious new facility offered a wide array of services for the community. We had our school, two theatres (one with over 1,200 seats that had been a movie theatre in its day), an industrial kitchen, space for banquets and receptions, many offices, and a large parking lot. The community was made to feel that *everyone* was welcome at Crossroads.

There was an excitement in the air as many celebrities came to Crossroads to perform in its theatres. The late Roxie Roker of *The Jeffersons* participated in fundraisers that included celebrity fashion shows. Some, like the late Edmund Cambridge, taught and acted, the late Lincoln Kilpatrick also performed, and there were those who simply found seats in the audience to support the many wonderful events at Crossroads.

Crossroads was on fire with its creative classes and events. Some, like Denzel Washington, Robert Townsend, and Vanessa Bell Calloway, sat on our program's "Hot Seat," offered to our students who were hungry to hear from successful Black entertainers.

The most memorable "Hot Seat" for me was the night Denzel Washington came to join our students. I had rarely run into Denzel since our ACT days as students, and it was nice to have him participate in our series.

As we ushered him inside the nearby Department of Water and Power space we had secured for that evening, I noticed Denzel was toting an armload of books from his car.

I said, "Denzel, you are only going to be talking to the students. Why are you bringing all these books inside?"

Denzel stopped me in my tracks when he said, "Because, Adilah, if they steal my car, I still have my research material."

True to form from his ACT days, Denzel was still meticulously preparing his work. He was more concerned about his research material than he was about his own car. Denzel had not changed.

He is one actor who invests the time to seriously do his homework and it shows in his work.

To actors in my classes, I hand out and expect they will complete their homework. I also stress the importance of doing the research. Actors I know personally like Denzel and Delroy Lindo are wonderful examples of actors who take the time to shade their characters in fully through their research. To that point, I remember well the time Delroy traveled all the way to Memphis, Tennessee, to research that city for his stage portrayal of Herald Loomis in the play *Joe Turner's Come and Gone.*

The more research and the better prepared we are in our work, the more defined and believable our portrayals.

Crossroads received numerous awards for its theatre productions. Even the television series *227* grew out of one of Crossroads' stage productions. Marla Gibbs had a name and was able to attract television producers who journeyed into "the 'hood" to see the successful *227* play that would soon become a successful television staple for audiences around the country.

One of the most significant byproducts of teaching at Crossroads, for me, was giving back. My students were now predominantly African American. Interestingly enough, most of my students when I lived in the Bay Area had not been. I now saw my calling as a teacher in a new way. In Los Angeles I had the opportunity and responsibility to use what I had gained as a teacher over the years to give back to my own. I felt my calling now was to continue to give the very best of myself as a teacher so that students would be well-equipped to fully compete on any level.

I had a vested interest in my new students, because they looked just like me.

The very first acting job I landed after making my permanent move to LA was a guest-starring role in the very popular television series *thirtysomething*. It also held my first guest-starring role on television.

I remember well the day in 1990 that I auditioned in the show's "producer's session" that included *thirtysomething* regular Melanie Mayron, who was making her directing debut on the series with that particular episode. Coincidentally, we both shared the same agent. I believe the latter played some part in getting me the appointment, but getting the part was on me.

I was excited to be working on the hit show *thirtysomething*. My character "Brenda," was a city official, and I was seen in a number of scenes. I also had great wardrobe, hair, and make-up for the substantial role.

What was uncanny about that episode was it was about the story of actor Tim Busby's character, "Elliot Weston," who was directing a commercial for the first time, and who had all the jitters that went along with it. Melanie was, in fact, directing her first episode on *thirtysomething,* and I was acting in my first guest-starring role.

There were many "firsts" surrounding that magical experience. From a business standpoint, I got "top-of-show" wages, meaning ceiling pay, on my very first guest-starring role. That does not always happen, but it spoke to the clout of my agent Jenny Delaney at Triad Agency.

In 1990, there would be another guest-starring role on *Roseanne* that would turn into a five-season role as the character Anne Marie. I would eventually step out on faith that same year as I left the security of Checkers Hotel.

The day finally came where I was forced to choose between my day job and my acting career. It came when my supervisor at Checkers Hotel told me she could not "allow" me to take time off during a slow period at the hotel to attend a booking conference with the Western Alliance Association (WAA). I had competitively been chosen by WAA to receive membership, a booth, airfare, lodging, per diem and an opportunity to promote my one woman show.

As I said before, sometimes you just have to step out on faith.

Since 1990, I have not worked outside my field. Like stepping out on faith to make the trek to Los Angeles in my old, funky, navy blue Volkswagen Squareback against all odds, I have also been blessed to "make it" on some level.

Chapter Ten

I Am That I Am: Woman, *Black*

I never forgot for a day, or for an hour, or for a minute, that
I climbed on the back of the courageous African American
men and women who went before me.
— Colin Powell, Secretary of State, Military Officer

"I was raped. Twice."

The young girl's words stung me. She could not have been more than eleven years old.

I didn't want to perform my solo show *I Am That I Am:* Woman, *Black* for fifth graders, but here I was onstage anyway, packing up my wardrobe suitcase following my two performances at a Las Vegas elementary school.

In 1992, I performed at the Las Vegas city facility Reed Whipple Theatre and a nearby middle school for the first time. Upon completion of my residency, the city of Las Vegas promised me they would invite me back in the future for a longer residency.

In 1996, four years later, they kept their word. They asked me back.

The City of Las Vegas offered me a week's residency that included excerpts from my solo show at two forty-five-minute assemblies at elementary, junior high, and high schools alike. I was also offered the opportunity to interface with a group of senior citizens, teen girls at a juvenile hall, and to teach acting classes for two teen acting companies. The centerpiece for the week was a closing finale performance of my solo show at the West Las Vegas Arts Center, a relatively new venue in the Black community of Las Vegas. This was quite an ambitious and rigorous proposal for a one-week residency.

There was only one catch.

The contract required me to perform at each of the venues proposed by the city. The *only* group I was hesitant about was fifth graders. I was only asked to do an excerpt of the show at each assembly, but I was adamant about not changing the writing to fit young audiences. A family-oriented and wholesome show, there were still sections of my show I felt were inaccessible and inappropriate for fifth graders. I knew some of the language was too elevated for that age group.

I had written the show with older audiences in mind and I was unwilling to compromise the integrity of my piece to accommodate younger groups. I was met with unpleasant visions of squirming, uninterested, and chattering students before me who would take away my enjoyment of performing and make the show feel like work.

I had a major artistic dilemma.

The opportunity to reach such a broad collective audience was inviting, the contract was a lucrative one, and I wanted to accept the city's offer to return. There was just this one matter.

Fifth graders.

I finally reconciled my hesitance. I opted to accept the residency. I decided I would only perform Sojourner Truth, Harriet Tubman, and Maya

Angelou for these multicultural elementary students. I further decided I would make the best use of the forty-five-minute assemblies by introducing each character with audience participation questions before performing.

I began with Harriet Tubman. I asked, "Who knows who Miss Harriet Tubman was?"

I paused.

Hands shot up.

I heard from one student, "She was a conductor on the Underground Railroad."

I further asked, "Who knows what that was? Was that like Amtrak?"

The more vocal, competitive, and sharp students were quick to answer, "No!"

They gave correct answers to everything I asked.

I thought, "Okay, this format is working."

After our brief dialogue, I ended by saying something like, "And now, Miss Harriet Tubman is here to join us today."

I moved to my coat rack to sing a cappella, "No More Auction Block for Me" while I changed into her costume.

I added Harriet's wooden stick that my friend Jemela Mwelu found back in 1990 during the early days of the show. She found it near her home as she walked along Redondo Beach one day. It is a beautifully curved stick that works perfectly as Harriet's staff.

I could feel the students' awe as they sat on the auditorium floor while I made the transformation to Harriet Tubman before their very eyes. Looking in their eyes, some seemed to accept the possibility that I actually might *be* Harriet Tubman.

Such is the imagination of children.

As I led into my portrayal of Maya Angelou, I decided I would use the opportunity to speak to the subject of molestation by sharing with these fifth graders the story that Maya shared in one of the volumes of her autobiography when she mentioned how she had been touched inappropriately when she was a young girl. I knew it was a risky subject, but I also knew it was likely that at least one child in that audience had been molested, and I needed to use my opportunity to broach the subject.

I took the liberty to say to those fifth graders, "There is a difference between a 'good' touch and a 'bad' touch. If any of you have experienced a touch that did not feel like it was a 'good touch,' if you have not already, please let someone know right away."

I went on to share with the students that as a result of Maya's report of what happened to her, the man who touched her in a "bad way" had been killed in retaliation. Maya felt it was her fault he lost his life. As a result, she refused to speak again for some years. She communicated only by a worn tablet and pencil that she carried on her person until one of her teachers who was very special to Maya refused to talk with her any longer unless she used her own voice to communicate.

Directly following that performance, a young fifth grade girl pulled me aside from audience members onstage as I packed my things up to leave. To my amazement, she told me she had been raped. I was absolutely shocked and unprepared for her openness.

I said, "Who did it?"

She said in a matter-of-fact tone, "Two boys. Teenagers."

I said, "Did you tell?"

She looked me squarely in the eyes and answered, "Yes."

I asked what happened after she told. She said, "They got in trouble."

I said, "See, you did the right thing by telling. They got punished for what they did to you."

Our conversation went on a bit further until we were interrupted by her teacher who said, "What does she have to say? She never has anything to say in class."

The young girl and I knowingly looked at each other as the teacher walked away.

What I had said about Maya Angelou onstage had spoken directly to that young girl.

The two of us alone again, I told her, "Thank you for sharing this with me. I know it is not an easy thing to talk about. Know that your body is a sacred place and you do not have to allow anyone to touch it unless you give your permission."

I added, "If anyone, including yourself, has made you feel bad or dirty about what happened, know that it was not your fault."

She listened intently as she looked directly in my eyes.

I gave her a big hug and told her that her healing had clearly already begun.

I ended our conversation by saying something like, "You called it exactly what it was—*rape*. How brave of you. You are a very strong little girl and you are going to be fine. And please, try not to be in any situation where that may happen again."

She nodded in understanding.

As I loaded my things in my car, I thought about how I had been used as a vessel that day. Had I had my way, I would *never* have performed for fifth graders. I was now very glad I had. I guessed that this young girl was probably only one of others in that room who had been touched inappropriately, including some teachers when they were children.

Maybe there was another in that audience carrying a vow of secrecy who would now also step forward to claim their freedom.

In 1989, shortly after making my permanent move to Los Angeles, I ran across an article in the *Los Angeles Times* announcing the deadline for the City of Los Angeles Department of Cultural Affairs' "Window Grant" applications. In addition to organizations, they were also accepting grant applications from individual artists. I saw this finding as a sign that this was my opportunity to finally create my very own solo show that I had been thinking of. However, the deadline was fast approaching.

I had just enough time to define the nature of my project, find a performance venue, create a budget, get letters of recommendation, and assemble anything else that was required. The idea of creating a solo show had been dancing around in my head for a while, but had I not run across that article, there is no telling when I would actually have created my own solo show.

I now had an opportunity and a deadline.

Little did I know at the time that that article would motivate me to create a historical solo show that would tour three continents: North America, Africa and Europe. To date, in North America the show has toured nationally from coast to coast in close to 40 U.S. states and excerpts performed on Tortola Island in the Caribbean. The show has also toured in Europe in Rotterdam, Holland, and excerpts have been performed in Africa in Abuja, Nigeria. I had no idea in 1990 that my show would span diverse venues that would include colleges and universities, elementary and secondary schools, juvenile halls, festivals, conferences, museums, libraries, churches, retreats, private gatherings, and city facilities.

For the City of Los Angeles grant proposal, I decided I would target senior citizen centers as my debut audience. I knew seniors were an underserved arts programming audience and I also felt seniors would be the least critical and most appreciative audience for my newly birthed solo show.

I was right.

Although *I Am That I Am:* Woman, *Black* would be *my* maiden one-woman show, performing solo work was not new to me. I had previously toured nationally in the mid '80s with the San Francisco-based African American Drama Company show, *Sister, Can I Speak For You?* I usually "opened" for the accompanying company show, *Can I Speak For You, Brother?*

I saw my own show as an extension of the work I had done with the company because I would still be bringing historical figures to life onstage. I did not know the African American Drama Company was, in fact, priming me for my own work.

Against my will, Artistic Director Philip Walker taught me I could, out of necessity, learn a solo show in seven days. In this case, Phil had bookings throughout the country to fulfill. Unexpectedly, he needed to replace his female actor.

He approached me.

I said, "Phil, I appreciate the offer, but I don't think I can learn a one-woman show in a week. I've never even performed a one-woman show."

After some persuasion, Phil assured me that I could do it. Once committed to the project, we worked feverishly ten hours a day for the next seven days using an ACT studio to prepare me for the road. I ate, slept, and thought about little else over the intense seven-day, seventy-hour rehearsal process. I literally closed myself off from most everything in my life as I entered the worlds of historical Black women who lived from the 18th century to the present.

As fate would have it, my first performance of that solo show was at my alma mater, UC Santa Cruz. My first audience included those who spanned my entire life. Jill Alpers, a woman I had known since Central Junior High School in Oroville, California was among them. Unbeknownst to me at the time, Jill was now a re-entry student at UCSC. She surprised me with her dimpled smile and warm hug.

I squealed, "Jill! What are you doing here?"

She returned, "I went back to school."

Fellow alumni and staff from my days as a student there who still lived in the area, including UCSC then staff member Brenda Brown, attended that performance. There were also current ACT students of mine who had made the sojourn all the way down from San Francisco to see their instructor perform.

Talk about pressure.

At one point in the show, I "went up" on my lines. That is, I could not remember the next line. I went totally blank. My training taught me to just keep going, but I am fairly certain my momentary babbling made no sense at all. However, I kept going until I clutched onto the line that got me back on track.

In that moment of disorientation, I was sweating bullets.

Going blank onstage is every actor's worst nightmare and most of us get our turn.

I could not wait to get off the UCSC Porter College stage. I graciously took my bow and quickly exited the stage. As I sat in my dressing room afterwards, beating myself up for what had just happened, Phil knocked on my dressing room door.

Dreading seeing him, I cautiously braced myself with, "Come in."

Once he was inside, I said, "Phil, I'm sorry."

Phil asked, "For what?"

"Because I failed you," I moaned.

Looking at me in bewilderment he said, "You didn't fail me."

He went on, "In fact, you got a standing ovation, but you never came back onstage to receive it."

I was appalled.

I never saw my first standing ovation for that solo show.

My mind was already racing ahead. My second performance was scheduled a couple of days later in California in the San Joaquin Valley town of Modesto. What I considered to be a failed night spurred me to give my very best the second time around.

I ran my lines over and over in rehearsal. I was incredibly focused in my preparation. I thought of little else before the next performance. My ego would not allow me a repeat of that first performance. I wanted to be sure I was ready for my next audience.

And I was.

I recovered well from my first performance. What I felt was an inadequate delivery the first time around, regardless of that standing ovation, fueled me.

To actors I say, *"No matter how good others say you are, develop an inner gauge that informs you when you are good and when you are not."*

I also say, *"Use what you consider to be a 'bad experience' onstage to force you right back up there to do better. Don't let a perceived failed performance make you give up. Use it."*

That is how my solo experience began. It was rocky, but I recovered.

I believe solo work is the most demanding work an actor can tackle. It tests what mettle an actor is made of. Being able to engage an audience alone, to temper and sustain energy onstage for a substantial period of time, and to stay fresh, show after show, by not going on automatic pilot is challenging.

Through the African American Drama Company, I touched many hearts and minds across the country. I would later come to do the same with my own show.

The biggest obstacle for me in the beginning when I began with the African American Drama Company was learning how to "break through the fourth wall." By that I mean learning how to relate to the audience by talking directly to them. In traditional theatre, the actor's reality generally does not go beyond the confines of the stage.

At one point in the show, I was required to join the audience. I looked directly in their eyes as I performed. It took some doing on my part to get comfortable with interactive theatre that required me to make eye contact and *use* my audience.

Interactive theatre is the most naked and challenging form of acting I have ever done.

I also learned the ropes on the road. I learned how to work with "presenters," or those who book shows. I learned how to pack economically, do one-shot tech rehearsals the day before or the day of a performance, to work in the best and worst of circumstances, and how to use frequent flyer cards in more ways than one. I could get frequent flyer mile credit from flights, hotels, and from rental cars. My frequent flyer miles multiplied quickly.

In 1989, seeing the *Los Angeles Times* article requesting grant proposals signaled the time had come for me to create my own vehicle. I had now moved to Los Angeles, far away from the Bay Area's African American Drama Company. Although I would perform one or two more shows with them after moving to Los Angeles, I felt I was *finally* ready to create my own work.

The upside was that now the African American Drama Company and Adilah Barnes Productions would both be a part of that cadre of Black actors who contribute to keeping Black History alive by touring work that we call "edutainment." We all teach, while entertaining our audiences at the same time.

I will forever thank Philip Walker and the African American Drama Company of San Francisco for positively influencing my training as an actor. The company opened the world of solo work to me and allowed me to see the country more than I ever dreamed I would.

In 1989, I approached four predominantly African American senior centers in Los Angeles that included the Betty Hill, Crenshaw, Lafayette, and Vineyard Friendship Senior Centers. The directors of each facility graciously drafted letters stating they would welcome me to perform at their centers if I received my grant from the Los Angeles Department of Cultural Affairs.

I got the grant.

I nervously performed my new show for my first four audiences. At the Vineyard Friendship Senior Center, I had a much-appreciated surprise. Sitting in the audience was my son's paternal grandmother, Rosetta Stuckey. Although Tariq had met her before in the Bay Area, I had not. I definitely knew her by name, but Mrs. Stuckey and I had never met personally. She had lived in Los Angeles for some time, and we lived in the Bay Area. She rose to identify herself and ask her post-performance question of me. I could hardly maintain my composure.

It was Mrs. Stuckey. We would finally meet.

My show in Los Angeles brought my son's grandmother and me together. Clearly, I received more from that performance than I ever imagined. I established a personal relationship with Mrs. Stuckey, and my son reunited with his father's mother.

Mrs. Stuckey is a woman I respect for her unfailing faith in God, her resilience, and her discipline in keeping her body in shape. Although well into her eighties and until recent health challenges, she used to walk daily. She remains an inspiration for me.

From the beginning, I received confirmation from those senior citizens that my work mattered. Many of those in the senior centers seemed proud and approving of the historical work I was doing. They nurtured my spirit and their appreciation encouraged me. They also served as my teachers. One elder at the Lafayette Senior Center had actually met my third character, Mrs. Mary McLeod Bethune when she was a child. She recounted their meeting and her personal impression of Mrs. Bethune.

She said in front of the audience, "I remember Mrs. Bethune was a very proud and stern woman."

One elder said, "Baby, we love what you have done for us, but the youth need to see this."

She further went on to say, "I am a member of Eastern Star. Would you come and perform for my group?"

That is how my touring began in 1990.

Not knowing what fee to set for my services, I asked Philip Walker what he would suggest.

He answered, "I cannot answer that for you. You will come to figure out what the show is worth to you."

Although Phil's cryptic answer gave me absolutely no help with my first paid booking, I did finally arrive at a fee. I practically gave the show away, but I later understood exactly what he meant. I eventually figured out what I felt the show was worth to me. Over time, I have periodically upped the fee for the show, because I feel I am worthy. I feel my many years as a performer, and the number of years I have invested in my show justify what I ask for.

However, for my first booking, the Eastern Star had no money, and I did not know any better.

My first touring came as a direct result of performing at one of the Los Angeles senior citizen centers. There have been many other performances that in turn have led to other bookings.

In 2000, I performed for the Association of American Colleges and Universities Conference in Pittsburgh, Pennsylvania. The exposure to their huge national membership opened the door to performances at yet other colleges. Venues included Berea College in Kentucky, repeat performances at the University of Wisconsin, Milwaukee, by way of Dr. Sandra Jones, and J. Herman Blake's Iowa State University. In fact, it was Herman who was responsible for me performing at the conference. That conference opened the door to performances in two new states for the show, both Kentucky and Wisconsin.

One presenter, Shari Clarke, began booking my show in 1995 when she was at Whitman College in Walla Walla, Washington. Everywhere she goes, she invites me. Because of her, I subsequently booked performances at the University of Maine, University of Nebraska-Lincoln, and more recently at Mansfield University in Pennsylvania. Shari is responsible for my show claiming two more states, Maine and Nebraska.

I also credit Shari with showing me how to eat a whole Maine lobster. Although I had on a paper bib at that Maine restaurant, it was still a very messy affair. However, the fresh succulent lobster meat was well worth the work. Even in Nebraska and Pennsylvania, Shari somehow found restaurants with good seafood.

When I once told Shari that my goal was to perform in all fifty states, she jokingly said, "Tell me which states you still need, and I will choose my next post from your list."

I cannot thank Shari enough for her graciousness. She was my link to three other performances in Nebraska: the University of Nebraska at the Kearney and Omaha campuses, and the nearby private school, Midland Lutheran College. She also guided me to new lifelong friendships with Dr. Kwakiutl Dreher and Dr. Venita Kelley that stemmed from my first performance in Nebraska.

At Midland Lutheran College, the presenter booked me in a chapel-like space on campus. When the head of the theatre department came to see the show and asked why I was not in their state of the art theatre, the presenter explained their theatre had always been off limits for outside programming.

I have found that rub is not uncommon. I have observed that theatre departments at many colleges and universities can be extremely territorial and snotty about their theatre spaces.

However, in this case, the theatre chairperson was new to his post and made it quite clear he would gladly have offered his theatre.

The lesson was, always ask for what you want. You just might get it.

The good news is that it is very possible that subsequent artists visiting that campus have now benefited by being in the college's beautiful theatre.

The National Association of Campus Activities (NACA) has been my biggest source of bookings over the years. It is a booking organization for both presenters and artists/managers. It caters to the "buyers and sellers" of college acts.

My niece, Venita Jacobson, was my original booking manager, and the person who helped build Adilah Barnes Productions. Not only did she perform duties as my booking manager, she also served as my publicist and graphic designer. Adilah Barnes Productions could *never* have been as successful as it has become without Venita's passion, hard work, and ability to relate so well with presenters. It is to her I owe a great debt for the success of my show.

In recent years, Brian Dennis of Diversity Talent has taken over where Venita left off. She was my booking *manager* and responsible for representing me at booking conferences, contract negotiations, marketing, public relations and providing my graphic design. He is a booking *agent* and responsible for representing me at booking conferences and negotiating contracts. Their roles have been different, but they both have ultimately booked the show. Many of my bookings now come from referrals or from those I know personally. In those instances, I handle the bookings myself and pocket my commission fees.

In 1994, during Venita's tenure, I showcased at a very competitive regional NACA conference in Birmingham, Alabama, for what was called then the Southeast Region. I actually booked thirty-eight performances from that *one* showcase.

Again, that was how I got the down payment for my home in North Hollywood.

There have been so many moments I have experienced along the way that have stayed with me. Many I have captured in my journal, and still others on my camcorder but all have been recorded in my heart. There is a complete book inside me on my touring journey alone. Because I am considering another book on the subject of my touring sojourn, I only wish I had kept a more formal journal along the way. With time, my memory has gotten a bit blurry. Still, the shows that most impacted me and that were not captured on paper or video are recorded inside me.

At the same time, to those who have not begun to tour yet, I strongly urge you to document every single one of your performances by keeping a journal.

Some of the memories that have stayed vividly with me include my performance at the University of Alaska in Anchorage to an audience I could not see because the "house" was so dark. I could only see the hot stage lights illuminating me. I least enjoy that type of lighting, not only because the lights are so warm, but more importantly, because I cannot see the faces of those before me. In the blackness, I can only commune with audiences by feeling and hearing them. Although not preferred, I have found it is still possible to commune with audiences in blackness.

When lighting allows me to see my audience, I can always identify at least one who is on my theatrical journey with me. I keep going back to that person to refuel. That person may nod in agreement, smile, laugh, or utter a "call-and-response" verbal talking back.

If that person approaches me after the show, I always acknowledge how he or she fed me. That audience member always seems surprised to hear how actively a part of the show they were.

At the close of my show in Anchorage, Alaska, the lights faded up and I was met with a packed audience of some four hundred African Americans. It was a mixed audience, but predominantly Black.

As I packed my things onstage after the show, one Black woman joined me.

In amazement of the audience's ethnic make-up, I asked, "Where did all these Black folks come from here in Anchorage?"

She said, "We get so few Black people here that when we *do* get Black performers, *everybody* comes out!"

She further went on to explain that many have settled there because of nearby military bases.

Another Black woman walked up and presented me with a book of poetry she had written. She is only one of many who have touched my heart by giving me mementoes along the way.

Although I almost froze in that snow-covered Alaskan city, I had a wonderful experience there. It just so happened that my son Tariq was on winter break and was able to accompany me there. We both got the opportunity to spend quality time together on the road as we visited a place we had never been. Although both in need of thawing out, we enjoyed Anchorage. We were struck by how virginal, safe, and new the city felt. There was also a noticeably larger ratio of men to women residents.

Somehow, my Harriet Tubman stick got checked elsewhere when my son and I separated at the airport to go to different states. I did not miss the stick until I arrived in Charleston, South Carolina, for my performance at the College of Charleston. Once I realized my stick was not with my bags, I immediately called the airline. I had two days between my two performances to either retrieve the stick or somehow get another one. I assumed the stick had accidentally traveled back to California with my son, and I was hopeful it would be tracked to Oakland.

The following day, I received a call from the hotel's front desk.

The voice on the telephone said, "Ms. Barnes, your sticks are here."

"Oh, no!" I thought. "They broke the stick!"

I quickly went downstairs and, to my surprise, found two separate sticks in two different plastic ski bags. It seemed to be some kind of karmic joke. Who else could possibly be traveling with a similar wooden stick?

I wondered if the universe was suggesting I keep the second stick for a back-up.

Since the stick was not mine, I decided to leave it at that hotel desk in Charleston. Although there was no identifying tag, I figured someone must have been looking for their stick, too. I have no idea what came of that second stick but I do hope it somehow found its way back to its rightful owner.

I love the city of Charleston. It is rich in history. Although much of it is a painful reminder of slavery, its aged architecture and moss-lined trees accent its beauty. It also has one of the best seafood restaurants I have experienced. From the restaurant, I was able to see the point from where I was told the Fifty-fourth Massachusetts Infantry, established in 1863 as the first Black regiment to fight in the Civil War, fought. I got to see basket makers who still weave in African tradition, passed on from generation to generation. Charleston College housed me in a beautiful Victorian building managed by Charleston College. Oddly enough, there were no other campus visitors there at the time so I had the huge Victorian all to myself.

I found out much later that a college buddy of mine, Sabra Slaughter, was living in Charleston at the same time I was there. Had I known that, I would certainly have invited Sabra and his family to my show.

I also remember performing at Grays Harbor College in Aberdeen, Washington. Again, I performed in a darkened theatre where I could not see my audience's faces. The lights faded up to a packed audience of, again, about 400 people. There was one Black woman—very attractive and well-groomed, with two young children. Nobody else in that theatre looked like me.

I then understood why that particular audience had been such a quiet one. My Grays Harbor College audience was typical of one of my "listening audiences," steeped in silence. I can always feel that type of audience learning as they listen.

In my customary question-and-answer period following that Grays Harbor College performance, the silence broke.

One older Anglo man stood up and asked with fury, "I just want to know why you included Angela Davis in this show. She was a Communist!"

I could feel his rage as I answered in a quiet tone, "Miss Davis is a political and social activist who came along during my time. She represents a period of change in American history that I personally lived through. She contributed much to this society, and although she was made out to be a criminal, she was not. She was acquitted of all charges in her trial in 1971. I feel very honored to portray her. In fact, she has sold the rights to her life story to a Hollywood studio and I am fortunate to be the only actor, to my knowledge, who has been cleared to portray her onstage."

The gentleman, along with the rest of that Anglo audience, quietly listened to my answer. I could feel that older man thinking. He did not say another word. I would like to think I challenged his judgmental thinking that day. That brief discussion represents some of the heated comments my show occasionally provokes.

In that same Washington town, I was lodged in the loving home of the Anglo family who brought me there. The teenage daughter approached me after my performance to say, "I'm really glad you came here. We don't often get exposed to anything like this. We really need it." Her comment underscored what I already knew. My show gave the audience a history lesson as they were being entertained.

In terms of history lesson audiences, there was also the time in a post-performance discussion at a college in Ohio where a student actually asked me, "Can you tell me again who Maya Angelou is?"

Mary McLeod Bethune I may have understood, but Maya Angelou?

In yet another venue along my way, an Anglo man stood up with tears in his eyes and said, "I fought in World War II and I fought with Black men I knew well who could not get in the same taxi with me when we came back to the States. We all fought for the same country, for God's sake. How could that be?"

He added, "How can we erase the racism in this country?"

The audience listened to the older man who spoke passionately from his heart. I told him I did not have the answers, but I also told him, "I believe that if each of us treated every person we come in contact with each day as if that person was the most important human being in the world, that would certainly be a good start."

As an exercise, I sometimes consciously try to do just that. When I do try to treat each person whom I come in contact with that kind of importance, I find I am met with wonderful responses.

I suggest we all choose a day to consciously treat everyone we come in contact with as if that person is the most important person in the world.

I remember well, following my performance at the University of Idaho, an Anglo woman who was the administrator of a women's shelter asked me if I would also come to visit the homeless women and their families who lived there. Surprisingly, in Idaho, the shelter was named after Sojourner Truth, one of the historical women I portray. I took that as a clear sign I was to visit that shelter.

Standing onstage next to the administrator, we were joined by a homeless, pre-teen, biracial girl who lived at the Sojourner Truth shelter with her mother and brothers.

Looking in that young girl's expectant eyes, I made my decision.

I was leaving Boise early the next morning for my next performance, but I said, "If we are going, we'd better go now."

Not everyone was open to meeting me, but I met all those at the shelter who wanted to be met, including the young girl's mother and brothers. The young girl proudly wore one of my show tee shirts that had been purchased for her that night. Upon my departure from the shelter, she walked me to the door.

She blurted out, "I want to be an actress."

I looked deeply in her eyes as I said, "That is wonderful. If you don't remember anything else from your experience tonight, I want you to remember that with hard work, you can become anything you want to be, despite any appearances right now."

I hope she has continued to pursue her dream of also becoming an actor and finds her way to this book.

On the road, I have also been able to sightsee.

In 2001, at the University of Wisconsin, Milwaukee, I was able to visit America's Black Holocaust Museum, the only museum of its kind in the United States. It felt profoundly eerie entering the darkened, tunnel-like entranceway. There were artifacts of slavery and photos of slaves along the way. African drum music accompanied the sounds of water and moans in the darkness. Past the darkened tunnel were display rooms depicting the atrocities of slavery and its horrific effects on African Americans along the Diaspora.

After my tour of the Black Holocaust Museum, I sat in on a talk given by the late James Cameron, founder of the museum. He spoke of how in 1930, he and two of his young friends had been wrongly accused of killing a young Anglo man. He watched while his two friends were beaten and lynched in front of a mob. He also spoke of how that early experience transformed his life, and led him to fight for civil rights, equality, and peace.

The museum began in his home. A fair-skinned man, he was quite old but still robust. He made it a point to make himself available to speak to tour groups, as he also preserved Black History.

I experienced a very sobering and enlightening reminder of the Black Holocaust as I walked through the museum. Millions of Blacks were lost during the slave trade from Africa to America.

My soul wept for my ancestors that day.

When I performed at Iowa State University, I stayed in the home of my mentor Dr. J. Herman Blake and his gracious wife, Dr. Emily Moore. I occupied the lower level of their beautiful three-story home.

A spacious home, we all had our own space, but we were bridged by the wonderful African American music that permeated their home. We also enjoyed wonderful conversations over meals that Emily lovingly prepared.

I became speechless when Herman asked me to guest lecture his Iowa State class. This was the same Dr. J. Herman Blake whose packed classes were legendary at UC Santa Cruz. I reluctantly agreed, although I was nervous about standing in front of him and his class.

On our way to class, I was puzzled when we stopped at a florist shop. He asked me to join him inside. Once inside the fragrant shop, he asked me to choose a boutonniere for myself. He told me that, like George Washington Carver, a student and later a faculty member at Iowa State University beginning in 1894, he also wore a flower each time he taught.

Herman asked me to do the same.

Herman and I arrived on campus and walked into the building where he taught. After his students had filed in, Herman gave me a very heartwarming introduction. Next, it was my turn to take the podium. I stole a glance or two at Herman as I began to lecture. Herman's smile gave me his approval.

His students, who represent a generation I still don't fully understand, came to learn a bit more about their professor that day. Before I began, he may have been seen as another graying professor in his senior years.

I could see them begin to sit up in their seats as I took them back in time to Herman's heyday. I shared his significant role as UC Santa Cruz's very first African American professor. He was on faculty when the campus opened its doors in 1965.

I spoke of how he meant everything to the twenty-eight Black students whom he was entrusted to lead. I recounted how he was our professor, father, therapist, friend, and even when needed, our disciplinarian. Many of us would not have made it at UC Santa Cruz, I shared with his students, without Dr. J. Herman Blake.

When I finished my lecture, silence spoke in the room. There was no question in my mind that his Black History class had gotten a full dose of Black History that day. I believe they came to see Dr. J. Herman Blake quite differently after that lecture.

My journey with my solo show took a thrilling turn in the year 2000. At the invitation of my Bay Area acting buddy Malumba Anderson, my show crossed over internationally. He asked me to perform at two venues in Rotterdam, Holland. One venue was the annual Fabrikaart Festival, and the other The Odeon, a city facility.

Malumba, an African American man, made Rotterdam his home in 1989. He now has a Dutch wife, Ils, and three beautiful children: Aisha, Malcolm, and Carmen. Remarkably, the Dutch language now rolls off his tongue. Having lived abroad so long, he now has a Dutch accent when he speaks his native tongue of English.

Stepping off the plane in Rotterdam, I expected to find a blonde, blue-eyed country. I was met, instead, with countless Black Dutchmen. Many had come across the waters from the former Central American Dutch colony Surinam during a major migration, following Surinam's independence from Holland in 1975.

Many of the Black Dutch speak English. However, the city facility presenter of the Odeon Theatre in Rotterdam wanted to make sure I would be understood fully during my performance. To prep my show, he set up a pre-show dialogue with a group of Surinamese women who were members of The Fifty Plus Club. He arranged a translator to accompany me as I spoke about the show the day before my Odeon performance.

In the audience of senior citizens was a tall, dark woman I had seen at The Odeon before. I was struck by her powerful, majestic presence, and the respect she commanded from everyone. She surprised me later, following my public performance, by giving me a beautiful ceramic Dutch windmill with chimes.

My interpreter that day was the daughter of the majestic woman. I was rather amused when she translated something I had just said and was corrected by one of the seniors who said, "What she said *was* . . ."

The interpreter blushed as she stood corrected. I knew then I would be understood well enough by my Dutch audience.

Directly following my performance at the Odeon Theatre, one young woman by the name of Reyna said, "As an African American, you are very lucky to know your history. We do not know our African history here." African Americans feel we do not fully know our history in America because it was virtually omitted in history books here, but Reyna's moving comment reminded me that self-knowledge is relative.

Since our meeting, Reyna and I have become pen pals by e-mail.

I have sometimes performed at venues with very meager budgets. One example was in 1999 at the Imperial Community College, a border town between California and Mexico. I was told that I was the first touring performer brought to campus from outside the area. They had so little money they could only afford an excerpt of my show on their campus.

A very poor and predominantly Latino community, they were so excited to have me that I decided to give them the *entire* show at a fraction of the cost. For that particular audience, it was not about receiving my usual fee. I knew they wanted the show in its completeness and I wanted to give it to them.

The show was very well-received, and I felt good about what I had done. I also received a very nice letter from the presenter after I returned home. The student body's enjoyment and acknowledgment after the show were payment enough for me.

It is not always about the money.

There have been times when I have not been at my best, but the show must go on. I once took a serious fall on a wet cafeteria floor at Georgia College in Milledgeville. My back was in excruciating pain, but I still went on.

At the Association of American Colleges and Universities Conference in Pittsburgh, Pennsylvania, I had a swollen knee. I could barely endure the pain, but somehow I performed the show, although I immediately collapsed afterwards in my hotel room.

Mind over matter is a miraculous thing.

My spiritual advisor predicted I would meet a significant man on that particular day. Perhaps if I had been able to walk to mingle more, I may have met him because there certainly were many attractive professional men at that conference. However, meeting someone was the last thing on my mind that day.

I have also had experiences that connected me closer to the women I portray in my solo show. I already mentioned in this chapter the elder at the Lafayette Senior Center who recounted in our post-performance audience discussion that she had met Mrs. Mary McLeod Bethune as a child.

Following my performance at the University of Central Florida in Orlando, I touched the soil of Bethune-Cookman University in nearby Daytona Beach. It was originally founded by Mrs. Bethune as a girl's school in 1904 and named the Daytona Normal and Industrial Institute for Negro Girls. She started the school with $1.50, a vision, and friends in high places. Those friends included Mr. Singer of Singer sewing machine fame, along with one of the men of the Rockefeller dynasty.

I want to return to Bethune-Cookman University so that I can take my time walking the halls of the college that still bears her name.

My first visit I had only enough time to step outside the car to see the outside of a few of the campus' buildings. I had pressed my University of Central Florida presenters to drive me there, and they had obliged. However, that fleeting glimpse only made me hunger to return.

I *will* return.

On that Florida tour, I asked a presenter to take me to the hometown of another of my women, Zora Neale Hurston. She knew how important it was to me and took me to nearby Eatonville, six miles north of Orlando. Eatonville, at one time, was an all-Black town, and the birth place that Zora spoke of in great detail in her writings.

I walked inside the tiny store Zora described in her autobiography *Dust Tracks on a Road.* The store porch is no longer there, but the store still is. I could feel the memories Zora spoke of as I walked down the aisles of the shoebox-sized store.

Zora heard countless yarns from the men who frequented that store porch. Those storytellers would directly influence and color her choice to become a folklorist, anthropologist, and novelist.

That store was not altogether unlike the neighborhood store I grew up near in Oroville, California, with its planked floors and packed shelves. At one time, ours also had a store porch that our town folk sat on to shoot the breeze.

I tried to breathe in Zora's essence as I walked down the two or three itsy bitsy aisles of the store. When I later stood outside, I tried to imagine the store porch that once stood there. I tried to picture the men she so descriptively spoke of as she dragged her feet past them so as not to miss a word when she tried to walk into the store unnoticed.

Children were not allowed at that time to sit with a group of adults on a porch unless invited, so she would take her time catching what she could as she went in and out of that store to buy sugar or coffee for her mother. The many tales she heard fascinated and stayed with her. They heavily influenced her later work as a writer.

Diagonally across the street from the store was the property that once held Zora's childhood home. I could see exactly the distance her mother would yell to Zora to bring back whatever she had been sent to buy.

The site of Zora's childhood home has now been transformed into the location of a fire station, but Zora has not been forgotten. The city has erected a granite stone dedicated to "Eatonville's Daughter." It claims, "She Jumped at the Sun."

Nearby, there is also the Zora Neale Hurston National Museum of Fine Arts, established by an Eatonville preservation group that holds an annual celebration to honor her name. I bought a tee shirt to remind myself that I had, in fact, been to Zora's birth place.

I wear it proudly.

What many do not know is that Zora Neale Hurston died in 1960 in Fort Pierce, Florida, where she was in later years a substitute teacher and somewhat forgotten by the public. Her last days were a far cry from her outrageous days as the controversial and bold female writer she came to be known as during the lively Harlem Renaissance, also known as the "New Negro Movement," that lasted arguably from

1919 to 1937. She was the toast of this Black intellectual elite that included the likes of writers like her one-time close friend Langston Hughes, Claude McKay, and James Weldon Johnson. The high point of this era of refined creative expression from African American literary figures also included poets, musicians, and performing artists.

Even with such notoriety, Zora returned to Florida, and in her last years worked anonymously as a maid. However, fellow writer Alice Walker, was led through overgrown brush by locals in Fort Pierce to Zora's approximate burial site many years after Zora's death to place a deserving headstone on her grave. When my travels take me to Florida again, I also want to honor Zora Neale Hurston by visiting her now-marked gravesite.

During one of my three sojourns to Birmingham, Alabama to perform, I was driven past the family home of activist Angela Davis. It is a beautiful two-story home, a world away from her family's early days in the Birmingham projects.

Following my performance at the Civil Rights Institute in Birmingham, a young man stood up during my post-performance discussion. He confirmed what Angela had remembered about her mother.

In Angela's autobiography *Angela Davis: An Autobiography,* she speaks of how her mother, a school teacher, would often give clothes to those who needed them, sometimes even before Angela and her sister had outgrown them.

The young man proudly declared, "I was also one of Mrs. Davis' students."

It is no wonder that Angela Davis became a communist. She has always looked out for the have-nots. She has given other examples in her autobiography of how her beliefs and actions to ensure equality for all have influenced her way of seeing the world. She has always been an advocate for the "underclass."

In one instance, Angela recounts how she stole coins from her father's bag of money he brought home from his service station each evening. The following day, she gave the stolen money to those children at her school "who did not have enough money to even buy a bag of potato chips."

I first met Angela Davis following a talk she gave at a convention sponsored by the Los Angeles radio station, *92.3 The Beat*. She spoke that day on welfare rights and prison reform for women. I sat in awe, hanging on to Angela's every word. After hearing her speak, I stood in line patiently with my show's promotional packet in hand. I excitedly waited my turn to speak with her. I shared with her that I was coming soon to perform at my alma mater, UC Santa Cruz, where she is now a professor. I told her I would be honored to have her in the audience to see my portrayal of her. She warmly asked that I follow up by telephone.

I called the campus several times trying to reach her to remind her of the date I would be coming. Unfortunately, I never received a confirmation of her attendance for the day of my performance. Her schedule took her out of town on the day of my performance. I felt disappointment, but what consoled me was having the audience stand and applaud after I performed her character. I had never received a standing ovation specifically for Angela until that night. I had received spontaneous applause for her character before, but not a standing ovation. Yet it was no wonder the Santa Cruz audience responded by standing. Angela Davis is very much loved and respected by the UC Santa Cruz community.

My second meeting of Angela was far more personally gratifying. In the fall of 2005, I approached her at one of the weekend events for the late Chancellor Denise Denton's investiture. I reminded Angela of our first meeting and shared with her that she and I would be the speakers at a luncheon to be held that weekend. Words cannot fully convey how proud and nervous I felt sitting next to *the* Angela Davis as a fellow speaker. She took the podium first.

When I followed her, I began with, "It is an absolute honor to be sitting next to Ms. Davis, because I also portray her in my one-woman show *I Am That I Am:* Woman, *Black."*

I went on to say as I glanced back at her, "So, Angela, I want you to know I am studying your every move!"

The audience roared with laughter as she shyly replied, "*Nooo.*"

We now have a context of experiencing each other in a very personal way.

I met Ms. Maya Angelou in 1989 during ACT's run of August Wilson's play *Joe Turner's Come and Gone.* Maya came to see the show at the invitation of cast member Roscoe Lee Browne's personal invitation. I felt honored to be in her presence after the show as we all went to a nearby restaurant on Geary Street. I was so awestruck, I did not even think to mention I had previously portrayed her in the solo show *Sister, Can I Speak For You?* for the African American Drama Company. Ironically, I had not yet begun to portray Maya in my own show.

What most impressed me about Maya is her powerful presence. She is indeed a woman of Southern grace. I also found her to be absolutely majestic in her metered eloquence, even though she appeared very shy. Her humility was unexpected, and for me, added to her greatness.

I have found that the truly great are oftentimes some of the most humble.

I *still* want Ms. Maya Angelou to see my show.

In 1997, at the now defunct Theatre Geo in Hollywood, playwright Lorraine Hansberry's sister Mamie and Mamie's daughter came to see me perform Lorraine during the Los Angeles Women's Theatre Festival. I knew of their coming in advance. I now wish I had not. I was a nervous wreck as I performed Lorraine for that matinee. My challenge was made no easier since Mamie and her daughter had center front-row seats directly in front of me.

I met and spoke with Lorraine's relatives following my performance. They were very kind in what they had to say of my portrayal. It was not my most relaxed portrayal of Lorraine Hansberry, but I was relieved to know my work was acceptable to them.

My performances have taken me to cities where I have friends and relatives. Many family members in Sacramento came to see my performances for Les Belle Artes, McClatchy High, and Valley High. My mother was in that number at the Les Belles Artes performance. My father Theoplis, my son's father and sister, and other family and friends were in the Oakland Museum audience in Oakland, California.

The latter performance felt like one of my two "coming home" shows, since I spent seventeen years of my life in the Bay Area. That audience stands out for me, because it is the *only* audience to date that stood while I sang the National Black Anthem, "Lift Ev'ry Voice and Sing." Many audiences have sung along *with* me, but the culturally-conscious audience of Oakland, California *stood*. It is no coincidence that Huey P. Newton founded the Black Panther Party in that same culturally and politically aware city.

Former student Karen Williams Harris came to see my show at Georgia Institute of Technology in Atlanta. Fellow UC Santa Cruz buddy Donald Nance came out to see my show at Kent State in Ohio and again at the College of Akron.

My acting buddies Ron Reed and Eugene Calhoun met for the first time when they came to see my show at Sonoma State in California. Eugene later invited me back to Sonoma State two more times to perform for the college preparatory TRIO Program, that includes Project Upward Bound, the program I previously mentioned that is so close to my heart.

The point I am trying to make is that it has been gratifying to look into audiences around the country (and even in Holland and the Caribbean) and see, over and over, those whom I personally know and love. It adds to my desire to give my very best, because I know family and friends have specifically come to see my work. It moves me to see their faces in the audience as they root for me to deliver a good show. Space does not allow full acknowledgment of *all* from my past whom I have seen along my touring journey. Those who have come out know who they are, and how much I appreciate their efforts to attend my performances.

At the same time, there is one performance I *must* single out. It is the one that most touched my heart. It included the most familiar faces from my childhood, and it had the most profound emotional impact on me. It took place at the State Theatre in my hometown of Oroville, California. I had been interviewed by the *Oroville Mercury* newspaper by telephone for an advance article, so my coming was well-publicized in the town paper before my arrival.

In the audience in 1996 were my elders. Some came on canes. There were those who were barely able to move because of their arthritis, but they made it a point to be in that audience to witness their daughter's performance. Classmates and family members were also in that packed audience. As I generally do, I acknowledged my family by asking them all to stand after the show.

My childhood girlfriend, Brenda Jackson Stovall, sped around the audience excitedly with a cordless microphone in hand. Our Oprah for the night, she held the instrument that allowed those who wanted to speak during that hearty post-performance discussion to be heard.

When Brenda took the microphone to Mrs. Chef, seated in the first row, I lost it.

Mrs. Chef, now a gray-haired older Italian woman, stood and said, "My name is Mrs. Chef. I was Lovey's third grade teacher."

She added softly, "I am very proud of you."

Until she stood up, I had no idea that one of my favorite grade school teachers had a front row seat.

I broke down in tears onstage as I acknowledged my third grade teacher who had also come out on that very rainy night. In the third grade I had tried my hand at acting in Mrs. Chef's class when we presented an Hawaiian luau skit for our families and friends. I can still see the class singing and dancing as we sang our Hawaiian song, "I'm Going on a Hukilau" in our grass skirts.

One older Anglo man in the State Theatre audience dampened the rainy night even more than the rain when he commented on how he could not believe how many Blacks had come out that evening. His comment did not sound complimentary. At the time, the city of Oroville offered season subscriptions to programs, and he was apparently a subscriber. He went on to say he rarely saw any Blacks come out to the theatre.

As I looked around the full house that mirrored me, I very gently told him, "When you offer programming that speaks to a particular audience, they will come."

I was on the stage of the State Theatre, the movie theatre to which I walked over a mile every Sunday to see the latest movies that came to town. It was the same place where I admired the art deco architecture as I walked up the carpeted winding staircase that led to the ladies powder room. It was the same staircase that took me to the exclusive loge seats I would sneak to sit in. This was the same theatre in which I occasionally sat next to boys I liked, hung out with my girlfriends, or just went to the movies alone to be transported to other times and places.

Finally, this was the same place where I ate my shoestring potato chips one by one as I admired Mr. Sidney Poitier. He lit up the stage, making me feel proud to be Black. I had absolutely no idea that one day I would also become an actor and perform on that very stage.

Now here I was, arguably Oroville's best-known daughter, hopefully also inspiring some little chocolate girl or boy sitting before me. That night I felt I had come full circle, and *I Am That I Am: Woman, Black* was the vehicle.

By returning to my birthplace where my entire village had indeed raised me, I felt that if I never gave another performance of my show, my touring was now complete.

Chapter Eleven

Chance Meeting

I'll tell you why I did all these things. It is very simple. I did all these things because they needed to be done.
—Marie Grace Augustine, social worker

In July of 1993, I attended a California Arts Council Touring Roster Conference in Pasadena, California. Little did I know then that attending that conference would open a new chapter in my life.

At the conference, I happened upon Miriam Reed. What we quickly discovered was that we had several things in common. We were both actors, we were both solo artists, and what connected us most was the fact that we both portray historical women in our solo work. Miriam portrays Anglo women who include birth control advocate Margaret Sanger and suffragist Elizabeth Cady Stanton, while I portray African American women that include abolitionist Harriet Tubman and political activist Angela Davis.

We found kinship that day.

Miriam and I attended some of the same workshops over that weekend and barely came up for air as we talked throughout the conference. As the conference came to an end, all participants were asked to assemble together in one large room to pow wow a last time as we gained closure.

When asked if there were any announcements from the floor, Miriam whispered, "What if I went up and asked all women solo artists to meet us in the back of the room?"

It did not take me long to respond with, "I think that is a *great* idea."

Miriam's question sprang from the idea of summoning all of the women solo artists who were present to see how we might collectively support each other. She identified me at the microphone as the point person in the rear of the wood-paneled room. I raised my hand to identify myself when named.

Much to our surprise, we were bombarded with a number of culturally diverse women from such disciplines as theatre, dance, storytelling, performance art, music, performance poetry and stand-up. If nothing more than out of curiosity, many of those multicultural and multi-disciplined women huddled together with us to find out what was going on.

We knew we were on to something when we saw the astounding number of solo artists we had attracted.

Without much forethought, we informed these women that we wanted to identify other solo female artists in our midst. Helene McCardle was one of two women who identified themselves as having a space at the Burbank Little Theatre and offered it for our first meeting. Many from that first day came back and joined us at the Burbank Little Theatre for our first meeting to figure out where we would go next.

By the end of that July night in 1993, the Los Angeles Women's Theatre Festival (LAWTF) was born.

The inspiration behind LAWTF was the Women's Theatre Festival of Philadelphia. At that time, it claimed itself as being the oldest solo women's theatre festival in the country. I came to know them in 1992 when they launched their first national satellite festival in Los Angeles at the University of California. Their vision was to create satellite festivals throughout the country and Los Angeles was the first. The Women's Theatre Festival dubbed the Los Angeles satellite as the "National Women's Theatre Festival."

I was fortunate enough to be selected as one of their performers at UCLA. Each performer was allowed one performance and I shared an excerpt of my solo show, *I Am That I Am:* Woman, *Black.* I was taken by the cultural diversity of the artists, range of personal stories, and the many disciplines they represented. I was mesmerized by seeing women of different ethnicities and disciplines all on one evening's bill, so much so that I returned as an audience member to experience other artists.

Following the 1992 debut of the National Women's Theatre Festival, much to my chagrin, the Women's Theatre Festival made the disappointing decision not to return to Los Angeles again. They felt Los Angeles was too "celebrity-driven." Their decision saddened me because they had left such a profound mark on me. That experience inspired me to suggest that our newly formed group pick up the torch and continue the work that had been initiated by the Women's Theatre Festival the year before.

The group heard my passion and took to the idea, favoring a festival that would belong to Los Angeles. We decided that evening to model ourselves after the Women's Theatre Festival.

As is usually the case, our group shrank as we began to roll up our sleeves to do the work. Those who did stay and commit made up our "Founding Circle." To pay homage to those deserving women, they are acknowledged by name on all of our LAWTF promotional materials. The Founding Circle includes Miriam Reed, Judith Heineman, Helene McCardle, Phylisé Smith, Joyce Guy, and Nina Kaufman. LAWTF will forever be indebted to each of them for carrying the torch in 1993.

Katie Goodman, co-founder of the Women's Theatre Festival, befriended the Los Angeles Women's Theatre Festival in its formative days. I asked her to guide us, and she did. At her invitation, I subsequently went to Philadelphia to perform in their annual festival. Katie has since married and moved on to Bozeman, Montana, where she and her husband Soren founded the Equinox Theatre. A spunky and energetic leader, I kept Katie abreast of the Festival's developments for many years.

When LAWTF began in 1993, we identified a need for a multicultural and multi-disciplined solo festival for women in Los Angeles. Other solo festivals have since sprouted up in the area. Both Highways Performance Space in Santa Monica and 2100 Square Feet Theatre in Los Angeles have offered solo programming.

In fact, in 2006 and 2007, Artistic Director Leo Garcia of Highways Performance Space invited LAWTF to partner with them as their "crown jewel" for Women's History Month. Our presence grew and by the second year we had standing room only audiences for our programs.

More recently, Bee-Bee Smith and Sloan Robinson launched *Solo Sundays,* an ongoing weekly event that took place at the Lucy Florence Cultural Center in Los Angeles. They featured solo women and changed shows monthly. Whitefire Theatre also produces solo performances. Wendy Kamenoff Hammers produces and showcases talented solo women performers, as well. It is heartwarming to witness all the venues that have now sprung up in Los Angeles to support solo women artists.

Our longevity and expansion distinguishes LAWTF from other solo programs that have come along since our inception in 1993. At the time of this writing, LAWTF has presented well over 400 solo artists from around the globe, and has honored over fifty LAWTF Annual Theatre Awards to deserving women.

Thanks to former Board member Tanya Kersey, we kicked off our First Annual Theatre Awards Ceremony in 1995 with Ms. Della Reese as our host. Ms. Reese said of the first awardees, "I am glad to be here with my friends."

Della was referring to the first award recipients who included the late Beah Richards (*Eternity Award*), Carmen Zapata (*Integrity Award*), Charlayne Woodard (*Maverick Award)* and both Ellen Geer and Theresa Chavez (*Rainbow Award*). It has been a pleasure to acknowledge yearly women who have contributed so substantially to theatre. It has also been heartwarming to hear their heartfelt acceptance speeches.

Three of the acceptance speeches that most stand out for me are Lily Tomlin's, for her humor and play on Webster's definition of the word "maverick," in describing the meaning of her *Maverick Award*, Lorraine Toussaint's, for her eloquence, and Loretta Devine's for her tear-filled acceptance speech from the heart.

Over the years, our illustrious roster has also included deserving women such as Marla Gibbs and Linda Hopkins (*Eternity Award),* Nichelle Nichols and Rachel Rosenthal (*Maverick Award*), Freda Payne, L. Scott Caldwell and Regina Taylor (*Integrity Award*), and Rosie Lee Hooks and Deborah Lawlor (*Rainbow Award*). Not every recipient is a household name, but each is known for her contributions in theatre, and each speaks sincerely as she holds her LAWTF plaque close to her bosom. Several have said their award raises the bar for them to live up to what the award stands for, especially the recipients of the *Integrity Award*.

In addition to presenting theatre, the Festival has also achieved its original educational outreach mission of 1993. LAWTF widened its programming net in 2002 to include *Wisdom Wednesdays,* a solo writing workshop that develops new solo works by new and established writers.

In 2003, the Festival began presenting Hot off the Press, organic works that have been nurtured in *Wisdom Wednesdays* workshops. Writers have embraced such themes as love relationships, murder, family, rape, the workplace, and religion. At least twenty performers have now been presented on LAWTF's mainstage.

In 2005, former Board member Lynda Reichbach opened the door of LAWTF's educational programming by taking LAWTF into public schools by way of the 31st District Parent Teacher Student Association's (PTSA) Creative Kids After School Program, a non-profit organization of which she serves on the Board of Directors. Over forty schools have now been served in the San Fernando Valley.

In 2007, LAWTF began another school partnership with Abraham Tetenbaum's Enrichment Works, an in-school arts program that offers theatrical assemblies in the Los Angeles Unified School District (LAUSD) and has served over half a million students since 1999. LAWTF's teaching artists prepare students for Enrichment Works' theatrical assemblies by meeting educational state standards.

Also in 2007, LAWTF expanded its outreach efforts to include a writing workshop, *Tellabration: Telling Our Stories!* for teens of the Gay and Lesbian Adolescent Social Services (GLASS) agency funded through a grant from the City of West Hollywood. This same year,

LAWTF performers took excerpts of their shows to Belmont High School students through a Department of Cultural Affairs grant in Los Angeles.

Well over 3,000 youth have now been served by LAWTF's many outreach efforts in the schools. By providing our arts outreach programs, we contribute to taking arts back into the schools.

In 2002, the Festival crossed mediums when it launched its public access cable television show *Los Angeles Women's Theatre Festival: On The Air!* Marla Gibbs, our original host, continues to grace the show accompanied by our able team that first included Fay Hauser-Price at the helm as producer, writer, director and editor. We expanded our production team leadership in 2007 to include editor Scott Pfeiffer who became producer in 2008.

Fay first took on the role of our Official Videographer in 1999. Making use of our archived tapings, she later went on in 2001 to produce a beautiful promotional video for the organization with funding provided by a Visibility Grant from the California Arts Council. In 2004, she joined the LAWTF Board of Directors. During her tenure, she served on practically every Festival committee, and still actively serves on our Screening Panel for our many annual performer submissions. Fay produced our Fifteenth Anniversary Awards Ceremony in 2008. She is an excellent example of one who has filled needs within the organization and grown with it.

When I look back, I am amazed that the Founding Circle actually pulled off our First Annual Festival in 1994 with only eight months of planning. Somehow we received enough submissions to choose from, and without a dime of public funding, curated our maiden Festival in the "black box theatre" at the Los Angeles Theatre Center.

Somehow, we raised enough money to bring the lights up. We did much of the work ourselves, and relied heavily on volunteers and in-kind donations to produce the first twenty-three solo artists. We made it happen, because underlying our passion was our mission to provide a place to give voice to exceptional women solo artists telling their own stories.

I say to anyone who has a vision, you can achieve whatever you will.

Certainly, the Los Angeles Women's Theatre Festival is one of my personal testimonials that we can have what we say we want if we are willing to work for it. It was Miriam Reed and I, joined shortly after by Judith Heineman, who were the early catalysts. At the same time, many others have bought into our vision along the way.

The first year, actor Angela Bassett joined us for our Opening Night performances. It was 1994, the same year Angela was nominated for an Oscar for *What's Love Got to Do With It?* She had become more and more in demand and we sat on pins and needles as we waited to receive confirmation that she would grace our stage on Opening Night.

Not only did Angela come to host the event in her black tuxedo and derby, she also surprised us by reciting poetry by Paul Laurence Dunbar. Her brief performance was the icing on the cake for LAWTF and the audience. A theatre-trained actor from the Yale School of Drama, Angela was in her element that night at the theatre.

I was downstairs preparing to go onstage with an excerpt of my solo show that first night when someone ran into the women's dressing room yelling, "Angela is performing onstage!"

In amazement and gratitude, I replied, "What?"

Both the Festival and the audience were thrilled by her fine performance. Hosting that night was Angela's moment, and she took it graciously and fully.

Angela did not win an Oscar that year for *What's Love Got to Do With It,* but she certainly received our grateful praises, and a fragrant bouquet of flowers as a gesture of our appreciation.

Starletta DuPois, another fine theatre actor, hosted our Closing Night program the first year. Starletta again honored the Festival by returning in 2003 to co-host our Tenth Anniversary and again in 2008 to co-host our Fifteenth Anniversary. It was very fitting for Starletta to host Closing Night of our first year and to return to host Closing Night as we celebrated a decade, and again as we celebrated fifteen years of theatre programming.

Starletta was so moved in 2003 by performer Kristina Sheryl Wong's theatre piece about finding her place as a Chinese American in *Laundry and Language* that Starletta tearfully "ministered" from her heart, directly following Kristina's moving performance. She was equally moved to tears in 2008 by Vanessa Harris-Adams' *Who Will Sing for Lena?* That piece is based on the true story of Lena Baker, executed in the state of Georgia for killing her employer who had raped her.

Clearly, the three areas of excellence that the Festival has maintained consistently over the years have been outstanding talent, a committed and hard-working Board of Directors and corps of volunteers, and beautifully-crafted promotional materials that visually capture the work we do.

At the same time, the Festival is in transition. This is an exciting time as our governing ranks and staff increase, but we are still endangered. We have expanded our programs far beyond our ability to adequately fund them.

We must strengthen our infrastructure in the areas of board governance, strategic planning, and organizational development. In order to survive, we must step up our fundraising efforts to increase our paid positions, and to meet our growing programmatic needs.

All in all, this is an exciting time of heightened possibilities for LAWTF. With our current Board members Jeanette Vines, Gayle Watts, Barbara Roberts, Donesther Dane, Attorney Kayretha Hale Willis, and Nancy Bauck, we have strengthened our governing leadership. They bring their own areas of expertise and are committed to growing our organization further.

In 2007, by becoming a new recipient of the Los Angeles County Arts Commission's Summer Internship Program, we were able to hire Los Angeles resident Shea Sullivan as our first full-time summer intern for ten weeks.

Marking another milestone, during the summer of 2007, LAWTF attracted six college interns from around the country who worked for LAWTF. They were Tonya Jones of Columbia University in New York, Joyce Joseph of Hampton University in Virginia, Jacki Martinez of the University of California at Santa Cruz (UCSC), Tunisha Singleton, also of UCSC/ Cal State University, San Diego, Shea Sullivan of Tufts University in Massachusetts, and Yazmin Watkins of Dickerson College in Pennsylvania. All were living in Los Angeles for the summer and chose to join our forces.

What an *amazing* team of college students LAWTF was blessed to have at one time!

We will be eternally thankful for their contributions that touched *every* aspect of our non-profit organization. They made a *huge* difference. Most worked on our public access cable show. Still others worked in the office. Our administrative interns even took the organization to a new level when they widened our knowledge and use of technology by creating a MySpace account and by placing LAWTF on YouTube.

I am hopeful that we will continue to sustain ourselves with our extended work force that included a second paid intern in 2008, Tehelah Edwards of Cal State LA, through another Los Angeles County Arts Commission Internship Grant. We also brought on another summer intern student, Shaniece Dinkins of Cal State Northridge.

Despite the Festival's many milestones, recognition, and some measure of success, the process has not been without many battle wounds. We were off to an exciting beginning in 1993, but we experienced our first big upset when co-founder Miriam Reed left the organization before our Second Annual Festival in 1995. I felt like we had been socked in the stomach with Miriam's announcement, because Miriam had been the driving force behind the organization.

Miriam planted the initial seed for the Festival, and it was also Miriam who handled the business side of the organization in the beginning. It was she who successfully established our 501c3 non-profit exempt status within our first year. Yet we had taken on more than we were able to handle without funding. Miriam began to grow weary as she questioned whether we could make it based on the loss of a particular much-needed board member, constant financial woes, and our underdeveloped business side. Her concerns were certainly well-founded and shared.

I mourned Miriam's leaving.

I was also unwilling to entertain the notion of LAWTF dying at such a young age. Our non-profit was only two years old, and I felt the organization had just begun to establish itself in the Los Angeles arts community. I also felt the organization had the potential to become bigger than any one of us. With Miriam's exit, co-founder Judith Heineman stepped into Miriam's big shoes to try to fill them as Managing Producer.

We forged ahead.

Miriam left Los Angeles, and Judith and I kept the Festival's doors open. After five years, Miriam surprised Judith and me by returning in 1999 for our Sixth Annual Festival. By then, the Festival had rotated around town and found its way to the 24th Street Theatre in Los Angeles. An emotional moment onstage, our original triad stood together once again in front of our audience for the first time since 1994. Not only did Miriam attend that program, she returned for yet another program that same year. She also insisted on attending as a paid audience member both times!

Miriam subsequently returned as a performer for our *Encore* program in 2001, the year we invited former performers to return. She has since returned year after year as a faithful donor and continually voices her pride in what LAWTF has become.

Miriam's return also opened the door for her to reunite with LAWTF co-founder Judith Heineman and perform in Judith's Tellabration Storytelling Conference in Chicago. Judith now resides in Chicago and Miriam in Oregon, but the bond of the founding "triad" remains. Miriam's return meant much to both Judith and me because we were the three founders who were the glue and light bulbs during the early days.

Our wounds were healed.

Despite differences, it is possible to work through them for the bigger good.

Even with our three vital roles with the Festival, the organization could not possibly have survived this long without the countless support of others the past fifteen years. In great part, it has also been the different evolutions of our Board of Directors over the years that have sustained LAWTF. Some of the organization's most devoted and long-term Board members include co-founder Judith Heineman, who left only because her husband relocated to Chicago, and actor Lynne Conner, whose passion and hard work have never been surpassed. An enthusiastic "doer," she also learned publicity with LAWTF and is now an established publicist in her own right with her own business, *Publicity 4 You*. She still supports the Festival by serving on LAWTF's Advisory Board, and gives back to the Festival through her public relations contributions.

The Festival has always been volunteer-driven, and it is the rank-and-file volunteers at all levels who have contributed to the longevity of the Festival. Volunteer Etoy Ridgnal Tharpe has worn many hats with the Festival, and we appreciate her for her giving over the years.

Advisory Board members such as Dave Shaw and Anne Peralta have been with the Festival for many years. They continue to lend their expertise and act as donors and ambassadors to the organization by their generous giving. They also continue to guide others to the organization.

There are *so* many others who have given to the Festival along the way. Some may have stayed for only a moment and others for years, but each left a lasting mark. Our early team included co-founder and actor Joyce Guy and CPA Ellen Donovan. It also included banker

Natalee Greene, who in 1999 opened the door to Union Bank of California's ongoing sponsorship, and Bruce Wilson of Tokai Bank, who lent his male energy to our team. Karen A. Clark of US Bank first brought Bank of America to us as an Official Sponsor and for the last two years has also guided US Bank to us as an Official Sponsor.

It was Brandilyn Amie who took us to the next level by finding a physical office for us in North Hollywood so that our office could move from my home in 2000.

There are many more I could call by name if space allowed. The danger, of course, in calling out only a few names, is that you invariably will forget some that are deserving of mention. Those who have given, mentioned in print or not, know who they are and so do I. On behalf of the Festival, I personally thank each and every one of those who have been in the Festival's trenches over the years.

I have successfully worked with many supporters over the years and I have also realized that being a founder of a non-profit organization is not without its own set of challenges. I have spoken with other founders and have found that one thing many of us have in common is the baggage that comes with the title of "Founder." Although we may be revered in our roles as initiators, we also may sometimes be seen as obstacles to moving the organization forward. Some come aboard to support the vision and mission of the organization, and some come with their own agendas.

In my case, it is a balancing act to try to welcome change. Many Board members, Advisory Board members, paid and unpaid staff, and contractors come with new visions, ideas and proposed directions. LAWTF in many ways is my baby, but it is not mine. I am continually trying to check myself to make sure others are given the opportunity, and encouraged to demonstrate their sense of ownership, while I stand as a gatekeeper for the original vision and mission of the organization. Fortunately, the organization has grown and expanded in ways that far exceed the original vision of the Founding Circle, and sometimes that process has not been easy.

Change can be painful.

One thing that revitalizes me each year and reminds me of why I keep doing what I do with LAWTF, is sitting in the audience and witnessing the remarkable talent and communion between performer and audience. I have witnessed audience members talk out loud to performers, laugh uncontrollably, weep, and rise spontaneously in unison to give a standing ovation. Being a part of that brand of magic somehow refuels me as I attempt to gear up for yet another year.

Seeing the joy in the eyes of our youth as they feel a sense of accomplishment with their work in our many classes, also touches my heart. I am reminded that LAWTF's work really *does* make a difference in the community.

Art is about personal expression. Like life, it may or may not always be about beauty in the conventional sense. Nonetheless, it can be about healing, esteem-building, edutainment, and can reach audiences socially and politically in ways that other forms of communication may fail.

Over the years, the Festival has given voice to such socially charged issues as rape, incest, death, homophobia, and racism. The Festival has also presented such light-hearted subjects as first love, family, womanhood, and cultural storytelling. The Festival's diversity also extends to those performers who are hearing-impaired and physically challenged.

Some performers have returned again and again.

Dancer Lisa Lock has the distinction of having performed in more Festivals than any other LAWTF performer. Until she and her husband Larry Coleman moved to Cleveland, she graced our stage with a different cutting-edge dance piece each year. We still look forward to Lisa's return. Our audiences love her work, because it is self-styled and demonstrates her incredible skill as a European-trained ballet dancer. I will never forget the year she performed *Human Huwoman*, a moving piece in a tutu and combat boots. Her work also makes audiences think, as they feel her visceral and unpredictable movements.

What amazes me is that as powerful as Lisa is onstage, she maintains a shy and humble spirit. When we began to pull our production team together for our public access cable television show, Lisa volunteered. When we went around the room to identify roles, we asked Lisa what she would like to do.

Lisa very quietly said, "I will do clean-up."

I said, "Lisa, I will do that."

We selected her, instead, to be interviewed on the show. Although extremely shy, Lisa gave herself permission to deliver a very rich television interview.

Lisa's husband, Larry Coleman, remains one of our most loyal Festival supporters, having created and maintained both the Festival's and my personal website. His joyful spirit and giving heart have been much appreciated over the years.

The Festival reached a major milestone in 1995 when the Festival received its first government grant. It was a City of Los Angeles Department of Cultural Affairs Small Organization Grant. Our Cultural Affairs grant was worth far more than funding. The city gave its stamp of approval, which translated into worthiness, legitimacy, and leverage for still more funding. The ripple effect brought government funding from both the Los Angeles County Arts Commission and the California Arts Council; amounting to city, county, and state funding.

We cannot thank the California Arts Council enough for its generous support, which began in 1996. The Festival, like many other non-profit arts organizations, lost funding awards when the California Arts Council (CAC) was hit with a ninety-five percent arts funding cut in 2003. The Festival lost its last year of funding from the CAC because there was no money to honor our grant. It was a devastating blow to LAWTF. However, funding has finally returned and in 2008, LAWTF received a "Creating Public Value Grant."

All who are artists and art lovers must apply pressure on our elected state officials to make sure state funding is never reversed again.

In 1998, the Festival began its fruitful relationship with the Flintridge Foundation in Pasadena. Our guardian angel there was Lena Kennedy, then Supervising Program Officer. Through Lena, LAWTF received numerous scholarships to attend workshops at Flintridge. We were awarded an LAWTF grant earmarked for a fundraising consultant to guide us forward in courting corporate sponsors. Fundraiser Dave Shaw was our man. We were able to land the Gas Company of Southern California as our first Official Sponsor in 1998 because of our fundraising relationship with Dave. Bringing aboard an Official Sponsor took the organization to yet another level of credibility.

Since then, our Official Sponsors have included our longtime supporter Union Bank of California, US Bank, Time Warner Cable, CRN Talk Radio, Bank of America, McDonalds, Breath Asure, Daily News, William Grant Still Center, Adilah Barnes Productions, and Gail Moore. Other funders have included Councilwoman Wendy

Greuel's office, the City of West Hollywood, Highways Performance Space, Artpeace Gallery, and the Trust for Mutual Understanding, which bestowed a sizable grant to LAWTF to bring Russian company Kamchatka to perform in the 2001 Festival, *Breaking New Ground*.

As impressive as this list may sound, funding is never promised from year to year. Like many other arts organizations, the Festival still struggles each year to stay afloat, especially since some funders are one-time contributors.

The year 1998 was a year of firsts in two ways. In addition to attracting our first Official Sponsor, the Gas Company of Southern California, it was also the year my longtime buddy Danny Glover came aboard as our first Honorary Chairperson. He has shown his support not only by lending his name each year, but also by co-hosting the Festival, becoming our first *UP CLOSE* celebrity guest, and by donating in a number of ways. Danny is one of the most generous humanitarians and actors I know. He continually gives back to the community and those he knew from way back when. His sense of loyalty is unsurpassed. However, I most respect Danny for standing up for the causes he believes in, and he has many.

In 1999, Hattie Winston joined Danny as our Honorary Co-Chair and usually co-hosts our Annual Awards Ceremony. We also appreciate her for her loyal contributions.

The year 2001 marked the Festival's global presence. We invited artists to perform from Brazil, England, and Russia. Our company from Russia even performed *in* Russian. That year, we also veered from the familiar by including *A One Night Stand*, a one night program of male solo performers. We invited several youth dancers, including the very talented, then pre-teen ballet dancer Aminah Flowers, who displayed extraordinary form for her age.

Considering the Festival began with women who were first and foremost performers, learning "the business side of the art" has proved to be an incredible challenge. What I personally know about producing and theatre administration I have learned by trial and error. It is now time to hire a committed Executive Director who knows more than I do to take the organization to the next level of sustainability.

I have learned it is important to surround yourself with those who know more than you do, and from whom you can learn.

In 2008, LAWTF celebrated its Fifteenth Anniversary, "ONWARD AND UPWARD!" at the EL Portal Theatre in North Hollywood. We were blessed to have international artists from India and the Netherlands, as well as artists from New York, Miami, Chicago, Oklahoma, and those from up and down the state of California who joined hands with us for this banner year.

We also received government recognition in the form of commendations, proclamations and presentations from the offices of Mayor Villaraigosa, Senators Diane Watts and Alex Padilla, Assemblyman Paul Krekorian, Councilman Tom La Bonge and Supervisor Zev Yaroslovsky. It was a huge honor to receive government accolades acknowledging our work over the last fifteen years from so many levels of government.

What began as a chance meeting with Miriam Reed at the California Arts Council Touring Roster Conference in 1993 turned into the formation of a solo festival that has attracted performers from all over the world, given voice to women and women's issues, provided outreach programming to children and youth, crossed mediums from stage to cable television, and filled a void in the theatre community of Los Angeles in a very solid and meaningful way. In this chapter, I wanted to acknowledge not only that monumental feat, but also by name many who have supported us along the way.

In 1993, I was a part of the Los Angeles Women's Theatre Festival's Founding Circle, and I am proud to be in that number.

Chapter Twelve

On My Own Terms

Success isn't about walking away. It's about facing things.
—Tommy Ford, actor

In 1994, I auditioned for a pilot that most every other African American female in Los Angeles was up for. Sitting in the lobby of that major studio was everyone from the late veteran actor Beah Richards to *A Different World's* Charnelle Brown. There were so many women in that waiting room that I literally had to step over some of them to find a space of my own. I was not only appalled by the sheer numbers and different ages of the women, but also the many types who were all reading for the *same* role.

Standing in that crowded room, it became immediately clear to me that the producers did not know what they wanted.

The "breakdown" description of the character I was reading for was described as a receptionist at a mail-order company who was a smoker with a hacking cough. Given the description, I decided to take a cigarette to the audition with every intention of smoking it as I read for the part.

I remembered what my fellow ACT actor Denzel Washington once said. He said he took his laundry to an audition because the scene called for him to have laundry. Although risky, he did it. He also got the part.

I decided to take my cigarette.

I was well-prepared to light it, but after pulling it out, one of the writer/producers panicked. "You're not going to light that in here, are you?"

I quickly changed my mind, but decided to use the unlit cigarette as if it *were* lit. I took long drags and held in the imaginary smoke. I talked as if I was releasing smoke with every word of my exhalation. I could feel the producers watching my ease with the unlit cigarette.

I worked that audition.

I knew the character, and I felt extremely comfortable with her. I was both confident and relaxed in that audition. Finished, I walked out the front door of that building the same way I had come in, stepping past other women. The difference was, on the way out, I had a very good feeling about what had just happened in the audition room.

I got the part.

As fate would have it, the same day I learned I got the part was also the day I learned my mother had passed away. My family all knew from her doctor that her passing was imminent, and we were as prepared as we could be for her death.

At 6:30 a.m. that February morning, the expected call came from my eldest sister, Dorothy. As soon as the telephone rang, I knew what I was about to hear.

Dorothy said simply, "Mother died."

After absorbing what I had just heard, I began grieving as my body heaved with tears.

Mom was gone.

Later that day, I heard I had been cast for the pilot I wanted. Earlier, I had been wailing. Now I was jumping up and down with the news of my new series role.

It was a day of very high highs and very low lows.

Before I auditioned, as is customary, "quotes" were discussed for the actor's pay. My manager at the time considered the highest offer too low for me to accept. Ironically, once the role was actually offered, we learned the role had been changed to a "recurring" role for budgetary reasons. When the billing changed, so did the weekly offer.

I ended up making less than I would have with the first offer.

My manager was one who did not make waves. Her strategy was if we accepted the recurring role, we would not have to go to the necessary "network" read to compete as a "regular" with others vying for the same role. She said she was trying to eliminate any further competition for me by accepting the ultimate salary offer.

She clearly wanted us to book that job, and she assured me that if the pilot got picked up, we would try to re-negotiate our contract to a regular.

It never happened.

By the time the pilot got picked up as a series that May, I was again offered only a recurring role. In retrospect, I probably ought to have held out. The role had originally been budgeted as a regular role, and more importantly, of all the choices the producers had at that crowded audition, I was their first. However, we didn't hold out.

Sometimes you have got to be willing to walk.

Just like every regular on the show, I shot all nine episodes of the series. By not standing up, I got paid significantly less. It was extremely demoralizing for me to see my billing as a "guest star" each week on the television screen when I *was* a regular. I wanted the role, and I had followed my manager's lead. Although I was hoping for more down the road, it never took place.

I got the lesson.

An actor's representation does not always make the best choice. I also realized that once a deal has been negotiated and the client has agreed, what is the incentive for the producers to offer more?

My recurring pay and billing was the downside.

The upside was I *did* have perks.

I had my own dressing room in one of the studio's bungalow buildings. It was like a studio apartment equipped with a telephone with voice-mail and a bathroom with a shower. I had studio lot drive-on privileges and my own parking space with my personalized name sign that read, FOR ADILAH BARNES ONLY.

Nobody could park in my space but me.

I had my own hair stylist who took the time to curl each of my many tiny braids in the fabulous styles she concocted each episode. My wardrobe was colorful, artsy, and in my opinion, very becoming. I had a rack full of clothing that we chose from for each episode. Everything was exclusively tailored for my petite frame.

However, as a recurring actor, I was not privy to *all* the perks. One of the regulars thought I already knew of one perk.

He said, "Have you ordered any tennis shoes yet?" as he perused the Nike catalogue.

I tried to play it off as I said, "Not yet."

Interesting to note, one of the hair and make-up artists had already put an order in for *her* tennis shoes. It appeared everybody else on the set was sporting complimentary Nike shoes except me. I also learned from one of the regulars that I could go to the amusement attractions on the same lot for free.

I did both.

I liked the perks. However, with all the trappings, I still did not get the pay and billing I deserved. I also did not get the exposure of doing television ads or print interviews to promote the series once the show was picked up.

I did ultimately earn the respect I wanted for both my character and myself, but it was not without a battle.

As written, my character had begun as a chain smoker with a hacking cough. I accepted that given, but I began to notice my role change daily with each re-write. She was beginning to look unrecognizable. She started to appear to be a little "ghetto" and started to spout too much attitude. I was getting uncomfortable with how she was starting to get shaded in.

She was starting to feel stereotypic.

I left that Thursday for my mother's funeral. When I returned the following day to shoot the studio tapings in front of two live audiences, I was met with the most unacceptable re-writes of all. As I read the profanity in the script and saw the large bag of potato chips left on her desk, presumably for her to eat during a scene, I decided I had had enough.

I asked the Assistant Director (A.D.) to get the producers. The writer/producer team immediately came to the set.

Baffled, one of them asked, "Yes, Adilah? What's the matter?"

I told them, "Each day I read my re-writes, I like my character less and less. I feel like I don't know her anymore." I went on to say, "My mouth cannot form these new words."

I could feel their panic.

Here we were on tape day about to shoot in front of two live audiences on the *last* workday of our pilot, and I was saying I did not want to go on camera with their final script.

One of them said, "We'll be right back."

They huddled.

I waited.

I had no intention of portraying my character using the latest version of the script. Putting my job and name on the line, I was prepared to walk. I was clear I was not going to portray my character on national television in the way she was written. I was unwilling to perpetuate yet another stereotype. The responsibility I felt to myself and my culture would *not* allow me to represent that way.

Although I had not deliberately planned to put the producers up against the wall, the truth was they would have been very hard-pressed to find another actor to take over my role that same day. They would have had to find someone in a matter of hours.

Well, they could have, but the question is, would it have been who they *really* wanted?

There was a lot riding on this situation on both sides.

The writer/producers joined me minutes later, and one said, looking through his glasses, "Okay. We are going to change the writing back to how it was."

I said, "Thank you."

The other writer/producer asked pointedly, "Do you know how many actresses we read for this role?"

I said, "Yes."

He went on to say, "Most of them would have done whatever we asked them to do."

I said, "I know that."

I further explained, "They would have done so not necessarily because they wanted to, but because they wanted to work. Some of them also wanted to please you."

I added, "If I never work a day in LA again, I *will* work. I have a one-woman show I tour all over this country."

They were silent.

We made it through that tape day. I gave my best. The tapings went well. Both live audiences seemed to enjoy the humor in our sitcom pilot. The producers got a strong performance out of me, and I got to play the role the way I wanted.

It was a win-win situation.

Interestingly enough, three months later, I got a telephone call from one of those same producers.

He exclaimed, "Guess what! Our pilot got picked up as a series!"

Since he was calling me, I presumed that meant I was being invited back for the series, too.

I said, "*We* did?"

The first table read of our new series included a former student of mine in the ranks of all the studio executives. It was comforting to know he was on the team of "suits."

I also got a second surprise I had not expected.

As all the actors went around the table introducing themselves, I immediately noticed our blonde lead from the pilot had been replaced by a brunette. I felt badly for the first actor, because she was so excited about the show. Like the rest of us, she helped sell the pilot. Her mother had even come from out of town for the pilot tapings to join her daughter.

However, just because an actor is used for a pilot does not mean the actor will be brought back if the pilot is picked up as a series.

She was now history.

Ironically, during the pilot taping, I stood up for what I believed in. I risked being fired, but I was still there. The other actor probably had no battles to fight, but *she* was gone.

They may not have liked me on that show, but I brought to the character what worked. I ended up appearing in every episode the show ever shot.

I have chosen my battles carefully, but I have fought.

Another battle I chose took place on a feature film I worked on. Oddly, no scripts were allowed at the audition nor on the set. All I had were my "sides," or audition pages, to read from for both the audition and on set to shoot the film.

I was very uncomfortable working that way. Had it not been for the reputable name of the writer/director/producer/actor of the project, I probably would have passed on the project. Based on his reputation, I trusted the movie would be a worthy project. At the very least, I knew *my* character was honorable.

While shooting my scene, the well-known director walked down from the church pulpit in our scene and whispered in my ear, "Too presidential."

Here I was playing a character on a school board and I was being asked to deny her stature. I had made the choice to play her with an articulate, cool dignity as she confronted his character. The director wanted me to bring something else.

I did not.

Unwilling to give the director what he wanted, we repeated the scene take after take. The director kept asking me to do the scene over and over, leaving out different sentences. For example, he'd say, "Give me the first sentence. Now the third sentence," and so on and so forth. I do not know how my mind remembered which line went where, but I hung with him without skipping a beat. I gave him the brief dialogue exactly in the order he asked for it.

In that church scene that included pews full of extras, a former acting student of mine was also on set. I refused to be called out and outdone, *especially* in front of one of my students. However, the end result was the director made me so flustered and angry, he got the rage he wanted for that character.

He won.

Never be controlled by emotion.

Nonetheless, my former student walked up to me after that exhausting tirade and gave me the nod.

He looked at me with admiration and burst out, "You hung with him, Adilah!"

Later, the director decided to add an improvised scene outside as his character was about to speed away in his limousine. I was told I would also be added in that scene. At first, I was glad to hear the news of a second scene in the movie because that meant more camera time for me.

We were told we could give the director script ideas for our new scene. I gave him what I considered to be appropriate dialogue suggestions for my character.

He vetoed my suggestion by simply saying, "Too deep."

Since he did not want my suggestions, I decided I would stay with my original short scene.

Given that I had completed my scripted scene, I said, "Okay. I'll sit that new scene out then."

He looked at me in disbelief.

I pulled up a director's chair, crossed my leg, and watched the new exterior shot that included a couple of African American female comedian/actors. I could feel their enthusiasm as they worked on the improvised scene. They seemed happy to have more camera time.

One of the two female actors actually yelled profanity to his character as he pulled off in the limo. She saw nothing wrong with that.

At one point, that same actor walked over to my chair and said in disbelief, "I heard you say to the director you weren't going to do that scene!"

I said, "Yes, I did."

She looked at me as if she felt I had passed up an opportunity. I continued to sit and watch. Based on what I saw, it became very clear to me it was best I was not in the new scene.

What I had shot was sufficient.

Later that evening, the director and I bumped into each on the set as I passed him on a very narrow walkway. Seemingly joking, he looked me in the face and gently placed his hands around my neck.

I removed his hands and looked him in the eyes as I asserted, "You know we are both Aries. I know you."

He said nothing.

I then walked past him.

There are some things I simply will not do.

Even though the network used me in almost all the trailers for the film's advertisement at movie theatres and on television, the irony is I was actually only in one scene in the film. I found it interesting that I stood up to the director *and* still got used in the trailers to promote the movie.

I stood my ground. I chose not to do a scene that would bring dishonor to my character. In what appeared to be poetic justice, I had been rewarded. I was used to advertise the movie.

When I saw the director again during a "looping session," an in-studio session to re-do a scene using voices only, he greeted me warmly as if our tense moment on set had never happened. I breathed a sigh of relief and moved on to the work at hand.

Since my arrival in 1989, Los Angeles has been many things for me. Through it all, one thing I have consistently refused to allow to be negotiable is my sense of integrity. There have been roles I have passed on because I found them stereotypic. There have also been roles I have adjusted without permission to make palatable. Then there have been roles, as in the case of that pilot I mentioned, where I have fought to bring honor to a character.

In the hands of another actor, the latter might not have happened.

The bag of potato chips on my character's desk and her use of profanity were never aired on national TV. Because of my stand, television audiences never saw that negative image.

Sometimes I have been more subtle in my fights. For example, guest-starring for a series on HBO, I played the role of a bank manager. To me, the language did not ring true, so I went through the scene and edited it. Among other things, I changed the "ain't" to "aren't." I even omitted one sentence completely.

On the set, the director did not seem to notice my grammatical changes until he got to the omitted sentence.

He said, "What about that other line? You didn't say it."

I said, "I know. I don't think she would say that."

The "star" of the show happened to be passing the director and me on the set at that exact moment.

Sensing in our body language and energy that something was not right, she said, "What's the matter?"

I said, "I don't think this character would say this line."

She looked at the line.

She paused as she thought about the line and said, "Oh, too street, huh?"

I said, "Exactly."

She said to the director, "Then cut it."

We did.

On that same series, "wardrobe" wanted to put me in polyester and loud colors, which I felt were unacceptable for the character. The choices were all wrong so I looked at some of the more conservative and tailored wardrobe pieces I saw on nearby racks.

Finding a suitable outfit, I said, "Now, I think *this* would look great on her!"

I got to wear what I chose.

Now, the matter of hair.

I do not always insist on how my hair is styled, but I did in one guest-starring role in a series. I was playing a teacher who had a somewhat youthful look. I wanted to wear my long hair down. The hair stylist wanted a more matronly look. She wanted me to wear my hair up. Reluctantly, I let her put my hair up. Called to the set to rehearse my scene, I walked on set with the updo. I stood next to the director. I decided to ask him what he thought of my hair.

Before he answered, I added, "I actually prefer wearing my hair down, but 'hair' wants it up."

The director looked at my hair, paused a moment, and then said, "I like your hair. I want you to wear your hair down, too."

I immediately relayed the director's wishes to my hair stylist. I said, "The director said he prefers my hair down."

She held her tongue and replied flatly, "Okay."

Against her will, she coiffed my hair in a very soft style that accented the length of my hair. The newly styled hairdo made my character look more feminine and more youthful. My hair now looked like it belonged to my character and it also went with the wardrobe I was wearing.

I know when hair, make-up, and wardrobe choices made for me are right and when they are *not* right for the character. In the early days, I silently accepted whatever was done to me, saying nothing. Over time, I have learned to speak up. Fortunately, most of the hair and make-up artists that have worked on me have been flexible in hearing me and taking into account what I want.

I believe every actor has the right to give input on how their character looks.

It has been my experience that the more comfortable I am with how I look on camera, the more I am able to relax and give my best work.

I had to fight for my hair with that one series.

On the other hand, I had a starring role in the Hallmark made-for-TV movie *Little John*. My hair stylist Julia Walker said, "Baby, you've got hair and *we* are going to play. When you've got it, flaunt it!"

To Julia's credit, my hair looked gorgeous in each scene. Julia has also been Whoopi Goldberg's personal hair stylist. I reminded her that we first met during *Kiss Shot*, the made-for-TV movie where I played Whoopi's mother.

I have at times been cast for television and film roles that have been in conflict with the touring schedule of my one-woman show. Although I do not ever want to pass on any role I might want, I also feel very strongly about honoring my contractual commitments.

I turned down a role on an Austin Powers sequel movie because of a possible touring schedule conflict. The Powers film had not yet penned the exact shooting dates for the film, but they were also not willing to work around my possible conflict dates.

I had to pass.

There are some in the industry who judge stage work as being less important. They seem to think that when there is a scheduling conflict, a stage actor ought to automatically choose film or television over a play. In my case, I am a touring artist who works primarily in colleges and universities. I have actually been asked to cancel my stage commitments completely or reschedule the dates at the last minute to take an on-camera role. However, touring does not work that way. The show has been promoted and audiences expect to see what has been advertised.

Many colleges and universities have booked artists a year in advance, and have advertised their coming in season brochures well before the performance date. Over the years, I have built a respectable name on the college circuit, and I am not willing to risk my touring reputation.

Not even for television or film.

In 2005, though, I began to double-cast my show with Valeri Parker Ross, a very fine stage actor. She and I have known each other since the 1980s when we worked together as Bay Area actors. She and I played opposite each other in Ed Bullins' play *The Taking of Miss Janie,* the production I mentioned earlier where I played a bisexual woman who kissed another woman onstage.

She was the other woman.

Before Valeri began as my double-cast actor, I used to gamble with bookings. The presenter at the University of Wisconsin booked me for performances in both 2001 and 2002 during both the shooting schedule for the movies *Little John* and *Murder by Numbers*, respectively. I took the risk to fly out the night before to Milwaukee for each of my stage performances because I did not want to choose one over the other. I was prayerful that I would make my red-eye flights each time. In a cold sweat both times, and in need of using frequent flyer miles at the last minute, I made it to my destination in time.

I accepted both offers but I do *not* like gambling that way.

Speaking of scheduling, I remember once a career-changing moment on the road with the African American Drama Company of San Francisco. Usually, if there was more than one booking during a week, I stayed out on the road and came home at the end of the week. This particular run out, I wanted to come home between my bookings, which were at both the beginning and end of that week. At the time, I did not know why I was being led home.

I later came to understand the payoff by listening to my intuition.

I came home and immediately got a call from my agents saying I had an audition for the top-rated ABC series *Roseanne.* The irony was the "producer's session" audition was scheduled for the same day I was to fly back out on the road. Fortunately, the casting director Karen Vice and her casting assistant Linda La Montagne were kind enough to change my appointment time so that I could make it to CBS Studios in Studio City to read the morning of my flight.

After my "pre-read" in front of casting, Karen said, "I want the producers to see you."

Looking at the time on the clock, I said, "Well, you'd better get them now because I have a plane to catch."

Because of her gut feeling that I was right for the role and because I could not change my flight, we were able to assemble the producers and writers of the show immediately. I had never experienced the likes of such quick movement before, nor have I since. In a matter of minutes, directly following my pre-read, I was in front of a room full of decision-makers.

I got the part.

Following the airing of my first, and arguably my best episode on *Roseanne,* I received a personal phone message on my answering machine from writer Don Foster, creator of my character.

He said, "Hi, this is Don Foster. I just wanted to say that we are watching your episode and we want to thank you for working on the show."

I said, "Thank you, Don."

Inside, my mind was racing.

I had never been directly called by a writer of a television series before. I thought it odd, but very promising. Based on Don's personal phone call and the on-camera chemistry between Roseanne and me, I thought there was a good chance I might be invited back.

Not only did they ask me back that season, the writers also created the character "Chuckie," my television husband. Chuckie was played by James Pickens Jr., presently a regular on *Grey's Anatomy.* We were eventually given a son. What began as one episode in a guest-starring role became a recurring character with a family. I returned as "Anne Marie" on *Roseanne* for five seasons.

Had I not followed my intuition to come home that week during my down time on the road, I would have missed an important role. The lesson in that experience was to listen to what my mother always used to call "our first mind."

If we listen, it will always guide us right.

An interesting story that indirectly relates to the *Roseanne* show took place on a pilot I worked on while I was still working on *Roseanne.*

One of *Roseanne's* former head writers had become a producer on the pilot. Roseanne's ex-husband was Executive Producer, and had offered me a role. No audition, just a phone call to my agents.

A straight offer.

I felt comfortable enough with the female producer/writer to give my feedback on re-writes each day. Some of the writing did not ring true for the Black characters, and I elected myself spokesperson. At first, my suggestions seemed accepted. At one point, however, I had apparently overstepped my boundaries.

To my surprise, I received a call on the set from my agent one day in a very fearful tone. He cautioned, "Adilah, whatever you are doing on that set, cool it!"

The producer/writer had called my agent. No one had ever called my agent on me. I knew then my comments were jeopardizing my job.

Some time later, after the pilot had been completed, the same producer/writer came to visit the set of *Roseanne*. Someone pointed her out to me across the set. I could only think of our previous incident and did not want to talk to her.

"Why don't you go over and speak to her?" someone said.

Because of our past run-in on the pilot, I was placed in a very awkward situation. We *had* made it through the taping of the pilot satisfactorily. I had even been given lines from another actor, because she felt I could deliver them the way she wanted them. At the same time, I was still wary of walking up to her.

I had two choices.

Either I would have had to explain my reluctance, or I could simply approach her. I took a deep breath and walked up to her.

She met me with that warm smile of hers and yelled, "Adilah!"

We embraced and talked as if nothing had happened on that pilot.

We ended our conversation by her saying, "I'm producing another show now. When I have something for you, I'll bring you on."

I thought, "Yeah, right."

Shortly thereafter, my agents called to tell me I had an offer to play a teacher on her new series. No audition, a straight offer.

I learned from our run-in that it had more to do with the stress of the situation than my suggestions. Once the pilot had been successfully shot, she released the incident. Since that time, I worked on yet another show of hers that was a very popular series with a long run.

We let bygones be bygones.

Regardless of my challenging film and television experiences, one thing that has always been a wonderful balance and constant for me on set has been having African American women support me as my "stand-ins." Time and again, they have looked out for me. "Stand-ins" are the extras who stand on a "principal" actor's "marks" on the set when camera shots are technically being created or "set up." Principals are allowed to take a break while they wait to shoot the next scene. They are spared standing on their marks while "camera blocking" is set up.

I remember one project I worked on where my stand-in guarded my wardrobe sweater between takes. She made sure it did not get wrinkled in any way, and she seemed honored to be standing in for someone who was also Black. Some stand-ins have offered to bring me food and beverages from craft services, get me chairs to sit in, and sit with me while I wait for scenes.

On one series, my stand-in watched the shots on the monitor and advised me how the camera was capturing me shot by shot. She also let me know how just one step one way or the other would give me a stronger camera shot.

She became my eye for the camera.

Because I am often the only Black principal working on a shoot, stand-ins often look out for me.

It is as if they are saying, "I see you as my role model. You represent me and I want to make sure you are fully taken care of, and that you look good."

I always appreciate my stand-ins.

It is usually a non-verbal understanding between us, but it is a powerful way of bonding, and it makes me feel very special and cared for. Although extras are often seen as lowest in our caste system, I value them in their roles, and for how they treat me.

No movie or television series could ever be shot without extras. They are sometimes treated thanklessly on sets, like second-class citizens. They sometimes have to stand in line last for meals, sit outside in the cold, and they usually have to bring their own wardrobe. The truth is, though, they are indispensable. Their "background" presence brings reality to a scene.

Now, about casting.

My feeling is that every role has an actor's name on it. I believe if a role is for me, I will get it.

For example, I was in the acting company at the American Conservatory Theater. I had a call from my agents regarding a made-for-TV movie that I spoke of earlier that Whoopi Goldberg was starring in called *Kiss Shot*. It was being shot in the San Jose area. I was asked to read for the part of Whoopi's mother.

Although I thought it odd that I would be asked to read for a role I was obviously too young for, I wanted to work with Whoopi. She and I knew each other, in part, because we both taught acting at the now defunct San Francisco School of Dramatic Arts. Whoopi eventually offered me the opportunity to take over her solo show *Moms,* playing the legendary comedian Moms Mabley.

The show was a huge success for her in San Francisco. It played to packed houses and had rave reviews. However, New York was now calling Whoopi's name to Broadway. The snag was she was under contract to do the San Francisco play.

She wanted out of her contract and offered me her role. She offered me the rights to continue performing *Moms,* even beyond that run. Although a potentially wonderful opportunity, I decided to pass. I did not want to follow in Whoopi's footsteps in a show that had become so closely associated with her. I did not want to place myself in a situation where I would be compared to her. More than that, I did not want to step into a role that had already been shaped by another actor and had her signature.

I wanted to go to that audition for *Kiss Shot,* but ACT was running its annual Charles Dickens play, *A Christmas Carol.* We were performing up to ten shows a week. I wanted to go to the audition, but they were being held in San Jose. I did not have enough time between shows to drive to San Jose to make the appointment and come back in time for my evening performance.

I asked my agents to have the audition moved to another day, and they obliged.

I timed perfectly my rescheduled trip to San Jose between my matinee and evening shows at ACT. I rushed to the freeway only to find out my Volkswagen Squareback would *not* go over twenty miles an hour. Try as I might, the car would not budge. A previous fuel injector problem presented itself at that exact moment. I feverishly tried to make the car go faster, but it choked its way off the nearest San Francisco freeway exit.

I could not believe it.

I called the agents to ask for a *third* audition time but I was told that was it. It was the last day of auditions. The director was scheduled to return to Los Angeles. Sadly, I released that missed opportunity from my mind as I went back to my ACT performances as "Mrs. Cratchit."

I soon found out that a fine Bay Area actor, Marguerite Robinson, had gotten the role. I felt some sense of consolation knowing she had been cast. Since I had not gotten the role, I was glad she had. I consider Marguerite one of the most talented Bay Area actors, and I have always appreciated her work. Moreover, I like and respect her personally.

I released the movie.

However, a short while later, I got a third call.

As fate would have it, the shooting schedule for Marguerite's scenes in the movie changed. She had committed to performing a play in New York and could not adjust her shooting schedule there. I was not surprised to hear Marguerite had passed on the film, because she is another actor who honors her contractual agreements.

I was asked if I could make a third audition.

The agent said, "Adilah, can you make it *this* time?"

I squealed, "Yes!"

My car was now repaired, but to be on the safe side, I went so -meet with the director, I ran into Whoopi on set. Seeing me, she asked what I was doing there. I told her I was reading for the role of her mother.

She jokingly said, "We are going to have to talk about this."

I chuckled, "We can talk about it now!"

With make-up, anything is possible.

I met with the director in his trailer and read for him. He then invited me to stick around and have lunch on set. I waited to find out if I had the role. I could hardly eat while I waited. He finally summoned me after lunch. I again went to his trailer.

I got the part.

If a role is for you, nothing can stop you from getting it, even if it has been given to another.

I have sometimes encountered subtle racism on sets that may have been purely unintentional.

For example, on at least four or five occasions, I showed up on a set and was told by a Production Assistant (P.A.) something like, "The extras are over there."

It is not a very welcoming way to be met on a set.

It has become ritualistic for me to say in return, "I am not an extra."

I am usually met with something like, "Oh, I'm sorry. I didn't know."

My patent answer remains, *"Never make assumptions. Always ask."*

I leave P.A.'s with that lingering thought, so that perhaps the next African American will be spared beginning a shoot with such unnecessary humiliation.

Interviewing fellow award-winning actor L. Scott Caldwell once, we touched upon some of our challenges, and stands we both have taken along the way.

At one point after we had shared some of our stories, I said, "Scottie, why is it you and I are always being placed in positions where we have to stand up?"

She answered simply, "Because we will."

Chapter Thirteen

Remember to Dance, Dance,
Dance Like Nobody's Watching

Enjoy your miracle today.

—Adilah Barnes

"Do you want to hear it?" Neil Blake asked me. My heart began to race.

I listened carefully to the soft background piano of Nina Simone's sultry "Here Comes the Sun" being played for me.

It was real.

I was about to launch my own internet radio talk show on BlakeRadio.com, and Nina's "Here Comes the Sun" was going to be my theme song.

After hearing my radio interview on *The Ted Terry Show*, Neil suggested to Ted that I might also make a good host on his BlakeRadio Network. When Ted first approached me on behalf of Neil, I got quiet. I also got scared. A professional actor I am. A radio talk show host I was not.

I said emphatically to Ted, "I don't think so."

I further asked why Ted thought I would be a good talk show host.

Ted said, "Because you're intelligent, you have a good voice, and a command of the English language."

He, being a veteran broadcaster of over thirty years, I listened.

I thanked Ted for his vote of confidence, but I also kept the subject at bay in our subsequent conversations. At Ted's continual nudging, I finally began to seriously entertain the thought of crossing over into yet another medium. I began to embrace the thought that radio could be another new frontier for me to pursue.

I began to daydream.

I started to brainstorm formats. I needed to figure out what my show might be about. Being one who operates from titles, I also began to wonder what my show might be called. I said, "Ted, what would I call my show?"

He said, "*Adilah.*"

I said, "*Adilah?*"

It sounded too egotistical to me. I said, "Who has a show with only their first name?" Then I caught myself mid-sentence as I answered my own question.

"Oprah."

Ted said, "Exactly."

I began to think more and more about format. First, I thought of leading into my hour-long show with a positive thought, followed by a celebrity interview, an excerpt of me performing something, and an interview with a book author.

All in *one* hour.

I began to share my format ideas with other talk show hosts. I also got feedback from lay people who represented my future audience. I quickly realized my initial format idea was unrealistically ambitious.

As Ted and I bounced around theme music ideas, he suggested I go with Pharoah Sanders' "The Creator Has a Master Plan." I considered that song because it is conscious, positive, and spiritual in nature, but it still did not seem quite right for *me*. I wanted a song that spoke to and represented me exactly.

I also wanted a *woman's* voice.

I began to run songs through my head from the a cappela group Sweet Honey In The Rock. I am moved by their harmony and consciousness, but it was Nina's voice that I kept hearing louder and louder in my head.

I said, "Ted, I've changed my mind about the Pharoah Sanders song. I've found my music."

With surprise, Ted said, "You have?"

I declared, "Nina Simone's 'Here Comes the Sun.'"

Knowing music, Ted immediately replied, "Good choice."

It had to be Nina.

I love Nina's consciousness and her deep, unbridled, raw voice. Nina passed away in 2003. By choosing her was also my way of paying homage to her. Hearing her voice daily on BlakeRadio kept her memory alive.

I intuitively knew I had made the right choice.

My music chosen, I was now ready to move on. I decided to segue from my opening music to an inspirational thought at the top of each show. For years, my home telephone voicemail trademark has held a positive quote of some sort for my callers. I decided an inspirational thought at the top of each taping would be *so* me. I have several books with a plethora of quotes from both the known and unknown. I knew I would have no problem finding quotes for each show.

That decision made, I would now need a "close." I knew I would have to include my outgoing voicemail message I am known for: "Enjoy your miracle today." I also decided to include my quote: "Remember to dance like nobody's watching." I put the two together and jazzed it a bit by coming up with, "Remember to dance, dance, dance like nobody's watching, and . . . enjoy your miracle today."

I had my show "close."

I was still uneasy with the thought of calling my show simply *Adilah,* so I took a poll. Having decided I would focus on industry guests whom I know personally, I began to choose possible show names that would embrace my format, because I did not think *Adilah* said anything about the content of the show. I shot an e-mail out to friends whose opinions I trust.

I listed other possible show names. I came up with titles like *Up Close, Up Close and Personal, Inside Hollywood with Adilah, Adilah's Hollywood, Backstage with Adilah, Fireside Chats with Adilah,* and many more.

Interestingly enough, *Adilah* actually rated pretty high with my sample group. Frankly, I was surprised. In the end, I decided to go with Ted's initial suggestion. So, truth be told, Ted chose the name of my radio talk show.

However, I was kicking and fighting all the way to the microphone.

The show name now chosen, I needed a "promo" to invite listeners to my show. I now had my show name, opening music, and format. I decided to create an enigmatic promo to give me wiggle room with my format, so I came up with, "Greetings! This is Adilah Barnes. Join me on BlakeRadio Network's "Rainbow Soul," Channel 5, where you will smile with me, laugh with me, and think with me. You never know who you may hear."

Although my intention was to only interview African American women in the business, I did not want to limit myself while trying to find my groove. I also did not want to limit who would tune in. I hoped the mystique in the promo served to perk interest, while allowing me freedom of format.

It is a good thing I made that choice, because after the 2005 Katrina Hurricane catastrophe in New Orleans, I interviewed Christopher Mayes, my first male guest. Christopher and I had history because I was the first person he interviewed while he was still a student at Michigan State University, and while I was performing on the road.

You never know how fate will guide you back to another in the future.

I was now ready to line up my guests for the show.

Despite Ted's opinion that only interviewing women might alienate male listeners, I knew I wanted to begin my talk show interviewing African American women. I also knew I wanted to interview women in the industry. In part, my choice had to do with my affinity for promoting women. It also had to do with my work with the Los Angeles Women's Theatre Festival.

Women are my niche.

I had *no* idea how easy it would be to secure celebrity guests. My publicist Allison Queen and I began compiling a list of possible guests. Allison then made contact with potential guests. She was invaluable in lining up my early guests. In the beginning she coordinated the scheduling with Neil Blake and my guests.

At that time, before changing over to the MP3 telephone-taping format, BlakeRadio hosts had set time slots to interview their guests. Neil connected hosts and guests together telephonically and recorded the show. He would edit, if needed, and then "stream" the show on the internet. Due to a basement flood where Neil's studio was located, all hosts were later required to record their own shows and give completed tapings to Neil so they could be aired.

I have much respect for Neil. He is an incredible entrepreneur. He is also one of the most positive human beings I have ever met. He and his family have built an empire on the internet that reaches 143 nations around the globe. Before Rainbow Soul's Channel 5 went off the air in January 2008 due to lack of funding, it was thrilling to be part of a radio network that focuses on African Americans and that is being heard on the internet literally around the world. Show topics included celebrity interviews, health, motivation, politics, sports, and metaphysics.

At the time of this writing, Rainbow Soul, Channel 5 is slowly returning. A mom and pop operation, I encourage listeners to become members. The revenue is needed to keep this innovative and socially relevant programming alive. I encourage everyone reading this book to visit our site at www.blakeradio.com and become a supporter. All donations, no matter the size, matter.

I needed to feel secure about my first interviews. For me, that meant choosing guests I felt I would have a rapport with. It also meant doing my homework. Allison made sure I had biographies on all my guests in advance. I began to do my own internet research to create questions that interested me, and that

I thought would interest our listeners. I read and highlighted each bio very carefully to compile my questions.

I enjoyed reading bios because they are so informative. I always learned facts about my guests that I was not aware of, and that contribute to their greatness. I generally came up with forty to fifty questions, although I *never* asked every one. Those I interviewed had so much to talk about that it was easy to come up with a battery of questions. Always concerned about having enough to discuss, I made sure I had more than enough to talk about during my hour with each guest.

What I learned from the start is that there is an "X" factor. Guests sometimes have a direction they want to go in, and things they want to cover. All the planning in the world cannot account for the spontaneity of two people talking.

I learned though, that, a good interviewer can very craftily steer interviews. I also learned my guests might take the interview where they wanted. Each guest is very different. Some are more guarded and others speak freely. I was protective of my guests and cared about how they presented themselves.

One thing is certain: most people like to talk about their successes.

As my broadcaster friend, the late Tobi Knight of KOST radio told me in the beginning, "You want to bring out the humanity in your guests. You want to always make your guests look good."

I always tried to do just that.

Ella Joyce, loved for her role as "Eleanor" on the television series *Roc*, was a perfect first guest.

She is vibrant, articulate, open, and has a wild sense of humor. I needed someone like Ella to be my first guest because I was unsure of myself in my new role as a radio interviewer. Ella helped relax me.

At the very least, I knew Ella could carry the interview if I fell short.

I will never forget my meticulous preparation for that first interview. I set things up in a way that would become my taping ritual. I placed a clock in front of me so I would constantly be conscious of time. I noted the twenty and forty-minute intervals within the hour to interject two station identifications during the hour. I laid my questions and my "by line" that indicated the name of my show in front of me. I also made sure all windows in the house were closed tightly, and that my Rottweiler Booch was outside. Now passed on, he had a huge bark, and I did not want to hear his unpredictable voice in the background.

The house had to be perfectly still, and my land line phone nearby. Living near the Burbank airport, I cannot control when airplanes will fly above my home. Fortunately, I never heard an airplane in the background while interviewing or during playback on the air. That does not, however, mean airplanes did not fly overhead.

Once the interviews began, I was totally present in my listening.

I heard the telephone ring at the appointed time for my first interview in 2003. I knew it was Neil. He greeted me and said, "Are you ready?"

I softly replied, "Yes."

When Neil patched Ella and me together, I could feel my heart palpitate. This was the real deal, and there was *no* turning back.

Although the shows Neil taped were pre-recorded, he generally taped the entire shows straight through. He only went back to sweeten the sound by increasing the volume, or to make technical edits on any glitches.

I knew after he wished us well and signed off, Ella Joyce and I were on our own.

The interview began.

I could not read my prepared opening quote correctly. My words kept getting twisted.

I called out for Neil. "Neil, are you there?" but he could not hear me.

Neil was gone and was not likely to return until the hour was up. Since my tongue twister was at the top of the taping, Neil and I went back after the completed interview to re-record the opening.

The beginning did *not* start out well.

Somehow, I made it through my first interview. Surprisingly, I experienced a rush afterwards that I had not expected. I was absolutely wired with excitement as I called Ted Terry to let him know how my first taping had gone.

I said, "Ted, I did it!"

I was delirious with joy because I had taped my first radio interview.

Ted listened to me with quiet amusement as he heard me spew every little detail.

After my interview with Ella, it dawned on me that I did not have to limit myself to actors. To that end, my later guests included actor/filmmaker Angela Gibbs, journalist/producer Tanya Kersey, producer/director/writer/actor Fay Hauser-Price, talent manager Dolores Robinson and the late Pat Tobin.

Other actor guests I interviewed included the late veteran actor Virginia Capers, Marla Gibbs, and Hattie Winston. I also interviewed vocalist/actor Freda Payne.

Neil was kind enough to place my first taping at the top of the new airing rotations the following morning. He had already played my promo announcing my show, so some listeners were aware of the upcoming new show.

My maiden airing was set for just after midnight, Pacific Standard Time. I had a splitting headache from the stress of the taping day. I did not want to listen to my show. I knew it would be in rotation to air again and again, and I was prepared to catch it another time.

However, Ted called to make sure I would be listening to my debut airing. I tried to get out of listening.

I said, "Ted, I've got a headache. I will listen another time," but Ted insisted I tune in.

I finally agreed.

To make myself more comfortable in my bedroom that night, I laid on the floor in total darkness with an ice pack on my forehead. Light of any kind during a migraine makes my head ache even more. I learned ice shrinks the vessels, so I had my ice pack in place.

I watched the clock.

Finally, I heard the piano and Nina's voice as she began singing "Here Comes the Sun." There was no mistaking it—my show was about to air for the first time. I felt both excitement and trepidation.

My head was also still throbbing.

My voice was about to go over the internet waves to 143 countries around the world.

Despite my fears, I began to listen. Nina's uplifting voice with that distinctive piano behind her began to soothe me. First, I was struck by the beauty of the show's opening theme song. I somehow felt protected having Nina as part of my show. She felt like my guardian angel, and I began to relax even more.

Then I heard my opening.

It went, "Greetings! This is Adilah Barnes. Welcome to my show *Adilah* on the BlakeRadio Network, Rainbow Soul, Channel 5, where we will get up close with our guests. Before I introduce you to our special, special guest today, I'd like to share with you my thought for the day."

I listened.

This is where I had botched my intro the first time. Through the magic of technology, Neil had seamlessly edited out my blooper.

I listened on: "'If you can't run, walk. If you can't walk, crawl. But by all means, keep moving.' Dr. Martin Luther King.'"

Miraculously, the delivery now sounded flawless. No one would ever have to know about the flubbed outtake.

Then I segued into my guest, Ella.

The show was now rolling.

Three of my broadcasting friends, Ted Terry, Tobi Knight, and Deardra Shuler were all listening in their homes right along with me. Their presence brought both comfort and intimidation. I later asked each of them for their feedback.

We all agreed upon one criticism of the show.

I would have to learn to allow my guests to complete their thoughts before barging in.

I sometimes tend to interrupt people, even in my day-to-day conversations. My mind tends to race ahead. Even still, I could not step on what my guests were saying in my interviews. It sounds rude, listeners can't hear either of us, and guests can lose their train of thought. It was painful to hear those places where I stepped on what Ella was trying to say in the interview.

Although I found our interview lively and informative, I cringed every time I heard myself interrupting Ella. Sometimes I would think she was done speaking, but she would have another spontaneous thought just as I was about to respond. It was purely natural, but it was also clear I would have to learn to hold back more the next time around. As Neil suggested, I would need to allow a moment after each time my guest spoke to make sure the person was done speaking.

Neil assured me that if I left space between my guest and me that he could tighten the "air" between our exchange. During my second interview with Tanya Kersey, founder of the publication *Black Talent News,* and founder of the Hollywood Black Film Festival, I forced myself to be silent until I was sure she was completely done speaking. The process felt extremely unnatural, but it worked. Listening to the playback, the rhythm flowed and Tanya was heard.

The thing I most enjoyed about interviewing people I know is learning more about them. I also enjoyed doing the research on guests I know. Structurally, during the interview, I began by allowing my guests to share their personal side with my listeners. I began by talking about their birthplace, family, and early ambitions. Although I eventually asked a few of the questions they are used to, many of my questions treaded on uncharted territory.

After my interview with Ella, she said, "I've done a lot of interviews, but I think this is the *best* interview I have ever had. I talked about things I've never discussed in an interview, and I felt relaxed and comfortable."

Ella gave me the highest compliment I could ask for as a talk show host.

To any "would-be" talk show hosts who are reading this book, I think Ella's comment speaks to one of the most important elements of successful interviewing: allowing the guest to feel safe and relaxed.

I tried to earn my guests' trust. That is why there were some places I would not go in an interview unless invited. In the case of my interview with publicist Pat Tobin, she mentioned that her mother died when she was an adolescent. Although she disclosed that fact, I did not feel I had permission to inquire about the circumstances of her mother's death, or what it was like growing up without a mother during her young years. I probably could have, but I did not feel led.

Hattie Winston mentioned during our interview that her daughter is adopted. We discussed advice she would give to those considering adoption and how to go about telling the child at some point. However, I did not feel it my business to ask why *she* chose not to have children. One broadcaster told me he would ask the "hard questions." In my case, I want a thought-provoking interview, but I want the interview to be relaxed. I am on the side of the guest.

I think smart interviewers know what to ask, how to phrase it, and intuitively when to move on. They also know what not to touch.

In speaking with one of my guests before our interview, she asked, "What are we going to be talking about?" Another said, "Do I get to see the questions before the interview?"

Those questions were red flags that I would probably want to be very mindful of where we went in our interviews. The former turned out to be someone guarded. Because of her intellect, we stayed in safe areas that allowed us to explore the business in very pragmatic terms. She hid behind her intellect. The latter was surprisingly open, going places I did not initiate. Both interviews proved informative and rewarding.

Interviewing Marla Gibbs was the exact opposite. I found her to be so open and candid, I began to feel I had to take care where we went in the interview. I have known Marla since 1990. My respect and loyalty made me want to take even more care in my questions because she kept shocking me with her naked answers.

I asked, "What brought you to Los Angeles, Marla?"

She said flatly, "I was trying to get away from my husband."

In the back of my head, I could hear talk show Tobi Knight's words: *"You want to always make your guests look good."*

I learned how to handle interview surprises.

One question that always yielded a surprising answer was, "As a child, what did you first think you might want to become?"

Ella Joyce said, "A nurse."

Pat Tobin said one fantasy she had was to become a stand-up comedian.

That question was one of my favorites because I was frequently taken aback by the unexpected answers of my guests.

Each interview was personally enlightening for me in different ways. The late veteran actor Virginia Capers was a walking history book. Her Broadway career began in 1957 in the musical *Jamaica* and she later won a Tony Award for Best Actress in 1974 for her role of Lena Younger in the musical *Raisin*. By her late seventies, she had countless stories to tell.

Being a "first" in many ways, she was a reminder that things were not always the way they are today. She spoke of days gone by when she was one of the early Black students at Julliard's School of Music (Julliard's former name). Her class had the first big influx of Black students. There were about a dozen of them.

She declared haughtily, "Darling, Leontyne Price was in *my* class."

She also spoke of working with the likes of Cab Calloway and Lena Horne.

Ms. Capers did not bite her tongue in what she had to say about some celebrities she worked with in the early days. At the same time, the one she most revered was Diahann Carroll.

In 1968, Ms. Capers recurred on Diahann Carroll's history-making television series *Julia*. She fondly spoke of how Diahann Carroll fought for story lines that were true to life and how she fought to maintain the integrity of the show.

My respect for Diahann Carroll grew as I listened to Ms. Capers.

I am quite sure the same was true for other listeners as we all heard of Diahann's triumphs and challenges. Diahann's character on the show was a single mother and nurse whose husband had died in Vietnam. I remember well watching her show. It was unlike most of what had been broadcast before depicting African Americans, with the exception of Cicely Tyson, who in 1963 played a secretary in the hour-long drama *East Side, West Side.*

Julia was one of the first weekly series to depict an African American woman in a professional, non-stereotypic role, and a lot was riding on that show.

With a number of interviews under my belt, I began to find my stride. I think it helped that I am an acting teacher. I have been entrusted with countless students who have given me permission to work with them in deeply personal ways to bring out their best work. I have also worked with countless personalities and temperaments. It serves me in my work that I have a background in clinical psychology because I better understand the workings of the human mind.

One of my favorite interviews was with Angela Gibbs, daughter of Marla Gibbs. She is a filmmaker and actor in her own right.

Surprisingly, I learned she was actually working in the business as an actor before her mother!

Because Angela is so sharp, warm, and funny, I had a ball interviewing her. We relaxed each other through humor, and there was an ease in our exchange. We have a long history with each other, and we admire and know each other well. Our relationship has dovetailed in many ways: we both worked at her mother's Crossroads Academy acting school, she was on the Board of Directors of my Los Angeles Women's Theatre Festival, and we were both in a women's support group together.

Angela loves to laugh and she made me laugh.

In our interview, we laughed continually. We are both Aries, and there is a wonderful fire in our chemistry. I can hear that interview over and over again in my head. The dynamic of having fun I aspired to in my interviews, again and again.

It was in my interview with Fay Hauser-Price that I discovered I actually knew her least of all, although I have known her since 1999 when she began to volunteer as the Official Videographer for the Los Angeles Women's Theatre Festival. It was much later that I came to know her as an actor who had, among many credits, originated a soap opera character on *Days of Our Lives*.

By way of her bio, I learned that Fay is one of the few people I have met who wears as many or more hats than I do. She is an actor, producer, director, editor, songwriter, artist, writer, and one of the first African American artists to begin marketing greeting cards.

Perhaps most telling about Fay are her roots. She comes from a family of hardworking, politically active parents who were forced to leave South Carolina and found refuge in Winston-Salem, North Carolina.

One of my most memorable interviews was with legendary vocalist Freda Payne. I came to know Freda because her son Gregory is a former acting student of mine. Freda came to co-host the Los Angeles Women's Theatre in 2005 and returned as an audience member for our *Melodies in Motion* musical celebration fundraiser at the Madrid Theatre.

In 2006, she performed in the Second Annual *Melodies in Motion* musical fundraiser for the Festival. Earlier the same year, the Festival awarded her with our *Integrity Award*.

Like Virginia Capers, Freda is also a walking history book. I, like others, have encouraged Freda to write *her* autobiography. There are innumerable career stories inside her that are begging to be shared.

For example, both Duke Elllington and Berry Gordy offered her a singing contract when she was a teen. In the case of Berry Gordy, that offer came before Motown existed. As a young adult, she subsequently worked with the likes of Quincy Jones, Bill Cosby, and Pearl Bailey. In our interview, she rattled off stories about legends she has worked with, seemingly without realizing the impact to a listener.

An interview that fascinated me was with successful talent manager Dolores Robinson, mother of Holly Robinson Peete. Dolores was brutally honest about so many things.

She shared with me that she came from a "hamlet" outside of Philadelphia that had 250 residents. All were servants who served the "blue blood" whites of the area. She said her father, grandfather, and uncles were all servants. She remembers outhouses and hand-me-down clothes from one wealthy girl named Penny. Being around the wealthy, she learned quality, etiquette, and how the "haves" live. She said she holds sacred the handle of a pump removed from her childhood home that she brought to her Beverly Hills home. Daily, as it pumps water in her soy garden, she is reminded where she came from, and how far she has come.

She said, "I came to Los Angeles because my husband left me for another woman. I had been a fake, pretending I had a good marriage. When he left, I had to leave Philadelphia."

It was her good friend, the late Cleavon Little, who introduced her to agent Maggie Henderson. Dolores answered phones for Maggie in her early Hollywood days. Dolores is another successful African American woman with countless stories that need to be told, including how she took Wesley Snipes' film quote from $100,000 a film to four million dollars in a matter of two years.

Speaking of Hollywood, Dolores said, "I have been fired for telling the truth. Most people don't want to hear the truth."

When someone once commented on how modest her Beverly Hills home is, she said, "I don't have anything to prove anymore."

I am very proud of my former talk show, *Adilah*. I was enriched by those who allowed me to interview them and share a part of their lives with others. My listeners were educated while being entertained.

As I mentioned earlier, the Rainbow Soul Channel 5 on BlakeRadio has begun its return. Some of my old shows are now being re-aired, and I am contemplating returning to tape new shows.

I tip my hat to Neil Blake for taking a chance on me.

I am the better for it.

Chapter Fourteen

Mother Africa Calls This Child Home

You must give of yourself in order to be worthy.
—Hattie Bessent, Nurse/Educator

"I see you doing global work. You can limit yourself to working in the United States if you want to, but I see you doing international work."

"Global work?" I repeated.

The woman talking from her Santa Barbara, California, home with the view of the ocean was spiritual advisor Pam Osley. It was during the early 2000s. What she said made no sense to me at all.

"Global work," I thought.

Fast forward to March 2006.

I received an e-mail from then-called Paul Robeson African Initiative (PRAI) organizer Sade Turnipseed, announcing a call for a "method acting" coach in Nigeria.

Two other people also forwarded me the same e-mail saying, "Adilah, this sounds like you."

I, too, had a good feeling about the opportunity, and knew with my training and many years of teaching, I fit the job description.

I submitted my cover letter and resumé. Within days, Amaka and Charles Igwe had invited me to teach acting for BOB-TV Marketplace in Nigeria's capital, Abuja. Amaka can be said to be the Steven Spielberg of Nigeria.

The teaching offer with their BOB-TV Marketplace was confirmation that the time had come to make my sojourn to the Motherland.

For many years I had wanted to go to Africa. I always imagined myself going as a tourist. Based on Maya Angelou's Ghanaian experience in her book *All God's Children Need Traveling Shoes* that I recount in my solo show, I thought Ghana was likely to be the first African country where my feet would touch the soil.

It was Nigeria.

The time had *finally* come.

I was going not as a tourist, but as a professional. I would be sharing my skills as an acting teacher. I came to learn that Amaka had contacted Sade by e-mail with a proposition to do some work together in Nigeria. She had found Sade by internet, presumably because of Sade's work with the Panafrican Film and Television Festival of Ouagadougou (FESPACO), the largest film festival on the continent of Africa. It takes place in Burkina Faso every other year.

Sade later told me that her original proposal for the BOB-TV Marketplace initially included only instructors in public relations, screenwriting, and television directing.

She said Amaka looked at her proposal and said, "But do you know anyone who can teach acting?"

That is where I came in.

I came to learn that Nigeria is one of the top three countries in the world that produces film and video. India is number one, followed by the United States. Nigeria holds third place.

It became very apparent to me that Nigeria's growing stature in the film, television, and video market now mandates more formal training of actors to meet the demands of excellence in the global marketplace.

My skills were needed.

I went to Nigeria with a sense of purpose.

In March of 2006, I taught three acting classes in Abuja at the BOB-TV Marketplace. I was overwhelmed by the response of my participants. My largest class held about 100 students. Most were actors, but some were also producers, writers, and directors throughout Nigeria. As I looked over a sea of eager students that I taught through lecture and demonstration, I could feel the hunger of these actors as they seemed to linger on my every word. They were appreciative and wanted to soak up everything they could in my acting intensives. In turn, I wanted to give them all the knowledge I could in the five days I spent in Abuja.

I also came prepared to perform an excerpt from my solo show *I Am That I Am:* Woman, *Black.* There was no way I was going to go all the way to Africa and not perform at *least* an excerpt of my show. As part of my demonstration, I shared the opening of my show by portraying Sojourner Truth. The participants listened intently as I brought to life an African American ex-slave before their very eyes.

I received comments like, "We never heard of this powerful woman, Sojourner Truth!" and "Now we know what acting is!"

While teaching in Nigeria, I created a visual display of my many acting books by lining them up behind me as I taught each class.

After each class, students came up to look closely at my resource books and thumb through my selection. One actor held a book as if it was gold.

He asked with wonder, "How do you *get* these books?"

I take my books for granted because they are so easy to come by in America. His question reminded me there is no Samuel French Bookstore in Nigeria for actors, and they do not have easy access to theatre books. My nearest Samuel French bookstore is only minutes from my North Hollywood home.

Upon my return home, I shared my experiences regarding the acting books with writer K. D. Greene.

Always one with novel ideas, she said, "Why don't you ask people to donate money so you can buy books to take back when you return?"

I listened.

I thought about K.D.'s suggestion, but did not feel comfortable asking anyone for money. However, I *did* feel comfortable asking actors to recycle used books. With my April press release announcing my return to Nigeria a month later, I added a personal note of appeal with my e-mail blast asking for acting books.

I had no idea the response would be so generous.

One published Hollywood acting instructor, Anita Jesse, donated an entire box of brand new acting books from a former edition of her acting book *Let the Part Play You*. Another writer, Angel Harper, donated her cold reading book *Master the Art of Cold Reading*, along with other recycled books. Still others donated their random used books and money. Clarinda Ross, a Board member of Actor's Equity Association (AEA), even offered the opportunity to explore how AEA might support my efforts in tandem since they were thinking of "adopting" an African country. She also invited me to write an article for the AEA magazine upon my next return back to the States.

Clarinda stressed, "And remember to take lots of pictures!"

One picture I took was of a beautiful Nigerian sister who was regally dressed in a green Nigerian outfit that included a fabulous head wrap. I first noticed her as she gracefully descended down a long staircase of the convention center where the BOB-TV Marketplace was being held. She signaled to me as she began walking down the winding staircase. I met her at the foot of the stairs.

With a warm smile, she stepped up to me and looked me squarely in the eyes as she said, "Sister, welcome home. You are always welcome in Nigeria."

I quietly replied, "Thank you."

We followed our exchange with a tight embrace as I fought my tears.

I had come home.

That moment sums up the emotional experience of returning to my roots in Mother Africa. From the moment I got off the plane in Abuja, I knew I was in a Black country. Most everybody looked like me and I was among the majority.

Surprisingly, I was also reminded of my many trips to different Caribbean islands. I thought, "Unlike America, how intact our culture was maintained in the islands."

To bring closure and underscore the power of my first trip to Africa, I had a very moving experience on my connecting flight home from London to Los Angeles.

I had gotten up out of my seat to stretch and check on my fellow traveler, television director and filmmaker Kevin Arkadie, who had accompanied my group. Kevin taught screenwriting and television directing at BOB-TV Marketplace. He was sitting in another section of Virgin Airlines, and I wanted to make contact with him. It was a *very* long trip, and I also needed to stretch.

As I tightly passed people in the narrow aisle waiting to use the tiny restrooms, I heard a deep voice say, "The restrooms are in use."

I turned around to say I was not going to the restroom and realized I was staring in the eyes of Reverend Cecil L. "Chip" Murray, who had served twenty-seven years at First African Methodist Episcopal Church (FAME). Founded in 1872 by ex-slave Biddy Mason, FAME holds the distinction of being the oldest Black church in Los Angeles.

A member of FAME, I said, "Pastor Murray, what were you doing in London?"

He looked at me with his huge, gentle eyes, and in his deep, metered voice replied, "My dear, what were *you* doing in London?"

I said, "Actually, I wasn't in London. I had a connecting flight from London. I am returning from Nigeria."

Pastor Murray met me with, "I am returning from Rwanda."

I repeated, "Rwanda?"

He said, "I am returning with a group from USC. We were there to meet with orphans and widows in Rwanda."

Pastor Murray did not need to say another word for me to get the impact of his sojourn. It is no secret that the 100 days of genocide in 1994 left over one million Rwanda residents dead.

He went on to say members of his group were lending their talents toward economically rebuilding the country. I felt something akin to electricity run throughout my body.

Pastor Murray reminded me of a conversation I had had with stage director Shirley Jo Finney. She recounted for me an experience she had on Goreé Island, a West African island off the coast of Dakar, Senegal.

Beginning in 1776, this haunting island was the principal entry point during American slavery. Until 1848, Africans were taken from nearby countries to Goreé Island's, "Slave House" before being shipped by some twenty ships across the Atlantic Ocean to meet their horrendous destiny along the Diaspora. Renderings of the ships are on display on Goreé Island, giving a visual reminder of the Black Holocaust.

Shirley Jo shared with me the devastating impact Goreé Island had on her. Like many other African Americans who have made that same sojourn, she shared how emotional the experience was for those returning to the port that transported our ancestors to the Western Hemisphere. She painted a picture of what affected her most. She described seeing the room where children were separated from their parents and stacked on top of each other like cargo. She also shared what it was like for her to see the well-known door that reads, "Door of no return."

Shirley Jo said she looked at that inscribed doorway and thought defiantly, "It's a lie. We're back!"

I finished my conversation with Pastor Murray by saying, "I think about you coming back from Rwanda, those in my group coming back from Nigeria, Oprah setting up her school in South Africa, Senator Barack Obama's AIDS-related trip to Africa, and a group of Black journalists that included my friend DeBorah who went to South Africa, and I know what Shirley Jo felt is true. We are back!"

Not only are more and more Black Americans returning to Africa as tourists, many of us are also returning with our acquired knowledge and skills. In some cases, we are even returning to make Africa our permanent home. I met a sister from Baltimore who has opened a private school for children in Lagos. We Black Americans are the descendants of African slaves who reigned from majesty and were thrown into the vile institution of slavery. We descendants have, in many cases, returned with an education, expertise, and a willingness to give back.

We *are* back.

On my second trip to Nigeria in April of 2006, I planned to give away to students all the acting books I had collected. I was slated to teach in Yenogoa, located in the Bayelsa State of Nigeria known as "The Glory of All Lands." I was invited this second trip by Peace Anylam-Fiberesima, CEO of the African Movie Academy Awards (AMAA).

However, once I arrived in Lagos, I eventually found out plans had changed. I was asked instead to participate as a judge in the African Movie Academy Awards, akin to the Academy of Motion Picture Arts and Sciences' Oscars in America.

Although I was disappointed I would not be teaching on my second trip, I was quickly told by Peace, "You can come back another time to teach."

That would mean returning a third time.

I agreed.

Plans had changed for me, but I was thrilled to be offered the opportunity to participate as a judge for the finalists in a prestigious event that brought actors, directors, writers, cinematographers, and nominees in technical categories together from around the African continent. I met others in the industry from South Africa, Ghana, Zimbabwe, Botswana, the Sudan, and other countries. I also received offers to bring my talents to those same countries.

In Lagos, I joined judges that included Ayuko Babu and his wife Asantewa, founders of the Pan African Film Festival in Los Angeles, and judges from other countries including Germany. I judged many films during our long screening sessions. Some faces onscreen were familiar to me because they had attended my acting workshops the month before. I had *no* idea until the film screenings that many in my workshops were celebrity Nigerian actors. I was also introduced, through their work, to still other professionals in the industry from around the African continent.

The exciting moments when envelopes were opened to name the AMAA winners were as breathtaking to Africans as the Oscars are to Americans. I looked around me. Africans were dressed impeccably, and I could not see an empty seat anywhere. There were thousands of attendees, and perhaps just as many outside the huge building who were unable to get inside. Many tried unsuccessfully to force their way in. In fact, it almost felt like we were about to have a riot, but the crowd was eventually contained.

I realized fully my creative journey had brought me home.

Vivica Fox and Lou Gossett also presented at the Awards. They had been invited to speak during the Ceremony, just as Danny Glover had the year before. It became even clearer to me how much Africans know the work of African Americans in film when Vivica Fox hit the stage. They went wild when she walked out. Their response was a reminder that Africans also watch our American movies. Judging by the audience's cheering response when Vivica Fox and Lou Gossett walked onstage, it was also clear that African American celebrities are very much welcomed at this annual African event.

The highlight of the Awards Ceremony was seeing and hearing the voice of the late South African diva Miriam Makeba. Known throughout the continent as "Mama Africa," I remember her well from her revolutionary music of the 1960s, especially after her exile from South Africa in 1963. She was banned from her homeland for speaking against apartheid at the United Nations.

A legend in her own right, the audience rose in unison, passionately yelling out, "Mama Africa!" when she graced the stage. Joining many other audience members, I ran to the lip of the stage to get as close to her spirit as I could.

I had met Ms. Makeba the day before.

I could not believe the woman I now witnessed onstage was the same woman I had met at our hotel. The day before, when I introduced myself to her, I saw an aging woman who was assisted by a walking stick. A survivor, she has risen above exile, several auto accidents, an airplane crash, and even cancer.

However, onstage, she was in her element.

Her walking aid was nowhere to be seen. She moved majestically and economically onstage. She even danced when the music moved her. She sang "Pata Pata" and other songs she is known for. Ms. Makeba is an extraordinary example of how artists are able to transcend challenges once the lights hit them onstage. She was not about to walk on that stage in front of an adoring audience of thousands with a walking stick.

There is something to be said about mind over matter.

After the Awards Ceremony and a private party held by the stylish governor Dr. Jonathan Goodluck, our envoy traveled back to our Port Harcourt Hotel. I sat in the back of our air-conditioned new bus and talked for over two hours to one of Ms. Makeba's band members. I felt a strong attraction to this South African man. I came to find out later he had been listening to a conversation I had with another band member on our hair-raising ride to Yenegoa for the Awards Ceremony.

You never know who may be observing you.

On the way back to our hotel, we shared a jewel of a moment as we talked nonstop and together watched the sun slowly rise the next morning. He kept saying, "You must come to South Africa."

I plan to.

Back at the hotel, he introduced me a second time to Ms. Makeba as she held court with her entourage. He wanted me to meet her in his presence. I shared with him that I wanted to take pictures with her the following day, and he wanted to make the introduction.

However, I blew it.

I walked up to Ms. Makeba in the dining room the following evening and approached her for my photo. She was again surrounded by her entourage as she enjoyed what appeared to be a rich seafood soup.

I began, "Ms. Makeba, I would like to take a photo—"

She interrupted me with, "My child, I am trying to eat my dinner."

I had not meant I wanted a photo at *that* moment, but she did not allow me to finish my sentence. Completely humiliated, I shrunk away from her table.

Not present, I was glad her band member had been spared from my embarrassing moment at Ms. Makeba's table.

A short while later, Ms. Makeba's assistant beckoned my new acquaintance Dorothy from Zimbabwe to come take a photo with Ms. Makeba.

Dorothy, unaware of my snafu said excitedly, "Adilah, come take pictures with us!"

I said, "Dorothy, you go. I walked up to Ms. Makeba earlier and she reprimanded me for approaching her while she was eating."

Dorothy said, "The same thing happened to me. Come with me and move beyond that."

Reluctantly, I slowly followed Dorothy and Ms. Makeba's assistant. Facing her, I apologized again. She seemed to have forgotten our incident as she graciously allowed me to pose with her and

Dorothy. Her assistant even encouraged me to get my own shots alone with Ms. Makeba. Finally, one last photo was about to be taken with Ms. Makeba and Dorothy. I was about to move away when Ms. Makeba reached out, and with strong arms, pulled me very close to her bosom.

She had forgiven me.

I learned in that moment that it is possible to work through an embarrassing moment.

I have many more rich memories in Nigeria. These are only a few.

I have met many whom I feel a close kinship with, including my spiritual sister Rosemary. I have seen the poorest of the poor, and experienced the contrast of Peace Anylam-Fiberesima's three-generation upper-class Nigerian family living in an elegant compound. This family possesses more knowledge of self, family, and dignity than most African Americans in America.

I have also had experiences that challenged me.

There were times I was a passenger in vehicles going so fast that the drivers had me sitting on the edge of my seat. The places I visited had no speed limits. I also remember feeling the nakedness of waiting for a guide momentarily on a very questionable corner where I knew no one, and where I felt extremely vulnerable because I clearly looked like an American without a chaperone.

Those few minutes felt like hours.

In Africa, I have also shared my talents with those who have invited me. I experienced many enlightening, nurturing, and unforgettable moments in Nigeria.

At the time of this writing, Peace Anylam-Fiberesima and I are now planning my third trip to Nigeria to offer the acting classes we spoke of in 2006.

I have been called back to Mother Africa, and like an obedient child, I have gladly come home.

I now understand what spiritual advisor Pam Osley spoke of when she said, "I see *you* doing global work."

Chapter Fifteen

What Next?

If I am going to do anything else, it better be now.
—Jane Pauley, Journalist

As I was driving home one evening in 2004, my longtime friend John Doyle asked me impatiently, "What do you want to do with your life?"

In traffic, I repeated from my cell phone, "What do I want to do with my *life?*"

He persisted, "Yeah. Do you want to get married or do you want to keep being godmother to all those kids?"

He was referring to the many I mentor.

Little did he know, I was pondering the same question.

I said, "Funny you should ask that. I have been giving a lot of thought to the same question lately."

He repeated, "So, what do you want to do with your life?"

I paused.

I took my time answering, "Well, I want to place my feet more gently on the earth. Maybe I'd like a companion to spend the rest of my life with."

He asserted, "You need to get you a companion first."

Then we got into our usual mating dance that always ends with our mutual self-conscious laughter. Ours is a long and complex relationship. We have a deep friendship and love for each other. We also banter back and forth regularly like an old married couple.

Driving, I kept thinking about John's question after we hung up.

"What do you want to do with your life?"

Four years later, I need to address the subject of death before I more fully answer the question of what I want to do next with my life. It has been said that until we deal with death, we cannot get on with living.

I agree.

On August 16, 2007 I lost my youngest brother, Edward, to terminal liver disease. In 2005, I lost my eldest brother Hollis to a tragic auto accident. I lost my sister Dorothy to an enlarged heart in 1999. In 1994, I lost my mother. Shortly before my mother's passing, one of my nieces was murdered by her husband in a murder-suicide, my nephew RJ died in a tragic auto accident, and my nephew Eugene died at age fourteen of asthma.

I *have* known death.

At the time of my baby brother's passing, I felt like the wind had been knocked out of me.

Not another sibling.

Collectively, the loss of my two brothers and sister are a sobering reminder that I need to get on with living as fully as I can, one day at a time.

Tomorrow is not promised to anyone.

So I exhale deeply to ease my aching heart. I have known sadness from the loss of family too often, and too many times. Still, I must move on as they would all want me to. I must try to learn life's lessons and allow some measure of wisdom to guide me, one day at a time.

So I leave for now the subject of death, and move on to the subject of *living*.

Many of the things I most want to do with my life right now seem simple by comparison.

I want to go back to my daily ritual of transcendental meditation twice a day, listen more to soothing jazz, experience more breathtaking views of nature at its absolute best, create the aroma of a home-cooked vegan meal in my own home more often, and allow more time to snuggle up on my sofa, wrapped in my purple throw in front of my fireplace during the winter, and watch beads of rain as they roll down my window panes. I want to listen more to the rhythm of the rain as it makes its way to the ground.

It has been the warmth and nearness of my grandson's young body near me when he has watched cartoons and played with his chosen toys that has informed me I am now, indeed, slowing down and placing my feet more gently on the earth.

I am learning to take my time with life more.

It warms my heart when I think of my grandson.

The first sixteen months of Malik Isaiah's life, I was the one who babysat him during the work week. Our early quality time together allowed us to bond.

I felt privileged that I was the one who witnessed those first unsteady steps firsthand.

I remember other firsts, like when my grandson wobbled alongside his father without his training wheels for the first time. Whenever Malik has mastered a success of some sort, he has yelled out, "I did it, Grandma! I did it!" I heard those exact words when he began to ride his bicycle without the protection and balance of his training wheels.

Malik also yelled out, "Look, Grandma! I did it!" at the YMCA near my home, where he took swimming lessons. He prides himself in his every new accomplishment. I have always praised him for each success.

It takes so little to encourage children to do their best.

My grandson has taught me how to live in the here and now.

As I look back over a career that began forty two years ago, it becomes increasingly clear to me that I need to look forward to my senior years. The truth is, I am *already* a senior. As I continue to lose those I know and love at an alarming rate, I am reminded again and again that the only time I know I have for sure is the moment I am living.

As my personal clock keeps ticking forward, I begin to notice a new gray hair here and there. I feel an ache in places I never felt before. I see my body form shifting involuntarily more frequently. Body parts once firm are now beginning to surrender to gravity. My body reminds me that I have surely passed the halfway mark of my years, yet getting old and dying does not frighten me. For me, it is the quality of life that matters most, not the length of time. Surely, I have done far more with my fiftysomething years of life than many who have lived much longer.

At the same time, I have begun to economize my energy. I give less to those I do not want to give to, and I try to surround myself with those who are real, positive, and who genuinely care about me.

I periodically walk around the Lake Hollywood reservoir. I use that time as my thinking and reflecting time. When others accompany me, I sometimes ask that we agree to walk in silence. I also maintain my YMCA membership to encourage me to work out more.

That commitment I am still working on.

Without fail, I do my morning yoga as I have for over thirty years. If time permits, I do my "morning ritual" I previously mentioned, that includes journaling, reading my thought for the day from Iyanla Van Zant's *Acts of Faith,* and pulling my "angelic cards" from my stack to see what thought the universe holds for me on a given day. I also enjoy my warm morning lemon water to cleanse my system as I start each new day.

Something I long to reclaim are my silence days for myself by taking a "talking fast." It may be for twenty-four hours. It may be longer. It is a time where I do not utter one word out loud. It is my time to totally go inside myself. That time spent inside not only calms me, it also allows me to hear spirit talk. I am always amazed at my personal discoveries during that time of solitude.

I now care less what others think about me. I have learned I cannot satisfy everyone, nor do I try. I tire of high maintenance people. Having relationships with complex, neurotic people is no longer worth my time, even with those I love. Being a part of real-life daily drama holds no benefits for me, nor does spending time listening therapeutically to those who, if allowed, will selfishly drain me. I don't have it to give like I once did, nor do I want to. I have learned I cannot *really* fix people. I can only try to fix myself.

Yes, more and more, it is becoming all about me.

Given that need, I am learning to ferociously protect my private time. I enjoy my quiet time, especially in my own home. I like that my inner circle is getting smaller and smaller as time passes. It is those

I've known many, many years, Jacki Scott from our college days at UC Santa Cruz and Mararice Bush Davis from childhood, who hold a sacred place in my heart. They remind me in different ways of my essence. Each has journeyed with me at different junctures, and in very different ways during my personal evolution.

I have done substantial theatre and television work during my professional life. I have also done film work I am proud of, especially projects like Universal's award-winning *Erin Brockovich* and HBO's *Iron-Jawed Angels*. I may not be a household name, but I have worked enough to make a living as an actor. Hallmark's *Little John* and the well-written episode "Strange Fruit" of the CBS series *Cold Case* that I worked on are examples of projects that have held a high degree of merit and personal satisfaction for me.

Television and film work is coming less as I age. It is *still* a reality that women over forty work increasingly less in my industry but I am more and more getting recognized for my body of work as an actor. I am one of those actors who has a familiar face, but people are not quite sure why. Some say things like, "I know your face. Do you go to my church?" Others may say, "Are you an actress?" Still others nail it by saying, "I like your work."

Invariably, those moments of recognition happen at the exact times I would prefer not to be noticed. I am learning to be more careful how I leave my house, because I never know who I may run into.

My humble beginnings took shape in a rural community, but the majority of my life has been spent living in big cities. However, I am still very much a country girl at heart. I feel very blessed to have known both the world of small-town living and city life, because each has nurtured me in a very different way.

The country taught me how to appreciate nature. I learned how to follow butterflies with my eyes and how to savor the taste of honeysuckle flowers while avoiding nearby bees. I learned how to identify trees like the mighty oak and weeping willow by name. I learned how to pick fruit, like prunes, blackberries, and mulberries. Sometimes, with other youth, I took the chance of raiding someone's yard for sweet, succulent plums, figs, and loquats over their fences. I learned how to enjoy the wind against my cheeks as I daily rode my blue and white Rollmaster bicycle *all* over town.

I also learned how to enjoy my own company.

My small-town life taught me a sense of community, respect for my elders, and the value of learning through role models. I learned from those who were not even aware they were teaching me. I mentioned some of them earlier, like our corner store owner and fireman Mr. Johnson, and our church leader for young girls, Mrs. Officer. There were many, many more along the way.

My hometown also taught me how to be resourceful and to appreciate the earth. Watching my mother plant her garden each year that yielded healthy fruit and vegetables she would can for our cold winters was a reminder we could live off the land and provide for ourselves. I enjoyed watching our produce sprout and grow. Watering the trenches of soil we laid our water hoses in made me a part of that gardening process.

I learned as a child how to travel beyond my life of being a have not by gazing through mail-order catalogs like *Spiegel's* and *Montgomery Wards*, wishing for what I did not have. Walking to the movies always allowed me to enter other worlds on the screen on Sundays after church.

The country also made me feel safe.

We did not have to lock our doors unless we wanted to. We could sit on our porches late into the summer nights, knowing everybody who passed by. We could even invite some of those same passers-by to join us at any hour, because we knew each other.

We were a community.

What an uncomplicated time I once knew.

On the other hand, the city has taught me how to navigate my surroundings with anonymity. Unlike Oroville, where everybody on my side of town knew everybody, I know far less people in the city. There are only a few of my present neighbors I have built a relationship with, although we do look out for each other when needed. My neighborhood in North Hollywood is a different kind of community than I knew as a child, now more private and invisible.

I have learned to survive in environments vastly different and far bigger than I ever imagined. The city has taught me that I can aim bigger and sometimes hit my mark, because I have more choices at my fingertips. The pulse of the city has kept me aware and alert. I wake up each day with a sense of expectancy, and that revs my motor for yet another day of surprises. I have learned that one telephone call can literally change the course of my day, and even my life.

Still, I have begun to long for a simpler life.

Looking out my living room window calms me. I have begun to appreciate watching the roses bloom in my front yard, one at a time. I enjoy moments of solitude as I look out my front window, past the birch trees that hover over me. I enjoy my protective trees and watch in awe as they change their appearance with the seasons. I see the squirrels running up and down them year-round, seemingly without a care at all.

I love to watch and listen to the birds. I see and hear the chirping sparrows that remind me that God's eye *is* on me. I see the nonstop hummingbirds suspended mid-air, and blackbirds lined up along my white picket fence. The blackbirds seem to stand guard along my fence in protection of me. There are also occasional cats that enter my yard. They stay for a moment, then they are on their way.

On two occasions, sparrows flew into my home. One I discovered at the start of a new day. He had been in my home throughout the night without my knowing. The sparrow's presence is a reminder that I, too, am being watched over.

When I take the time to notice, I am reminded of life around me, even in my front yard. I appreciate that time of stillness.

I have given much to my creative world in which I have touched hearts, minds, and spirits. Some are still in my life and others stayed such a short time I do not even remember their names or faces. Yet I do remember their momentary impact on me.

I have taught countless students and co-founded two arts organizations, along with one theatre company and a reading circle. I have been an initiator and a trailblazer. However, all I have done has not been without a price. I have made costly sacrifices in my personal life that I would not make again if I knew in advance the cost I would pay, especially with my son.

Fortunately, there has been some value in paying such a high price. In the long run, my professional life has been a relatively successful one. For that I am exceedingly grateful, and yet I yearn for something more.

I am beginning to be pulled more and more toward my writing, bringing me full circle back to my first love. Writing is a solitary expression, and one that relaxes and fulfills me. I love the quiet as I seek the right words and manipulate language to translate my thoughts and feelings on paper.

I have taught writing from time to time with the Los Angeles Women's Theatre Festival. I have also been invited to teach a solo writing class at the Alliance Theatre in Atlanta. It brings me great satisfaction to watch others pick up the pen and begin to connect the inner dots of their personal stories. I love feeling the energy of active minds as moving pens work in unison in the quiet of our writing space. I also participate in the writing exercises during class. In those moments of mental creativity and imagining, we are one.

This industry thing called "making it" has no real power over me. Success can be measured in so many ways. Making money does not drive me. It never has. I rarely make decisions based on money. I have never longed to be either famous or rich. As a result, I am neither. However, I am proud of my body of work and I do live comfortably without compromising my integrity.

Money always seems to come.

I now feel some degree of freedom in my life. I also feel more and more I want change. My life is relatively predictable in that I am an actor, acting teacher, producer, writer, and now a writer's retreat proprietor. Although each day holds surprises for me, I spend my time pretty much doing those same five things. I keep asking myself which hat I will shed to make room for more personal time.

That is a tough question because I do not want to choose and yet, I need to cut back even more on all that I do.

I am trying to position the Los Angeles Women's Theatre Festival in such a way that it can survive if I choose to step down. I am working with our current Board of Directors to identify and attract more funding so that our non-profit can begin to be staffed more by paid staff, and depend less on me. I have volunteered fifteen years for the organization, and it needs new leadership to advance it. I also need more time for myself to explore my writing further, and to do other things I want to do with my life.

I tell myself maybe I can exchange teaching classes by offering only private coaching. That way, I would work exclusively with actors on a one-on-one basis. That choice appeals to me, and that is what I have begun to do more since 2007.

I have enjoyed being able to travel while working. Being on location as an acting coach with vocalist Toni Braxton in Toronto in 2005 for *Kevin Hill* and San Diego in 2002 for *Play'd* was very satisfying. Also, directing Roz Browne's solo show *Fried Clams with Bellies* in 2005 sparked my interest in directing solo shows. I love directing and want to do more of it outside my acting classes.

Roz invited me to go on location with her to Martha's Vineyard that year to direct her again in *Fried Clams with Bellies*. I directed her for that venue, but I got ill before the trip and could only be there in spirit. I give thanks to both Toni and Roz. They believed my guidance valuable enough to their work to take me on the road with them.

It was an illness in 2005 that caused me to cancel my trip to Martha's Vineyard with Roz Browne. Although I fought as long as I could, I had to undergo a colon surgery in November of that same year. That long-time illness that resulted in hospitalization and surgery was a very painful wake-up call. I have begun to appreciate life more, and I am pacing myself better.

Stress can attack the body with illness.

In June of 2006, I participated in a twenty-one-day detox diet in Santa Monica with Dr. Richard DeAndrea and John Wood. I had begun this highly regimented cleansing diet in November 2005, but was unable to complete it due to my health. I was determined to return to complete it, and successfully did so in July of 2006.

I came off of the detox diet that year and never went back to animal products. I feel better now than I can remember feeling in years. Although I have not eaten red meat in over thirty years, I am now even more disciplined in my diet. What I eat now is vegan and often organic, pure, and completely free of animal products.

Sometimes restless, my Aries nature feels like I want to become a filmmaker. I want to tell stories that matter to me; stories that ought to be told. I also feel I would like to found a performing arts school somewhere where artists can receive professional conservatory training, both adults and children.

I now want to make time to take classes for the sake of pure learning. It is not necessary to seek another degree. I just want to learn to learn. I love languages. I am thinking of brushing up on my Spanish and French. Travel would be easier having the confidence of speaking other languages more fluently. I have traveled extensively for work, touching the soil of most of the United States and three continents, but I still love traveling for pleasure. I want to see still more of the world, especially other countries in Africa beyond Nigeria. Ghana seems to be calling me next. I also want to take another writing, yoga, and acting class.

I realize I have many, many choices in my life.

Although I love the comfort of my humble North Hollywood home, in 2006 I purchased a home in the Atlanta area. It sits on 1.8 acres of lush land and is literally surrounded by taller trees than any I have seen in California. I knew the moment my realtor Veronica Dodson and I drove down the private road at the end of a cul-de-sac, that *this* was the house calling my name. It is serene, beautiful, and a place where I am able to recharge my batteries, as I also create. It has its own nearby creek that I have explored while walking through my many Georgia pines, oaks and maple trees. Although I have never walked the entire property, the former owners showed me from afar my property lines that extend to a road where I can see cars passing by.

This may be the place I choose to retire.

I began to see Atlanta with new eyes when my astrologer Loda Shaw and my feng shui adviser Milan, also an astrologer, independently said the same thing. Each saw me living in Atlanta based on my astrological chart. Given their advice, I decided to consider the possibility of becoming bi-coastal. I am content that I made that decision because doors have begun to open very naturally in a city where I can contribute my talents to the community in a number of ways.

Atlanta has grown on me.

I love the people who represent, on the one hand, a kind of simplicity. On the other hand, there are those who represent a Southern aristocracy. I now claim Atlanta my Southern home, a place where I can write in peace and get away from the hustle and bustle of the business world of Hollywood. Atlanta is also a thriving city, but it is slower. I can breathe freely at my residence, which is slightly removed from the city. I can claim both the country and the city—the two worlds I have known throughout my life.

I have begun to move forward with my vision of turning my home there into a writer's retreat for women. I have named it "*The Writer's Well.*" I joined The Writer's Retreat, a network that represents a number of literary retreats around the world, so my vision is now becoming a reality. Many thanks to my National Advisory Circle that includes Assuanta Collins, Nia Damali, Dr. Kwakiutl Dreher, Marcia Ellis, Adrian Hill, Jonae Jackson, Venita Jacobson, Dr. Venita Kelley, Keryl McCord, Iona Morris, Crystal V. Rhodes and Sandra Seaton. They have all contributed their creative input for *The Writer's Well.* I strive to provide a warm, safe and inspirational place where creativity will flourish.

At the same time, the Palm Springs desert continues to summon me. I find great peace when I go to my timeshare in Palm Springs. The rock formations, open space, and palm trees soothe my soul and rejuvenate my spirit. I find more clarity and relaxation there.

Life is easy in Palm Springs.

I love any place with a strong Native American presence, and Palm Springs offers that. I ritualistically visit the Indian Canyon most every time I go there. I love the hikes along the streams and the boulders that silently sit near me. I watch the lizards as they run past me, and I listen attentively in silence to the spirits of the ancestors.

The canyon renews me.

When not in North Hollywood, I split my time between Atlanta and Palm Springs. Each feeds me in very different ways.

About love.

That is the area of my life I feel less surefooted about. I mentioned earlier that most of my relationships have been long-term, and I have had marriage proposals along the way. However, at the time of this writing, I am very much single and celibate. I once joined an online dating site but I am still not convinced that is the way I will meet my next love.

Pam Osley's spiritual reading in Santa Barbara that I spoke of in the last chapter revealed that my "global" work will bring another benefit. She feels my soul mate is connected with that global work. I was told I had not met him yet, but he will be ready to meet me when I am ready to meet him.

It appears that for now, he awaits me still.

I am now beginning to look at men with my eyes wide open. As my astrologer Loda Shaw said, "Like a taxicab, you have to make sure you leave your light on." I am now beginning to take the risk of occasionally turning my light *on.*

What next?

We shall see.

Afterword

As her one-woman show concluded and she accepted her standing ovation with her usual grace and humbleness, I could not help but see what others perhaps could not of her. I listened to the crowd fill the theatre with elevating applause, but it was upon her that my eyes remained. How beautiful she was with deep, glowing radiance from within, emanating from a spiritual place that could only be visited, nurtured, or blessed by the characters she earnestly portrayed. They anointed her, and you could feel it.

Her long black hair was twisted up and pinned in steadiness with her final character. She appeared, as she does in life, of tiny stature, yet phenomenal in talent and in spirit of the ages. She performed profoundly with what seemed to be no effort—the kind you accomplish from a complete and total surrender to "the art." She was an angel to me, with dark, sparkling eyes that danced toward you from the stage, if she wanted them to. The crowd still applauded as my heart captured all this in reverent remembrance, for this moment will live within me forever as I carefully immortalize each detail.

But for me, it was the smile and the outstretched arms, beckoning me to come, that transformed the stage to another place in time. As we drew closer, I could visualize us younger and younger until we were but children again, on our grandmother's wooden porch in summer dresses and oiled legs. We had sticky faces from melon slices and were exhausted from the millionth game of "tag"—a scene we cousins remember so very well.

The profound love and deep respect for each other became clearer to all with each approaching step until we met in the middle and the tears began to flow, remembering those summer evenings at Granny's where the night air smelled of jasmine and the streetlights chased us home. The crickets ended our mother's lullabies each night, and the moon promised to replace itself by the morning sun, giving us yet another day to be thankful we had each other.

This world was Adilah's stage back then. She fervently shared it with us and took us places our young hearts could scarcely visualize. Through her enchanting eyes and her vibrant imagination, she shared adventures with us all, and touched my soul with a fire that would not go out until I could see for myself, as a young woman, what lay beyond our grandmother's rose-petaled walkway.

Marilyn Theresa Colvin